The Dover Bronze Age boat in context: society and water transport in prehistoric Europe

The Dover Bronze Age boat in context: society and water transport in prehistoric Europe

Béat Arnold, Mike Baillie, Peter Clark, John Coates, Edwin Gifford, Joyce Gifford, Christopher Green, Flemming Kaul, Kristian Kristiansen, Frode Kvalø, Thijs Maarleveld, Peter Marsden, Seán McGrail, Robert Van de Noort, Keith Parfitt, Francis Pryor and Owain Roberts

Edited by Peter Clark

Oxbow Books

Oxford & Philadelphia

Published in the United Kingdom in 2004 by
OXBOW BOOKS
10 Hythe Bridge Street, Oxford OX1 2EW

and in the United States by
OXBOW BOOKS
908 Darby Road, Havertown, PA 19083

Reprinted 2014

Paperback Edition: ISBN 978-1-84217-139-4
Digital Edition: ISBN 978-1-78297-680-6

A CIP record for this book is available from the British Library

For a complete list of Oxbow titles, please contact:

UNITED KINGDOM
Oxbow Books
Telephone (01865) 241249, Fax (01865) 794449
Email: oxbow@oxbowbooks.com
www.oxbowbooks.com

UNITED STATES OF AMERICA
Oxbow Books
Telephone (800) 791-9354, Fax (610) 853-9146
Email: queries@casemateacademic.com
www.casemateacademic.com/oxbow

Oxbow Books is part of the Casemate Group

Cover image: Reconstructing the Dover boat
Design by Mark Duncan
Photography by Damien Sanders

Contents

Foreword *Frank Panton* vii

1. The Dover boat ten years after its discovery *Peter Clark* 1

2. Evidence of a marine environment associated with the Dover boat *Christopher Green* 13

3. Reconstructing the Dover boat *Peter Marsden* 17

4. The legacy of Ted Wright *John Coates* 20

5. Some thoughts on boats as Bronze Age artefacts *Francis Pryor* 31

6. Round the headland or over the horizon? An examination of evidence for British prehistoric efforts to construct a seaworthy boat *Owain Roberts* 35

7. North-west European seagoing boats before AD 400 *Seán McGrail* 51

8. The use of half-scale model ships in archaeological research with particular reference to the Graveney, Sutton Hoo and Ferriby ships *Edwin Gifford and Joyce Gifford* 67

9. Dover to Bevaix, from the Middle Bronze Age to Gallo-Roman times, from lashing to nailing: a page of naval archaeology illustrated by the evolution of techniques, tools and the discovery of new materials *Béat Arnold* 82

10. The Humber, its sewn-plank boats, their contexts and the significance of it all *Robert Van de Noort* 90

11. A search for the prehistoric harbours of Kent *Keith Parfitt* 99

12. An environmental context for the Dover boat? *Mike Baillie* 106

13. Sea faring voyages and rock art ships *Kristian Kristiansen* 111

14. Social and religious perceptions of the ship in Bronze Age Northern Europe *Flemming Kaul* 122

15. Finding 'new' boats: enhancing our chances in heritage management, a predictive approach *Thijs Maarleveld* 138

16. Facing the sea in Bronze Age Norway: the ship, the sea and society *Frode Kvalø* 148

Foreword

Dr F H Panton CBE, Chairman, Dover Bronze Age Boat Trust

The discovery of the well preserved remains of a Bronze Age boat in Dover in 1992 was one of the most important post-war archaeological finds in Britain, and an event of national and international archaeological and historical significance. The boat, a stitched oak plank structure dated to 1550 BC, has been preserved and conserved by the Dover Bronze Age Boat Trust (DBABT), and is exhibited in a specially designed, multi award winning Gallery in the Dover Museum. Conservation was achieved in two and a half years by a hitherto untried process of impregnation of the timbers with soluble wax, followed by freeze-drying.

A full account of the discovery and treatment of the Boat, together with reports of studies by British experts on many aspects of the Boat and the light it sheds on the technology and life of the Bronze Age Community that built and used it, is in course of preparation under the aegis of English Heritage. In the meantime, to explore the impact of the boat on European Bronze Age studies, and also to mark the tenth anniversary of its discovery, the DBABT organised a two day Conference in Dover in 2002 on 'The Dover Bronze Age Boat in Context: Society and Water Transport in Prehistoric Europe'. Seventeen experts from six different European countries delivered an impressively wide range of papers, and the Conference was attended by some 130 people, including students and members of the community. The high quality and pertinence of the papers was such that the DBABT resolved that the proceedings of the Conference should be made available by publication to a wider audience, and we are grateful to Oxbow for the achievement of that in this collection of the contributions to the Conference.

I should also like to register our thanks to donors whose support made it possible to stage the Conference, namely, Pfizer Ltd, British Academy, Dover Harbour Board, P & O Stena Line, Kent County Council, Kent Archaeological Society, Hammond PLC, and Dover District Council.

1. The Dover boat ten years after its discovery

Peter Clark

The conference was held ten years and 33 days after Keith Parfitt made his dramatic discovery of the Dover Bronze Age boat; those exhausting days of sodden toil to excavate, record and salvage the vessel must rank as one of my fondest archaeological memories (Figs 1.1–1.5), and it was enormously heartening to see so many people from all over Europe come together to celebrate the tenth anniversary of the find.

In the decade following the discovery, we have studied the boat, conserved its fragile timbers, re-assembled the vessel in its multiple-award-winning gallery at Dover museum and written a detailed account of these activities (Clark 2004). From the earliest days of our endeavours to study the vessel, I was determined to do something more than simply produce a technical report on the hull itself. The boat was made and used by people living three and a half millennia ago, and it was to better understand these people, their society and the world they lived in that was as much a focus of the analysis team's work as the study of the vessel itself. That desire is, I hope, reflected in the splendid gallery at Dover museum and in the pages of the Dover boat monograph.

Whilst no other complex prehistoric sewn-plank boat has been found since 1992, our understanding of Middle Bronze Age society has been transformed over the last decade. A light has been turned on the world of the Dover boat, allowing a more sophisticated appreciation of that world and the boat's place in it than was possible when it was found.

First, our understanding of the chronology of the Bronze Age has become far more refined, largely through absolute dating and the increasing use of Bayesian statistics in calibration. This has allowed us not only to glimpse the fine grain of continuity and change during the period but also to allow more

Fig. 1.1 (far left) The first section of boat revealed at the base of the shaft for a pumping station. Note the gaping hole in the hull caused by machine damage.

Fig. 1.2 (left) The boat was cut into sections and lifted out by crane.

Fig. 1.3 A boat 'piece' immediately after lifting, undergoing initial cleaning and treatment prior to being immersed in a temporary water-filled holding tank.

Fig. 1.4 The excavation and recording of one end of the boat (probably the bow), revealed in the second shaft.

convincing temporal correlations between societies with different cultural expression across Europe.

Perhaps most importantly, new data have allowed the exploration of exciting and sophisticated models of explanation; the relationship between the sacred and the secular, monumentality, the perception of landscape and people's place within it, placed deposits and fragmentation, issues of gender and social organisation, economy and environment. More satisfying theories of people, their societies and the world they lived in have been mooted, often describing trajectories at odds with older chronological divisions based on the technology of material culture. Whilst debates will continue for years to come, the last decade has been a fascinating and exciting time for archaeologists in NW Europe, especially for students of the Bronze Age.

The boat itself can contribute to these broader discussions, offering a rare example of complex, large-scale and sophisticated woodworking that may stimulate further reflection on Middle Bronze Age society. In this short note I shall look briefly at how the Dover boat might contribute to our present understanding of social organisation in the Middle Bronze Age. We should note here, of course, that terms such as the 'Middle Bronze Age' are useful but imprecise labels. The beginning and end of the Middle Bronze Age were not precise, historical events but gradual processes of change that occurred in different places, at different times and with different duration. Thus the Dover boat, dated to 1575–1520 cal BC (Bayliss *et al* 2004), is considered to be of Middle Bronze Age date, whilst across the water in Pas-de-Calais, the triple enclosure at Frethun, dated to 1736–1466 cal BC (from an inhumation within the central ditch) is deemed to be of the Early Bronze Age (Bostyn *et al* 2000, 122).

Middle Bronze Age Settlement

First, then, we may wish to consider where the people who built and used the Dover boat lived, and how were their settlements were organised. For this, we shall have to look further afield than the immediate environs of Dover. Notwithstanding over 10 years of commercially funded archaeology in Kent, there is still very little evidence of middle Bronze Age settlement in the County. Little has changed since Tim Champion's survey in 1982, though one exception to this was the discovery in 2002 of a single Bonze Age roundhouse at East Valley Farm, just a few kilometres north east of Dover (Fig 1.6; Parfitt 2002; Parfitt and Corke 2003). The site overlooks a dry chalkland valley running down to the sea at Kingsdown. The house, slightly terraced into the valley side, was nearly 6 metres in diameter, with a ring of central post supports within an arc of paired stakeholes that presumably supported the outer wall of the building. Other

Fig. 1.5 (left) The end of the boat, after cleaning and recording, prior to dismantlement. The superb preservation of the timbers and toolmarks can clearly be seen on the inboard surfaces of the planks.

stakeholes outside this arc may have marked where the presumed pitched, thatched roof touched the ground. To the south-east was a porched entrance about 1m wide. It did not appear to be associated with any other building or structure, but this may be because only a small area was opened.

Similar examples of such roundhouses can be found throughout southern England, though they are often found in small groups and there are differences in the details of construction technique. At Varley Halls, near Brighton in East Sussex, four 'huts' of similar size to the St Margaret's example were set slightly terraced into the hillside, two with central support posts and lines of stakeholes marking the outer circuit of the hut wall within the terrace cut (huts 1 and 2; Greig 1997), though not as symmetrical and set in pairs. These stakeholes, as at St Margaret's, suggest the outer wall of the roundhouse was of wattle and daub construction; construction debris from the terrace of hut 3 suggested a similar arrangement here. The fourth hut appeared to be built in a different style, with no wattle wall adjacent to the terrace cut and perhaps a low masonry wall supporting the roof downslope, in the manner suggested for hut 4 at Black Patch, also in East Sussex (Drewett 1982, fig 12).

These four hut terraces, together with a rectilinear four-post structure (possibly a granary or helm; Gent 1983, 245–50; Zimmermann 1992), a pond and a number of ditches, appear to constitute a single settlement, possibly occupied by an extended family group with each structural element having a

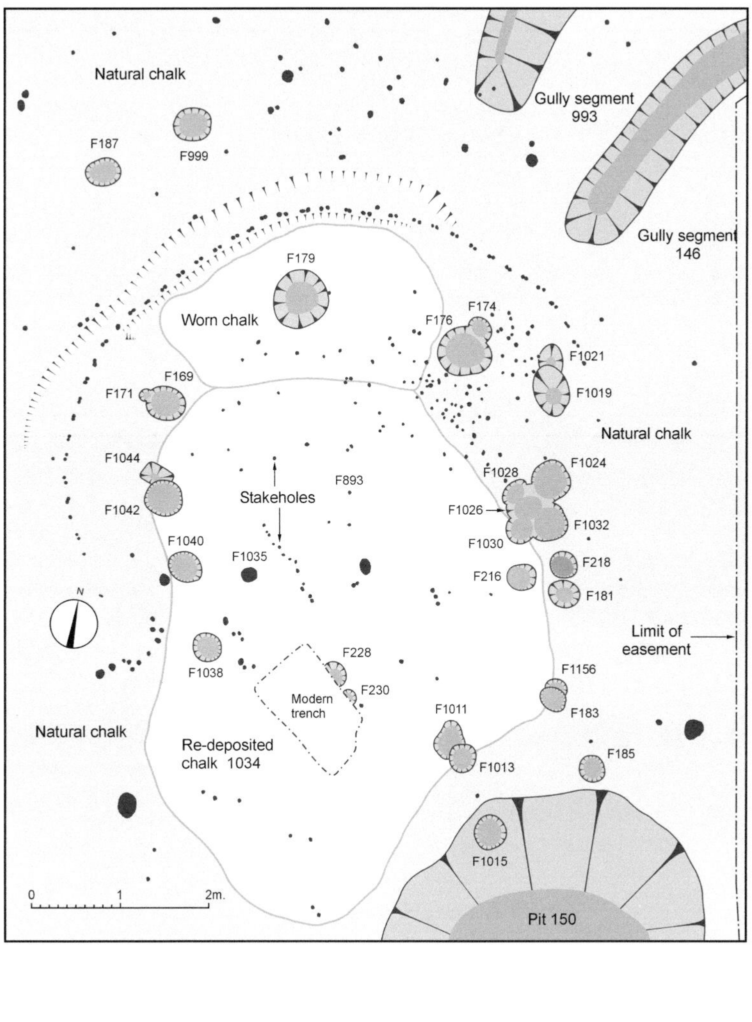

Fig. 1.6 (below) The Bronze Age house at East Valley Farm, St Margaret's-at-Cliffe.

different function. Similar small groups of roundhouses and associated features have been found across southern England, such as those at Black Patch (East Sussex; Drewett 1982), Chalton (Hampshire; Cunliffe 1970), Patcham Fawcett (East Sussex; Greatorex 2002; forthcoming), Downsview (East Sussex; Rudling 2002), Eldon's Seat (Dorset; Cunliffe and Phillipson 1968), Thorny Down (Wiltshire; Ellison 1987), Itford Hill (East Sussex; Burstow and Holleyman 1957; Ellison 1978; Holden 1972; Russell 1996), Mile Oak Farm (East Sussex; Russell 2002) and many others. Although constructional details and the number and disposition of the associated structural features vary, these small settlements, usually comprising a few roundhouses accompanied by a number of pits, a pond and perhaps one or two four-post structure, often set within an enclosure and associated field system, are typical of the middle Bronze Age and offer important insights into social structure at the time. Most sites appear to have been occupied for a limited period; Joanna Brück's analysis of 76 middle Bronze Age timber buildings suggested that some 75% showed no evidence for repair, refurbishment or rebuilding (Brück 1999, 146), and she has suggested that the settlements were 'single-generational', occupied by a small extended family and perhaps abandoned on the death of the 'head of the household'.

Social Hierarchies

Recent work on middle Bronze Age social structure has focussed on this model of small isolated settlements housing an extended family group with a somewhat peripatetic relationship with the landscape, moving on to a new settlement site with each generation. How does the Dover boat square with this model of social structure? Constructing the boat would involve a huge investment of labour and material; harvesting the raw materials, including at least two oak logs weighing 7.5 tonnes apiece, over a hundred yew withies, not forgetting the large quantities of moss and beeswax required to make the boat watertight would surely have been beyond the capability of a single family group. Estimates of the labour required to build the boat after harvesting this material vary from 250 to 600 person days (Darrah 2004; Goodburn 2004). Once built, the size and capacity of the boat would seem excessive for a single such settlement; it would require a crew or perhaps sixteen people, and be able to carry a cargo of up to three tonnes. Although we have no evidence for what kinds of cargo the Dover boat carried, it is widely assumed that bronze would have been carried, either as ingots or scrap metal for recycling. If, say, a third of its potential cargo was of bronze, this would constitute enough metal to manufacture 2,000 palstaves of the same type as was used to create the boat itself; surely more than enough for a single family group.

The boat therefore seems to imply that the small settlements we see in the archaeological record were articulated into higher level social groups that enabled the mobilisation of labour and the pooling and distribution of resources. We currently have little understanding of these higher level social groups; were they local communal arrangements negotiated through consensus and *ad hoc*, intermittent agreement? Or were territories controlled by ruling elites who wielded political power through the control of resources, including perhaps the knowledge of building sophisticated boats and the seamanship to navigate them across long distances? If so, there seems to be little trace of such a hierarchy expressed in the settlement evidence (though some potential candidates such as Rams Hill and others may be suggested towards the end of the 2nd Millennium BC; Bradley and Ellison 1975; Bradley 1986, 47; Needham and Ambers 1994).

There is, of course, plenty of archaeological evidence that these small family settlements worked together and were capable of undertaking large-scale communal projects. Looking first at the agricultural basis of the family settlements, it would appear that both arable farming and the exploitation of livestock were major factors in their subsistence strategy. But were these co-residential groups self sufficient in subsistence terms, or did they work together as part of a co-operative strategy of food production? Occasionally, considerable quantities of charred cereal grain have been recovered from storage pits associated with such settlements. At Black Patch, for example, a pit in Hut 3 (House Platform 4) contained around 2 million cereal grains (21kg, mostly barley), whilst in Hut 1 (House Platform 1) a pit was found to contain a similar quantity of charred grain (19.5kg), a mix of barley, wheat and beans (Hinton 1982, 387). A pit in Hut E (Enclosure IV) at Itford Hill, Sussex (Burstow and Holleyman 1957, 177) produced over 5kg of barley (about half a million grains, based on the Black Patch analysis). In 1970 Barry Cunliffe attempted to calculate the cereal production of a single such settlement by making a series of assumptions based on the capacity of three storage pits excavated at the middle Bronze Age site at Chalton, Hampshire (Cunliffe 1970, 12–13). The capacity of the pits totalled 1.5m^3 (53 cubic feet or 44 bushels). Assuming grain consumption of 0.4m^3 per year (based on Cato's figure for the intake of a Roman slave; Bowen and Wood 1968), Cunliffe suggested that the settlement could have supported a community of up to four individuals, 'the minimum figure one might expect for a family unit' (*ibid*, 12). He then adopts Bersu's assumed figures of an output of 1m^3 per Hectare (11 bushels per acre) and the need to store 33 percent of the grain above ground (Bersu 1940) to estimate the area of arable land associated with the settlement at 2.2Ha (5.5 acres) or 6.5Ha (16 acres) assuming a two-third fallow system was practised. This is an interesting avenue of supposition, though the relationship of the pits to the structures at Chalton is not unequivocal (Cunliffe 1970, fig 3) and there is no guarantee that they were in use at the same time. However, a similar approach might be adopted where there is a clear relationship between storage pits and roundhouses and a reasonable assumption that the pits were in use contemporaneously, as at Hut 3, hut platform 4 at Black Patch (Drewett 1982, 326, fig 4). Here three oval pits were set at the perimeter of the house, on the opposite side to the porched entrance. Calculations based on the capacity of these pits with an assumed density of grain and a revised estimate of grain yield from arable land might suggest some useful conjecture regarding the amount of arable land associated with each settlement (particularly when compared against any associated field system). We may thus gain some insight into whether each settlement was self-sufficient in grain production, or if some produced a surplus for redistribution.

Studies of animal bone, particularly from Varley Halls and Black Patch, suggest that there was some interdependency between these scattered family groups. At Varley Halls, situated close to a valley bottom that would provide sheltered grazing, the majority of animal bones were of mature cattle, suggesting that they were largely raised primarily for milk and perhaps additionally used as draught animals. However, they were chiefly represented by the skeletal extremities, suggesting on-site butchery with 'the remainder of the animal…taken to other sites on the downs, which were less suitable for cattle, with only a small proportion of the meat cuts retained for local consumption' (Greig 1997, 31). The majority of juvenile animals were of sheep or goats, perhaps suggesting that animals raised in settlements on higher ground were exchanged in the reverse direction. At Black Patch, an upland settlement, the cattle bones came from all parts of the skeleton, suggesting that these animals were slaughtered and consumed in the general vicinity of the site with no exportation of meat to other settlements. However the low numbers of bone at the site (187 identifiable fragments of domestic animals compared to nearly 800 at Varley Halls) led the excavator to suggest (as one explanation) that 'stock was kept on lowland pasture, slaughtered and jointed there, with only the meat being brought up to the settlement' (Drewett 1982, 341).

There is some suggestion, therefore, that these isolated settlements were not completely self-sufficient, but had some degree of interdependency, with settlements in lowland areas exploiting cattle and those in upland areas exploiting sheep or goats, and a reciprocal exchange of these animal products between them. Such an exchange may have been through trade or may indicate close familial ties or a political affiliation such as tribe, perhaps overseen by an elite individual or group.

We may also see evidence of higher level social organisation in the field systems that often surround these settlements. The development of large, co-axial field systems during the middle Bronze Age, with several separate blocks of fields laid out on the same alignment again indicates a higher level of social organisation than the extended family group, with the laying out and ordering of the agricultural landscape a communal endeavour undertaken by a number of neighbouring household settlements (Brück 2000, 290–291; Fowler 1983, 104; Yates 1999, 158–160). Similarly, the construction of monumental architecture, primarily the ubiquitous round barrows prevalent throughout southern Britain (Ashbee 1960; Ashbee and Dunning 1960) must have involved some communal mobilisation of labour to construct, even if it appears that they were related to individual domestic settlements over a relatively short period (namely the lifetime of a 'single-generational' settlement), as suggested at Itford Hill and elsewhere (Burstow and Holleyman 1957; Ellison 1980; 1981).

There are other indications that these individual domestic groups co-operated and worked communally; the importation and distribution of metalwork during the period must have been an enormous operation, judging by the apparent ubiquity of metal tools and the possibly associated decline of a developed stone tool technology during the second millennium BC (Clark 2004, 316–317; Rowlands 1976; Saville 1981), and one which of course necessitated contact with other communities at considerable distances.

We may therefore posit that there was a considerable degree of inter-group co-operation and communal endeavour during the middle Bronze Age, at a time when there seems little evidence of nucleated settlement or indeed of 'settlement hierarchy' whereby we might suggest 'central places' that might be interpreted as redistribution centres or foci of political power or the residences of a social elite. We do not appear to have a clear understanding of how this co-operation and communal effort was organised, or how it was regulated. Joanna Brück (2000) has argued compellingly for the 'fragmentation of society' during the middle Bronze Age, and this is clearly reflected in the archaeological record of southern Britain. She suggests that the mobilisation of communal labour and the inter-group co-operation implied by the archaeological record were articulated by 'inter-group alliances', 'reciprocal labour obligations between households…at certain times of the year' and 'the sharing of particular resources or facilities between several households' (Brück 2000, 290–291). It might be useful to develop these ideas further; different scales of co-operation (local, regional, inter-regional) may require different mechanisms of organisation; the perceptual horizons of a single domestic group may facilitate co-operation between a number of communities (perhaps linked by family ties) at the local scale, say to build a family tomb, but how were large scale, long distance communal activities negotiated? Is it necessary to posit a higher level political polity, a 'social elite' whose perceptual horizons were perhaps wider than the individual farming families in their scattered homesteads?

The need for Bronze

The Dover boat may have some contribution here. We have touched on the material and human resources required to construct it, and this investment of time and effort could no doubt be undertaken by an 'inter-group alliance', a number of neighbouring communities coming together to build the vessel. But there are other questions. Who would have commissioned its construction? Who would possess the skills to make what is an undeniably complex and sophisticated example of woodworking and nautical design? Who would possess the skills to navigate the vessel, and knowledge of the sea conditions it would encounter on its voyages? From where was its crew drawn? What kind of settlement would constitute its 'home base' (if indeed it needed any)? If it brought home cargoes of bronze and other 'exotic' goods, where were these unloaded and how were they distributed amongst the dispersed settlements of the middle Bronze Age landscape?

First, it is clear that there was substantial movement of large quantities of material over large distances during the middle Bronze Age (McGrail 1985; Muckelroy 1981; Scarre and Healey 1993). The raw materials for bronze, for example, are not to be found in south-east Britain, and need to be imported from the far west of Britain or from distant sources in Continental Europe, e.g. from eastern and southern Brittany or the Massif Central south of Argenton (Nash Briggs 2003, fig 1).

As has been suggested above and explored elsewhere in more detail (Drewett 1980; Drewett *et al* 1988, 87), these small domestic settlements were not self-sufficient, but worked together both as a subsistence strategy and in social terms, most evident in the realisation of large communal construction projects and in the securement and distribution of 'exotic' materials (particularly metal). Finds of bronze tools and scrap metal from British coastal waters such as Langdon Bay, Moor Sands and elsewhere have been interpreted as evidence for the importation of bronze to Britain from the Continent by sea (McGrail 1993; Muckelroy 1981; Needham and Dean 1987). Indeed, the small communities of southern Britain were linked by boat to communication networks that stretched across Europe, to the eastern Mediterranean and perhaps to North Africa. McGrail (1993) has suggested four principal sea routes from Britain to the western seaboard of continental Europe; from the Rhine to the Thames; from south-eastern Kent to Pas-de-Calais; mid-channel routes from Wessex to the estuaries of the Seine, Normandy and northern Brittany; and from the estuaries of the Loire and Garonne to south-western Britain and south-eastern Ireland via western Brittany. It seems likely that bronze was a major component of these long-distance connections, and the tin sources of western Britain and Ireland were hugely important to the bronze-using communities of Western Europe and beyond. Although bronze technology appears to have had its origins in Mesopotamia in about 3,700 cal BC and spread across Europe over the next two millennia, it appears very early in Britain (around 2,500–2,200 cal BC), perhaps suggesting an autonomous centre of innovation in these islands (Pare 2000, 25–27, fig 1.14). The consistency (in metallurgical terms) and widespread distribution of tinned bronze in the Early Bronze Age has led some to suggest that 'within Britain, we do seem to have a consistent, well-organized, long-distance tin movement dating to around 2200 BC' (McKerrel 1978, 11). In addition, the earliest evidence for a transition to 'full bronze use' is to be found in NW Europe, specifically the British Isles, from where it spread to Central and latterly Southern and Eastern Europe (Pare 2000, 27). This long-distance movement of material continued for several centuries until the latter part of the 2nd millennium BC, when there appears to be a decline in the activities of the British copper mines, and the increasing appearance of scrap metal in the archaeological record (Pare 2000, 29). This dramatic change in the composition of bronze hoards appears to occur across Europe (e.g. the 'Bühl-Ackenbach' horizon in Central Europe; Kimmig 1955; Mayer 1977; Rittershofer 1984), perhaps associated with a change in social structure and the adoption of a 'Weighed Currency Economy' (Pare 1999, 510–514).

Thus for the first half of the 2nd millennium BC the co-residential groups of southern Britain were linked through the exchange of copper and tin to extensive communication networks that stretched to the western British Isles and ultimately across Europe. Later, 'with the increased quantity of copper, tin and bronze which was now in circulation, it seems that the earlier high level long distance (directional) trade in copper and tin was undermined by a low-level short distance (down-the-line) exchange in scrap bronze' (Pare 2000, 29).

Whether long-distance, directional trade or short-distance down-the-line exchange (though we should be wary of such modern economic models to explain middle Bronze Age activities), such contact had to be made by boat. The shortest of McGrail's (1993) sea routes between Britain and the continental seaboard is that between East Kent and the Pas-de-Calais in northern France. Although there is no evidence as yet from France for prehistoric seafaring, we might suggest that landfall might be made on the broad beaches of Wissant, or perhaps even south of Cap Gris Nez at the mouths of the Rivers Canche or Authie, which further provide navigable routeways into the interior.

'The people of La Manche'

Recent excavation and survey work in Pas-de-Calais and Somme have revealed a number of Bronze Age sites with close parallels with southern British evidence, such as the great triple-ditched enclosure at Frethun (Bostyn *et al* 2000a), the roundhouses at 'le Chateau d'eau' just north of Roeux (Desfossés *et al* 2000), the ring ditch cemeteries at 'le motel', west of Fresnes-lès-Montauban (Desfossés and Masson 2000), 'la Frénésie' at Conchil-le-Temple (Piningre 1990) and Coquelles (Bostyn *et al* 2000b), the funerary ring ditch and enclosures at Étaples (Desfossés 2000) and the ubiquitous ring ditch cemeteries in the valley of the River Somme (Billand and Talon 2000) all suggesting a social structure very similar to that suggested for southern Britain. Indeed, it is not just the structural evidence that has similarities to British material; both ceramic material and metalwork recovered from these sites would not be particularly out of place if found in a British context.

Of particular interest to our subject is the great site of Étaples (Desfossés 2000). Situated near the mouth of the valley of the River Canche, an extensive settlement of Bronze Age date has been excavated in what is a natural port where marine currents from the south lead naturally to the southern British coastline.

In the earlier Bronze Age to the beginning of the middle Bronze Age, a huge oval enclosure ditch (Zone I), around 130m in diameter was constructed. Though heavily truncated, this seemed to be a large settlement, with many cut features in its interior that may relate to roundhouses, one clear example of which was found on the periphery of the site. It was replaced during the later middle Bronze Age by an even larger settlement enclosure (Zone II), around 160m in diameter, with ditches 4 to 5 metres wide and up to 2m deep. This may have been associated with a large funerary Ring Ditch (Zone III) lying to the north.

The circular house plan at Étaples is very familiar to students of the middle Bronze Age in southern Britain. But unlike the evidence for Britain, here there is a suggestion that they may have been concentrated in a large nucleated settlement; is this the settlement evidence for the 'higher level social groupings' that we have been looking for? Is this the kind of place that would commission a boat, where bronze, copper and tin would have been imported and redistributed to the more scattered settlements inland?

On either side of the English Channel we find strong similarities in the form of funerary monuments, house structures and in styles of pottery and metalwork. The French material recovered from along the coast ('l'entité culturelle d'affinité atlantique') contrasts sharply with that found further inland ('l'entité culturelle d'affinité continentale'; Billand and Tallon 2000). Indeed, the close affinities on either side of the channel have led many authors to suggest that there were very close and regular contacts across the sea (Brun 1990; Mohen 1968; Rowlands 1976, 152); rather than being a barrier, the sea was a 'pathway for ceaseless exchanges' (Briard 1965, 11). Some French scholars perceive the settlement at Étaples as a 'colony', and the development of the settlement as a response to 'implanting' a different cultural tradition (i.e. southern British) into an alien environment (Desfossés 2000, 186–187). However, the evidence suggests that this community of cultural expression existed for hundreds of years, and that such a cultural identity must have been maintained by regular social and economic intercourse by sea. We may therefore suggest that there was a higher level social grouping that straddled the channel, that rather than 'trade' or 'exchange' between different groups either side of the water they were a single 'people' or 'tribe' bound together by close social (perhaps familial) and economic relationships; 'the people of La Manche'. Whether the Dover boat is an example of one of the boats that maintained contact across the seas is moot, but it is clear that these journeys were made in a boat of some sort. Dover and Ferriby are all that we have (Clark 2004; Wright 1990).

So we seem to have evidence of a community with similar cultural expression in terms of funerary and domestic architecture, ceramic and metal artefacts, lying on both sides of the English Channel, stretching inland from the coasts and seemingly existing for many centuries. At Étaples we may for the first time be seeing a complex, nucleated settlement of small round houses that as yet has not been found on this island, but may reflect the settlement evidence of higher level polities in the middle Bronze Age.

If further research can help confirm the existence of a maritime community along the lines of 'the people of La Manche', this will help inform a more general understanding of the social structure of middle Bronze Age society. In addition, it would provide an important, if indirect, insight into the range and capabilities of water transport during this period. The journey from Dover to Étaples (ignoring the effects of current and tide) is around 30 nautical miles (55km). From Dover to Roeux, some 75 nautical miles (140km); there is some suggestion that the possible territory of this maritime community extended further to south into Normandy and northern Brittany (Briard and Nicalardot 1985; Yves Desfossés *pers. comm.*), and to the north, into the Low Countries, requiring voyages of even greater length.

What is perhaps significant here is that we are not suggesting occasional, intermittent contact by sea, but rather regular, routine contact between members of an extended community with a strong social identity. How regular is 'regular' is, of course, another matter (Clark forthcoming a). In addition, there is evidence that longer journeys were made, perhaps reflecting contact between other wider level communities.

Distant Contacts

At the ring ditch cemetery at Monkton-Mount Pleasant on the Isle of Thanet, one of the Ring Ditches (Ring Ditch X) offered a surprise for the excavators (Clark forthcoming b). Most of the fills of the ring ditches were largely devoid of finds, despite the total excavation of ditches. However, the policy of total excavation (as opposed to partial sampling of the ditches) was to prove worthwhile. Lying in a secondary fill of Ring Ditch X was the largely complete, though fragmented, remains of a large Trevisker urn, which was radiocarbon dated to around 1600–1320 cal BC (Gibson *et al* 1997; Gibson forthcoming). The vessel (now undergoing restoration by UCL) was originally 0.6m high with a rim diameter of 275mm, with a capacity of over 30 litres (about 7 gallons). It had been brought to Thanet from Cornwall, in the south-west of Britain. The most obvious method of transporting such a large, fragile and cumbersome object over such a distance would be by sea; the date of the pottery vessel corresponds well with the date of our wooden vessel.

Fig. 1.7 The Ringlemere gold cup.

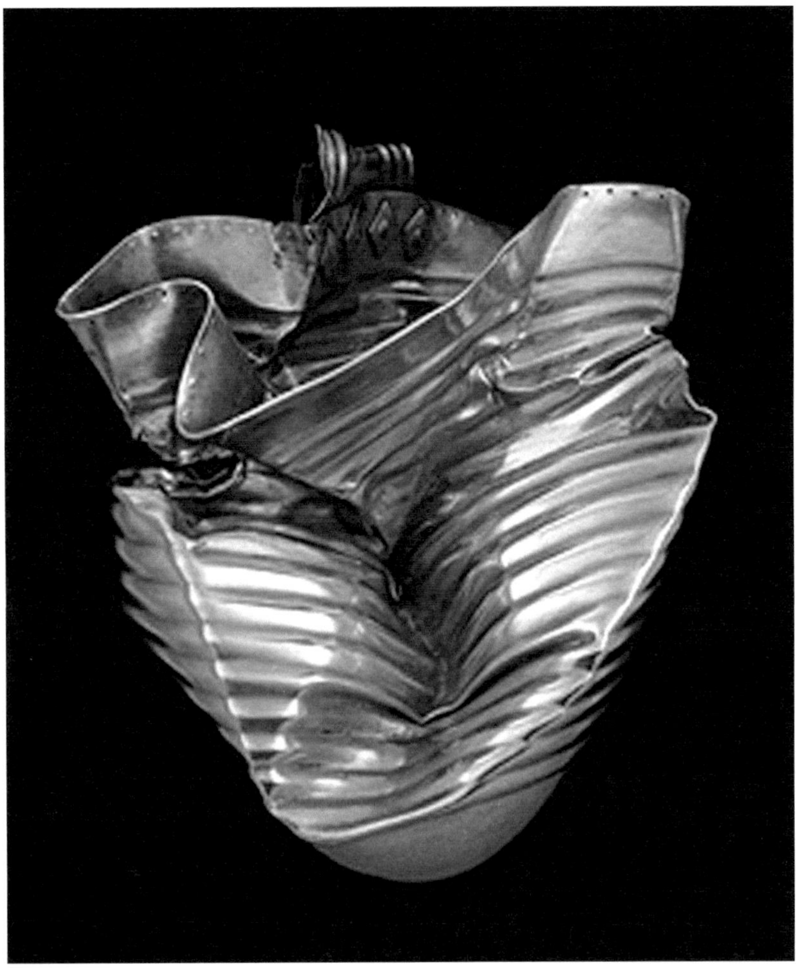

Just 25 km to the south, a small piece of unworked shale was found on the inboard surface of the Dover boat, which on laboratory analysis proved to originate from Kimmeridge Bay, on the central southern coast of Britain (Bown *et al* 2004). Whether this was a vestige of the boat's original cargo or not, it is further evidence that goods were transported considerable distances during the middle Bronze Age.

Dover to Kimmeridge is about 120 nautical miles (220km); the Trevisker urn must have been transported nearly 250 nautical miles (465km) to its final resting place. Of course such journey could have been made hugging the coast, whereas other archaeological evidence suggests longer journeys over open sea. To what extent this was intermittent contact is moot, but clearly the reality of long sea journeys was not alien to the people of the middle Bronze Age.

Another burial mound at Ringlemere in East Kent, about 15km north of Dover, was the find spot of further evidence of long-distance European contacts (Fig 1.7; Parfitt 2003). In 2001 a local metal detectorist recovered a Bronze Age gold cup, dated to 1700–1500 cal BC and one of only five previous findings in Europe, including Rillaton in Cornwall (held at the British Museum; Ashbee 1960, 117–18; Grinsell 1953, 125–6; Smirke 1867), Fritzdorf in Germany (Ashbee 1960; Piggott 1965, 134; von Uslar 1995), Eschenz in Switzerland (Ashbee 1977; Hardmeyer u. Burgi 1975; Kinnes 1975), and from Golenkamp in north-west Germany (Ashbee 1977, 157), though part of a gold cup has also been found at Ploumilliau, Cotes-du-Nord, Brittany (Briard 1965, 75–77).

Further east, a remarkable object discovered in 1999 (recently radiocarbon dated to around 1600 cal BC, approximately the same age as the Dover boat) gives us a further glimpse of the sophistication

Fig. 1.8 The 'Himmelscheibe' *(Sky Disc) from Mittelburg, near Nebra in Eastern Germany; diameter 320mm.*

and geographical contacts of the people of the middle Bronze Age (Meller 2002). The Nebra Sky Disc, found at the Bronze Age site of Mittelburg, near Nebra in Eastern Germany, is 320mm in diameter, and bears the images of the sun (or full moon), 32 stars and a crescent moon embossed on the disc and covered with gold leaf (Fig 1.8). One cluster of star symbols is thought to represent the Pleiades star cluster, which appear at the time of the autumn equinox.

Mittelburg Hill, 252m high and around 1000m in diameter is currently being excavated by Harald Meller from the Institute for Archaeological Research University in Halle who has suggested the site is an important religious or symbolic site. Opposing edges of the disc are highlighted with arcs of gold leaf, which are thought to mark the arc on the horizon separating sunrise and sunset on 21st June and 21st December.

Of interest to us here, though, is what appears to a boat symbol, again marked out with gold leaf, familiar from many depictions on other portable artefacts from northern Europe, and though to be a highly important religious symbol in Bronze Age religion. Some have suggested (with good cause) that this iconography ultimately derives from the religion of the Eastern Mediterranean and perhaps ancient Egypt (Kaul 1998, 277–284; this volume; Kristiansen 2001; this volume).

From the isolated extended families in scattered farmsteads of southern Britain we have moved to an extended community connected by the waters of La Manche, long distance transportation of goods along the breadth of southern England, to cultural similarities southwards to the Alps, northwards to Scandinavia, eastwards to Germany and ultimately to the eastern Mediterranean and North Africa. Of course, these contacts worked at very different levels and through very different mechanisms. Articulating the wider levels of social structure in the middle Bronze Age remains an exciting challenge for the next ten years.

List of references

Ashbee, P 1960 The *Bronze Age round barrow in Britain*, London: Phoenix House

Ashbee, P 1977 'The Gold Cups from Rillaton, Fritzdorf and Eschenz', *Cornish Archaeology*, **16**, 157–159

Ashbee, P and Dunning, G 1960 'The round barrows of east Kent', *Archaeologia Cantiana*, **74**, 48–57

Bayliss, A, Groves, C, McCormac, C, Bronk Ramsey, C, Baillie, M, Brown, D, Cook, G and Switsur, R 2004 'Dating', in P Clark (ed), *The Dover Bronze Age boat*, English Heritage, 250–255

Bersu, G 1940 'Excavations at Little Woodbury, Wiltshire', *Proceedings of the Prehistoric Society*, **6**, 30–111

Billand, G and Tallon, M 2000 *Nécropoles de l'Âge du Bronze: Rue (Somme) et Thourotte (Oise)*, Archaéologie en Picardie, Amiens: DRAC Picardie and l'Afan Nord-Picardie

Bostyn, F, Blancquaert, G and Lanchon, Y 2000a 'Les enclose funéraires de l'Âge du Bronze de Coquelles 'R.N. 1' (Pas-de-Calais)', *Habitats et Nécropoles à l'Âge du Bronze sur le Transmanche et le T.G.V. Nord*, Société Préhistorique Française Travaux I, Joué-lès-Tours: La Société Préhistorique Française et l'Association pour les Fouilles Archéologiques Nationales (A.F.A.N.), 129–144

Bostyn, F, Blancquaert, G and Lanchon, Y 2000b 'Un enclos triple du Bronze ancient à Frethun (Pas-de-Calais)', *Habitats et Nécropoles à l'Âge du Bronze sur le Transmanche et le T.G.V. Nord*, Société Préhistorique Française Travaux I, Joué-lès-Tours: La Société Préhistorique Française et l'Association pour les Fouilles Archéologiques Nationales (A.F.A.N.), 109–128

Bowen, H and Wood, P 1968 'Experimental storage of corn underground and its implications for Iron Age settlements', *Bulletin of the Institute of Archaeology*, **7**, 1–14

Bown, P. Bristow, C and de Silva, N 2004 'The shale', in P Clark (ed), *The Dover Bronze Age boat*, English Heritage, 216

Bradley, R 1986 'The Bronze Age in the Oxford area – its local and regional significance', in G Briggs, J Cook and T Rowley (eds), *The Archaeology of the Oxford Region*, Oxford: Department for External Studies, 35–48

Bradley, R and Ellison, A 1975 *Rams Hill: a Bronze Age defended Enclosure and its Landscape*, British Archaeological Reports (British Series), **19**, Oxford

Briard, J and Nicolardot, J-P 1985 'Un habitat de hauteur côtier de l'Age du Bronze en Bretagne: La Grosse Roche a Saint-Jacut-de-la-Mer', in D Spratt and C Burgess (eds), *Upland Settlement in Britain*, British Archaeological Reports (British Series), **143**, 365–374

Briard, J 1965 *Les dépôts Bretons et l'âge du bronze atlantique*, Travaux du Laboratoire d'Anthropologie Préhistorique de Rennes, Rennes: Faculté des Sciences de Rennes, Centre National de la Recherche Scientifique

Briard, J 1978 'Das Silbergefass von Saint-Adrien, Cotes-du-Nord', *Archaeologisches Korrespondenzblatt*, **8**, 13–20

Brück, J 1999 'Houses, lifecycles and deposition on Middle Bronze Age settlements in southern Britain', *Proceedings of the Prehistoric Society*, **65**, 145–66

Brück, J 2000 'Settlement, landscape and social identity: the Early-Middle Bronze Age transition in Wessex, Sussex and the Thames Valley', *Oxford Journal of Archaeology*, **19/3**, 273–300

Brun, P 1990 'Le Bronze Atlantique et ses subdivisions culturelles: essai de définition', in C Chevillot and A Coffyn (eds), *L'Âge du Bronze Atlantique: ses faciés, de l'écosse a l'andalousie et leurs relations avec le Bronze Continental et la Méditerranée*, Actes du 1er colloque du parc archéologiques de Beynac, 11–24

Burstow, G and Holleyman, G 1957 'Late Bronze Age settlement on Itford Hill, Sussex', *Proceedings of the Prehistoric Society*, **23**, 167–212

Champion, T 1982 'The Bronze Age', in P Leach (ed), *Archaeology in Kent to AD 1500*, Council for British Archaeology Research Report, **48**, 31–9

Clark, P (ed) 2004 *The Dover Bronze Age boat*, English Heritage

Clark, P forthcoming a 'Shipwrights, sailors and society in the Middle Bronze Age of NW Europe', in D Croes (ed), *Wet Sites Connections: Linking Indigenous Histories, Archaeology,and the Public,* 10th International Wetland Archaeology Research Project (WARP) Conference

Clark, P (ed) forthcoming b *Monkton–Mount Pleasant: Prehistoric, Roman and medieval discoveries on the Isle of Thanet 1994–95*

Cunliffe, B 1970 'A Bronze Age settlement at Chalton, Hampshire (site 78)', *Antiquaries Journal*, **50**, 1–13

Cunliffe, B and Phillipson, D 1968 'Excavations at Eldon's Seat, Encombe, Dorset', *Proceedings of the Prehistoric Society*, **34**, 191–237

Darrah, R 2004 'Woodland management and timber conversion', in P Clark (ed), *The Dover Bronze Age boat*, English Heritage, 106–123

Desfossés, Y (ed) 2000 *Archéologie Préventive en Vallée de Canche: Les sites protohistoriques fouilles dans le cadre de la réalisation de l'autoroute A16*, Nord-Ouest Archaéologie, **11**

Desfossés, Y and Masson, B 2000 'Les enclos funéraires du 'Motel' à Fresnes-lès-Montauban (Pas-de-Calais)', *Habitats et Nécropoles à l'Âge du Bronze sur le Transmanche et le T.G.V. Nord*, Société Préhistorique Française Travaux I, Joué-lès-Tours: La Société Préhistorique Française et l'Association pour les Fouilles Archéologiques Nationales (A.F.A.N.), 19–58

Desfossés, Y, Martial, E and Vallin, L 2000 'Le site d'habitat du Bronze Moyen du 'Château d'eau' à Roeux (Pas-de-Calais)', *Habitats et Nécropoles à l'Âge du Bronze sur le Transmanche et le T.G.V. Nord*, Société Préhistorique Française Travaux I, Joué-lès-Tours: La Société Préhistorique Française et l'Association pour les Fouilles Archéologiques Nationales (A.F.A.N.), 59–108

Drewett, P 1980 'Black Patch and the Later Bronze Age in Sussex', in J Barrett and R Bradley (eds), *Settlement and society in the British Later Bronze Age*, British Archaeological Reports (British Series), **83**, 377–396

Drewett, P 1982 'Late Bronze Age downland economy and excavations at Black Patch, East Sussex', *Proceedings of the Prehistoric Society*, **48**, 321–400

Drewett, P, Rudling, D and Gardiner, M 1988, *The South-East to AD 1000*, Longman

Ellison, A 1978 'The Bronze Age of Sussex', in P Drewett (ed), *Archaeology in Sussex to AD 1500*, Council for British Archaeology Research Report, **29**, 30–37

Ellison, A 1980 'Deverel-Rimbury urn cemeteries: the evidence for social organisation', in J Barrett and R Bradley (eds), *Settlement and society in the British Later Bronze Age*, British Archaeological reports (British Series), **83**, 115–126

Ellison, A 1981 'Towards a socio-economic model for the Middle Bronze Age in Southern England', in I Hodder, G Isaac and N Hammond (eds), *Patterns of the Past: Studies in Honour of David Clarke*, Cambridge: Cambridge University Press, 413–438

Ellison, A 1987 'The Bronze Age settlement at Thorny Down: pots, postholes and patterning', *Proceedings of the Prehistoric Society*, **53**, 385–392

Gent, H 1983 'Centralised storage in Later Prehistoric Britain', *Proceedings of the Prehistoric Society*, **49**, 243–267

Gerloff, S 1975 *The Early Bronze Age Daggers of Great Britain and a reconsideration of the Wessex Culture,* Munchen

Gibson forthcoming 'The imported Cornish vessel', in P Clark (ed), *Monkton–Mount Pleasant: Prehistoric, Roman and medieval discoveries on the Isle of Thanet 1994–95*

Gibson, A, Macpherson-Grant, N, and Stewart, I 1997 'A Cornish vessel from farthest Kent', *Antiquity*, **71**, 438–41

Goodburn, D 2004 'Assembly and Construction Techniques', in P Clark (ed), *The Dover Bronze Age boat*, English Heritage, 124–162

Greatorex, C 2002 'Appendix 3: Excavations at Patcham Fawcett: A summary', in D Rudling (ed), *Downland settlement and land-use: The archaeology of the Brighton Bypass*, UCL Field Archaeology Unit Monograph No 1, Institute of Archaeology, University College London, Glasgow: Archetype and English Heritage, 271–276

Greatorex, C forthcoming *The excavation of a Bronze Age downland settlement site at Patcham Fawcett School, Carden Avenue, Brighton, East Sussex*, 1993–1994

Greig, I 1997 'Excavation of a Bronze Age settlement at Varley Halls, Coldean Lane, Brighton, East Sussex', *Sussex Archaeological Collections*, **135**, 7–58

Grinsell, L 1953 *The Ancient British Burial Mounds of England*, London

Hardmeyer u. Burgi, J 1975 'Der Goldbecher von Eschenz', *Zeitschrift fur Schweitzerisches Archaeologie u. Kuntstgeschichte,* **32**, 109–120

Hinton, P 1982 'Carbonised seeds', in P Drewett, 'Late Bronze Age downland economy and excavations at Black Patch, East Sussex', *Proceedings of the Prehistoric Society*, **48**, 382–390

Holden, E 1972 'A Bronze Age cemetery-barrow on Itford Hill, Beddingham, Sussex', *Sussex Archaeological Collections*, **110**, 70–117

Kaul, F 1998: *Ships on Bronzes. A study in Bronze Age Religion and Iconography*, Publications from the National Museum, Studies in Archaeology and History Vol. 3:1 and 3:2, Nationalmuseet, Copenhagen

Kimmig, W. 1955 'Ein Hortfund der frühen Hügelgräberbronzezeit von Ackenbach, Kr. Überlingen', *Jahrbuch des Römisch-Germanischen Zentralmuseums*, **2**, 55–75

Kinnes, I 1975 'A Gold Beaker from Switzerland', *Antiquity*, **49**, 132–133

Kristiansen, K 2001 'Rulers and Warriors: Symbolic Transmission and Social Transformation in Bronze Age Europe', in J Haas (ed), *From Leaders to Rulers. Fundamental Issues in Archaeology*, Kluwer Academic/ Plenum Publishers, 85–104

Mayer, E F 1977 'Die Äxte und Beile in Österreich', *Prähistorische Bronzefunde*, **9**, 9, München, 66–71

McGrail, S 1985 'Early landing places', in A Herteig (ed), *Conference on waterfront archaeology in North European towns, No 2, Bergen 1983*, Bergen: Historisk Museum, 12–18

McGrail, S 1993 'Prehistoric seafaring in the Channel', in C Scarre and F Healey (eds), *Trade and Exchange in Prehistoric Europe: Proceedings of a Conference held at the University of Bristol, April 1992*, Oxbow Monograph **33**, Oxford: Oxbow Books in association with The Prehistoric Society and the Société Préhistorique Française, 199–210

McKerrel, H 1978 'The use of tin-bronze in Britain and the comparative relationship with the Near East', in A Franklin, J Olin and T Wertime (eds), *The search for ancient tin*, Washington DC: Smithsonian Institute Press, 7–24

Meller, H 2002 'Die Himmelscheibe von Nebra', *Archäologie in Sachsen-Anhalt*, **1**, Halle, 7–20

Mohen, J 1968 'Bronzes protohistoriques de Paris et sa région au Musée de l'Armée (Invalides)', *Bulletin de la Société Préhistorique Française*, **65**, 119–816

Muckelroy, K 1981 'Middle Bronze Age trade between Britain and Europe: A maritime perspective', *Proceedings of the Prehistoric Society*, **47**, 275–297

Nash Briggs, D 2003 'Metals, salt, and slaves: economic links between Gaul and Italy from the eighth to the late sixth centuries BC', *Oxford Journal of Archaeology*, **22/3**, 243–260

Needham, S and Ambers, J 1994 'Redating Rams Hill', *Proceedings of the Prehistoric Society*, **60**, 225–243

Needham, S and Dean, M 1987 'La Cargaison de Langdon Bay à Douvres', Actes du Colloque de Bronze de Lille – R. A. P./S. P. F.

Pare, C 1999 'Weights and weighing in Bronze Age Central Europe', in *Eliten in der Bronzezeit. Ergebnisse zweier Kolloquien in Mainz und Athen*, Monographien des Römisch-Germanischen Zentralmuseums, **43**, Mainz: RGZM, 421–514

Pare, C 2000 'Bronze and the Bronze Age', in C Pare (ed), *Metals make the world go round: The supply and circulation of metals in Bronze Age Europe. Proceedings of a conference held at the University of Birmingham in June 1997*, Exeter: Oxbow Books, 1–38

Parfitt, K 2002 *Excavations at East Valley Farm, St Margaret's-at-Cliffe, Kent*, unpublished archive report, Canterbury Archaeological Trust

Parfitt, K 2003 'Ringlemere Farm, Woodnesborough', *Canterbury's Archaeology*, **26**, Ashford: Canterbury Archaeological Trust, 34–35

Parfitt, K and Corke, B 2003 'The Deal–Dover bulk supply water-main', *Canterbury's Archaeology*, **26**, Ashford: Canterbury Archaeological Trust, 35–36

Piggott, S 1965 *Ancient Europe,* Edinburgh

Rittershofer, K F 1984 'Der Hortfund von Bühl und seine Beziehungen', *Bericht der Römisch- Germanischen Kommission 1983*, **64**, 139–415

Rowlands, M 1976 *The production and distribution of metalwork in the Middle Bronze Age in southern Britain*, British Archaeological Reports (British Series), **31**, Oxford

Rudling, D 2002 'Excavations adjacent to Coldean Lane', in D Rudling (ed), *Downland settlement and land-use: The archaeology of the Brighton Bypass*, UCL Field Archaeology Unit Monograph No 1, Institute of Archaeology, University College London, Glasgow: Archetype and English Heritage, 141–201

Russell, M 1996 *A reassessment of the Bronze Age cemetery-barrow on Itford Hill, East Sussex, and its place in the prehistory of southeastern England*, Bournemouth University School of Conservation Sciences Research Report, **2**, Bournemouth: Bournemouth University

Russell, M 2002 'Excavations at Mile Oak Farm', in D Rudling (ed), *Downland settlement and land-use: The archaeology of the Brighton Bypass*, UCL Field Archaeology Unit Monograph No 1, Institute of Archaeology, University College London, Glasgow: Archetype and English Heritage, 5–81

Saville, A 1981 'Iron Age Flintworking – Fact or Fiction?', *Lithics: The Newsletter of the Lithics Studies Society*, **2**, 6–9

Scarre, C and Healey, F (eds) 1993 *Trade and Exchange in Prehistoric Europe: Proceedings of a Conference held at the University of Bristol, April 1992*, Oxbow Monograph **33**, Oxford: Oxbow Books in association with The Prehistoric Society and the Société Préhistorique Française

Smirke, E 1867 'Some account of the discovery of a gold cup in a barrow in Cornwall, AD 1837', *Archaeological Journa*l, **24**, 189–195

von Uslar, R 1955 'Der Goldbecher von Fritzdorf, bei Bonn', *Germania*, **33**, 319–323

von Uslar, R 1956 'Der vorgeschichtliche Goldbecher von Fritzdorf, Landkreis Bonn', *Rheinisches Jahrbuch*, **I**, 71–79

Wright, E 1990 *The Ferriby boats: Seacraft of the Bronze Age*, London: Routledge

Yates, D M 1999 'Bronze Age field systems in the Thames Valley', *Oxford Journal of Archaeology*, **18/2**, 157–170

Zimmermann, W 1992 'The 'helm' in England, Wales, Scandinavia and North America', *Vernacular Architecture*, **23**, 34–43

2. Evidence of a marine environment associated with the Dover boat

Christopher Green

Previous research

Whether the Dover boat was a sea-going vessel or not remains a matter of debate. The argument that it was intended solely as a river craft seems to have gained significant support from the palaeo-environmental evidence in the sediments on which the boat lay and by which it was enclosed. Marine indicators are almost entirely absent from this setting, and the final resting place of the boat was undoubtedly the floodplain or channel of a river, upstream of any tidal influence. However, in assessing the significance of this evidence, it is necessary to recognise the challenging circumstances in which the boat was discovered, the sediment sampling procedures that were possible in those circumstances and the aims of the subsequent palaeoenvironmental investigations.

Palaeoenvironmental studies concentrated on the depositional environment in which the boat was found. These studies, both of the sediments themselves and of their contained flora and fauna show that the setting is the product of river activity, and that the boat came to rest, or was emplaced, near the edge of a channel of the Bronze Age River Dour. Although the sea was at most a few kilometres away, there is almost no evidence of its proximity. A few plants that normally occupy coastal habitats are sparsely represented in the pollen flora, and the shells of marine molluscs, or their broken remains, occur in the sediment, but only rarely and not in typical faunal assemblages.

The possibility that physical traces of a sea-going past might still be associated with the boat does not seem to have been systematically explored. Such traces might be materials or organisms adhering to the timbers of the boat, or preserved in joints in its structure or cracks or other openings in its timbers. Bearing in mind the unknown lapse of time between any hypothetical sea-going use of the boat and its arrival at its final resting place, and bearing in mind also that it was affected by fluvial processes and processes of decay once it had been abandoned, traces of a marine context are likely to be small and patchily preserved.

When ArchaeoScape, based in the Geography Department at Royal Holloway, University of London, assumed responsibility, in 1997, for detailed sedimentological and stratigraphical investigations, the sample material still available that could be assigned to a context in contact with the boat's timbers was limited to one 0.5m column sample and one bulk sample. Both these samples came from sections in the northern coffer dam (Coffer Dam 1; Fig 2.1). The column sample (Monolith 10) was taken from Section 6 (S136) which formed the southern face of the excavation and exposed a

Fig. 2.1 The boat excavation; position of sections and sample positions.

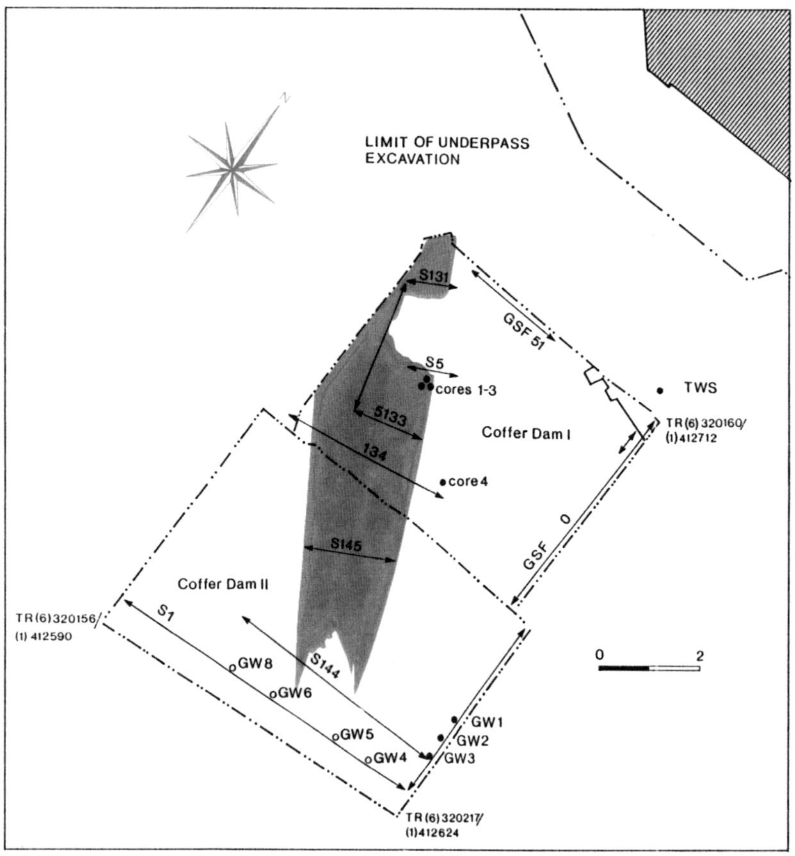

complete cross-section of the boat's remains. The column reached down to the inboard surface of the timbers forming the bottom of the boat. The bulk sample came from Context 4933 recorded in Section 4 (S134), which also exposed a cross section of the boat's remains (Fig 2.2), at a distance of *c.* 0.5m to the north of Section S136.

Context 4933

Context 4933 (Section S134) is the sediment resting directly on the inboard surface of the timbers forming the bottom of the boat. It extended across the boat as a layer nowhere exceeding 64.5mm in thickness. A similar (but un-numbered) context was present in Section 6 (S136).

A 0.5m column sample (M05) from Section 4 (S134) was examined by Bates and Williamson (1997) and the lowermost 65mm, equivalent to context 4933, was described by them as a sandy coarse silt. A sharp contact separated this unit from a darker overlying layer of coarse silt. This column sample was no longer available for inspection in 1997 but the basal lithostratigraphic unit in column sample M10 (S136) is closely similar and it seems reasonable to regard it as equivalent to archaeological context 4933. This unit, examined at Royal Holloway, consisted of a thickness of 68 mm of silty clay.

A sub-sample of sediment from context 4933 was also examined by Dr Enid Allison as part of her investigation (1998) of the insect faunas preserved in the sediments enclosing the boat. She described the sediment as clay silt.

In the present account the particular significance of the fine-grained character of the sediment forming context 4933 is the evidence it provides for quiet water deposition within the boat during the initial stages of burial. This contrasts with the evidence of sedimentation outside and adjacent to the boat where scouring appears to have taken place, undercutting the boat on its riverward side, and where much of the sediment around the boat is in the form of tufa gravels, indicating flow velocities greater than those affecting the inside of the boat. Thus in terms of the burial history of the boat, the inside is the more likely place for materials to be preserved that relate to its pre-burial history.

Sedimentology

No sedimentological investigations were undertaken that set out specifically to identify materials relating to the use of the boat prior to its arrival in the Dour valley, and adhering to or trapped among its timbers. More than 30 core and column samples were described, either by Bates and Williamson (1997) or in the ArchaeoScape studies, but the original sampling strategy provided few opportunities to examine material in immediate contact with the boat's timbers, and detailed attention was not particularly directed to these opportunities. The principal sedimentological evidence, outlined in this paper, that the boat had a sea-going history, comes from a more general study of the composition of sediments within and outside the boat. Over 2 tonnes of sediment were sieved by Dr Enid Allison and yielded just over 100kg of residue, mainly retained on a 5mm mesh. However, although this work contributed significantly to an understanding of the environment in which the boat was found, apart from the sub-sample from context 4933 (mentioned above), none of this material came from contexts adjoining the inboard surface of the boat's timbers.

In the less extensive investigation described in this paper, 8 samples from contexts both inside and outside the boat were wet sieved to 1mm, and the 1–2mm fraction was examined under a low power binocular microscope. This was not a quantitative study and the results were recorded in terms of presence or absence. In all samples the main components were tufa and flint together with particles of wood and pieces of terrestrial or freshwater mollusca. Other components present in some but not all samples included quartz, chalk, moss remains, seeds, charcoal and bone. While all the samples are broadly similar in character and can be explained almost entirely in terms of derivation within the catchment of the River Dour, the sample

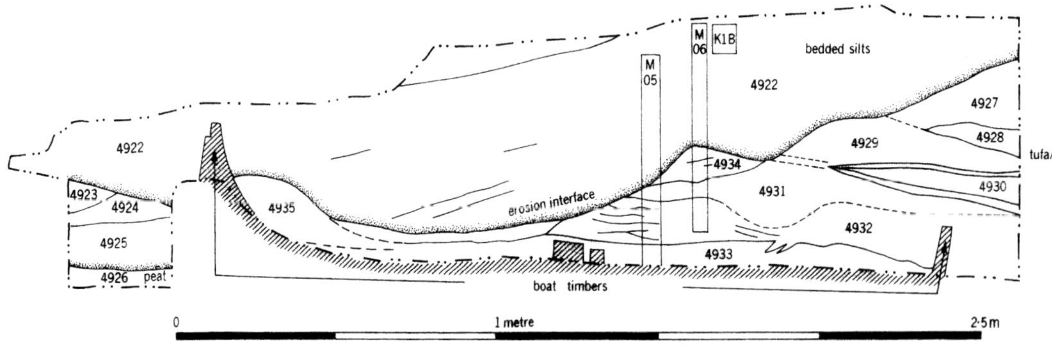

Fig. 2.2 The boat excavation; Section 134.

from context 4933 contained a distinctive and conspicuous assemblage of components that was not present in any of the other samples. This consisted of well rounded grains of glauconite, well-rounded and polished grains of quartz and well-rounded and polished particles of mollusc shell. These components are interpreted here as having been derived from marine beach sand that had been preserved on the inboard surface of the boat's timbers. This interpretation is based on the following evaluation of the nature and possible source of the distinctive components involved.

Marine shell

Particles of well-rounded and polished mollusc shell were present only in the sample taken from context 4933. They are unlike the shell remains of terrestrial or freshwater species and comprise pieces of thick-walled shell in which growth layers are recognisable. They have a slight iridescent sheen, typical of the shell of many marine species. They are unlikely to be the remains of large freshwater species as none is present in the mollusc fauna recovered from the sediments enclosing the boat, and none would normally be expected in a river as small as the Dour. The rounded and polished condition of the shell particles is also unlike that of the freshwater and terrestrial shell material in the samples, which is only lightly abraded and has a matt surface texture. Thus these distinctive particles appear to be the shell remains of marine species. Such material is often present in marine beach sand.

The shells of marine molluscs, or their broken remains, are present elsewhere in the sediments that enclose the boat. They are recorded from several of the bulk samples examined by Dr Allison, and marine shell was noted by the author in a column sample (M11) taken from the east side of Coffer Dam 2 (Section S143) at a distance of *c.* 2m from the boat. However, in no case is there any indication of a marine faunal assemblage, and where the probable species of the marine molluscs was recorded, they are edible species. It seems likely that this shell material is domestic waste, and this possibility is supported in the residues examined by Dr Allison, where marine shell is almost always associated with burnt flint, charcoal and probable flint debitage.

Glauconite

In the study described here, glauconite was recorded only in the sample from context 4933. There are no obvious sources of abundant glauconite in the basin of the River Dour. The bedrock underlying the entire catchment is the Chalk. Hancock (1975) notes that glauconite is present in the Chalk only in 'minute quantities' and he quotes figures from Weir and Catt (1965) recording 0.077 per cent as an exceptionally high content. Hancock (1975) states that 'greater quantities of glauconite occur very locally in hard-ground-chalks', but he does not say where or provide any quantitative data.

Despite this background, Bates and Williamson (1997) found glauconite in the sediments enclosing the boat. Altogether they recognised 183 litho-stratigraphic units but they recorded glauconite in only 17. In 16 cases the glauconite was described as 'rare' or 'very rare', but exceptionally in one unit it was estimated to form 5–10% of the sediment. Glauconite was not recorded by Bates and Williamson (1997) in the sands and gravels by which the boat was initially buried. All but two of the glauconite-bearing lithostratigraphic units were in the body of mainly silty sediment that overlay the sand and gravel that initially buried the boat. This silty sediment was deposited after erosion had partly removed the sand and gravel around the boat and had probably partly re-exposed the boat. The remaining glauconite-bearing units were in sediment beneath the boat.

Thus, although a source of glauconite is apparently present in the basin of the River Dour, glauconite was not found in the sediments that enveloped the boat, except in context 4933, immediately overlying the inboard surface of the boat's timbers. If, as is argued here, the glauconite in context 4933 originated not in the basin of the Dour but elsewhere in marine beach sand, a potential source is present only a few kilometres away near Fokestone where glauconite-bearing geological formations in the Lower Chalk and the Lower Cretaceous Greensands reach the coast.

Quartz

There are no obvious sources of abundant quartz in the basin of the Dour, but like glauconite it was recorded by Bates and Williamson (1997) as occasionally present in the sediment associated with the boat and it was present as a minor component in some samples examined in the present study. However, the quartz content of the sediment forming context 4933 is remarkable for the size, shape and surface texture of the grains, which, as noted above, are large, well-rounded and well-polished. Quartz having these characteristics was not noted in any of the samples examined in this study except the sample from context 4933. The shape and surface texture of the grains is typical of quartz that has been a component of marine beach sand.

Conclusion

Thus, in the sediment forming context 4933 there are three components that might be expected to occur in nearby marine beach sand. In this respect, context 4933 is unique among the sediments recorded around the Dover boat. The setting of this material, resting directly on the inboard surface of the timbers forming the bottom of the boat, suggests that it might represent traces of sediment adhering to the boat at the time that it came to rest in the valley of the Dour. It is not difficult to visualise that such components could have entered the boat while it lay on a sandy beach – possibly on the feet of people using the boat, possibly on cargo or equipment that had rested temporarily on the beach, perhaps only a few kilometres away near Folkestone. The quiet-water conditions that prevailed during the initial stages of sedimentation within the boat as it lay in the valley of the Dour would have particularly favoured the survival of such traces of a previous sea-going history.

List of references

Allison, E 1998 *The Insect Remains from the Dover Bronze Age Boat*, unpublished archive report, Canterbury Archaeological Trust

Bates, M R and Williamson, V D 1997 *A report on the stratigraphy associated with the Dover Bronze Age boat, excavation phases I and II*, Geoarchaeological Service Facility, GFS Technical Report 96.02 (unpublished report prepared for the Canterbury Archaeological Trust)

Hancock, J M 1975 'The petrology of the Chalk', *Proceedings of the Geologists' Association*, **86**, 499–535

Weir, A H and Catt, J A 1965 'The mineralogy of some Upper Chalk samples from the Arundel area, Sussex', *Clay Mineralogy*, **6**, 97–110

3. Reconstructing the Dover boat

Peter Marsden

One of the objectives of investigating the Dover boat has been to establish how and where it was used. This is not an easy task for the answer depends not only upon a reconstruction of the boat's structure, but also upon an understanding of the environmental circumstances in which it was found.

All that survived of the boat were its two flat bottom planks, the corner planks between the bottom and each side, and the lower part of one sloping end. The upper planking of the sides was missing, and the other end could not be excavated (Marsden 2004). Even before its missing timbers could be reconstructed it was necessary to establish the original form of the squashed and distorted planks (Darrah 2004).

It was a substantial vessel, about 2.25m wide and at least 14m long, and seemed to have been too large for use entirely in the shallow freshwater river in which it was found. Consequently, it seemed more likely that it was used at sea, but this required that it should be reconstructed with strengthening structures which were not found. It has been suggested that the boat originally had an upper plank on each side, a flat transom stern, was paddled by a crew possibly sitting on the gunwale, and was used on coastal routes at sea and might even have been used to cross the Channel (Roberts 2004).

As a member of the analysis team my task was to describe the boat as it was found, and as a result I studied each piece in very great detail. I came to know the skills of the boatbuilder very well and the process that he and his colleagues used to fashion the logs with axes, and to twist the stitches through holes at the plank edges. He was a clever man, who managed to create the most complex scarf between the bottom and the end that I have ever seen in any ancient vessel.

But doubts about its supposed primary use at sea have lingered on in my mind for the boat has all the characteristics of a punt-like river vessel of recent times. Moreover, it was found in a wholly freshwater river. Therefore, before considering adding hypothetical structure to the vessel, for which there is no evidence, so as to place it in a maritime environment, I feel that it is important to examine its use as primarily a river craft.

An enormous number of illustrations exist of similar eighteenth and nineteenth century punt-like river vessels, both ferries and working boats, with flat bottoms and sloping ends (e.g. Chaplin 1988, 40, 47, 66). Indeed, this form of river craft with sloping ends has one of the longest ancestries in Europe: Roman vessels are found at Zwammerdam, Netherlands (Weerd 1988, 155–161), and a gold model of an Iron Age boat of the fifth century BC has been found at Dürrnberg in Germany (McGrail 1987, 213).

The size of the Dover vessel is not necessarily a reflection of it having been used at sea, for size is also a feature of function – in this case perhaps as a ferry. The Later Bronze Age boat from Brigg, for example, was larger than the Dover boat, but it was found in the River Ancholme, a tributary of the Humber (Fig 3.1; McGrail 1981).

The Dover boat certainly has weaknesses that would make it dangerous to use on extended voyages at sea. Its bottom planks might pull apart in rough water, the wooden wedges holding them probably being insufficient as fastenings, particularly as the planks themselves evidently flexed along the centreline as is shown by the outboard wear only occurring on their outer longitudinal edges (Marsden forthcoming). Extra strengthening was certainly necessary if the boat was to be used at sea.

Had treenails been used to fasten the bottom planks to the 'transverse timbers', which might be termed embryonic frames, the bottom of the vessel would have been far stronger. Treenails and a flat transom stern could have been used in the Dover boat had the boatbuilder known of them, especially as treenails, stitches and a transom stern were used at a slightly later date in the Appleby dugout canoe from Lincolnshire (Fig 3.2; McGrail 1978, pt. 1, 147–8). This has been radiocarbon dated to 1525–1315 BC (95% probability; Switsur 1989, 1016). As far as I can tell this is the earliest dated use of either wooden nails or a separate transom found in Britain.

However, the absence of treenails in the Dover

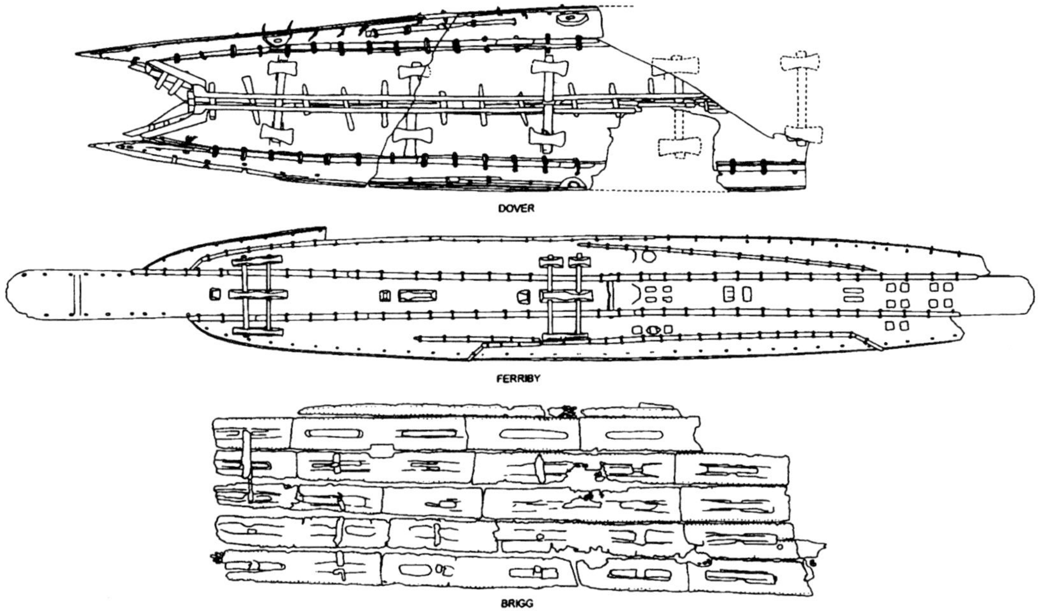

Fig. 3.1 Plans of Dover, Ferriby and Brigg boats for comparison.

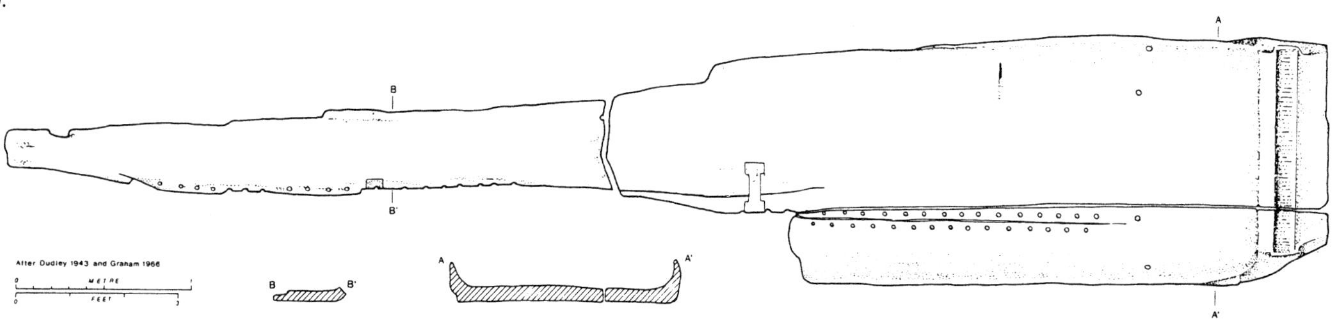

Fig. 3.2 The Appleby boat (from McGrail 1978, pt. 2).

boat suggests that the boatbuilder did not know of them, so to incorporate them in a reconstruction would probably be incorrect. The same might apply to a transom stern, and the unexcavated end could have been sloping like the discovered end, but would not be as strong as a transom. We should keep to what we know the boatbuilder used, otherwise we would break the rule that underlies all scientific modelling – that 'one should not make more assumptions than the minimum needed'. This rule propounded by the medieval English philosopher, William of Occam, is important since it separates fact from speculation – even though the latter may eventually be proved correct.

In spite of this, the primary reason for thinking that the Dover boat was seagoing is not so much based upon the boat, but rather upon its reconstructed environment – thought to have been a small shallow river. The fact is that the boat was found in the river, and that we know nothing of the width or length of the river or of the location of any of the Bronze Age settlements that presumably existed along its banks. Consequently, we cannot be sure that the boat was unsuited to that environment. But maybe it had a use carrying goods both in the river and on short trips along the coast to nearby communities.

In the discussion that followed my presentation Chris Green, who had undertaken the analysis of sediments in and around the boat, drew attention to an extremely important silt deposit, lying immediately on the bottom of the boat, which seems to reflect a sea trip. The sediment included marine shell fragments with unusually large amounts of quartz sand, and also grains of glauconite that are 'foreign' to the Dover area. These were presumably introduced from a marine beach whose nearest location is the glauconite-rich sediments of the Lower Cretaceous Greensands in the Folkestone – Hythe area about seven miles west of Dover. Small river valleys exist there also, and on their banks could have been Bronze Age settlements. We can therefore postulate that the Dover boat was used to carry goods and people on the day-long trip between communities in the Folkestone and Dover areas, enabling them to bypass the high chalk hills and sea cliffs between.

This crucial evidence has changed my understanding of the boat, and a combined river and local coastal use seems to me to fit the evidence. This would account for the boat's wide flat bottom, giving it a shallow draft for work in rivers; its sloping end giving easy access to river banks for loading and unloading; and its size enabling it to carry a substantial load. Longer voyages, particularly across the Channel to France, were probably out of the question unless the vessel had very substantial strengthening – for which there is no evidence.

Short calm-weather day-long sea and river trips of about six nautical miles (11km) between the Bronze Age communities at Dover and Folkestone may even help explain the curious diagonal wear marks on the outside of the boat. These suggest that sometimes the boat had been moored beside a stone quay and that waves had lifted the boat up and down and back and forth causing the score marks.

List of references

Chaplin, P 1988 *The Thames from source to tideway*, London: Whittet Books

Darrah, R 2004 'Illuminating the original shape of the Dover boat timbers', in P Clark (ed), *The Dover Bronze Age boat*, English Heritage, 46–105

Marsden, P 2004 'Description of the boat', in P Clark (ed), *The Dover Bronze Age boat*, English Heritage, 32–95

McGrail, S 1978 *Logboats of England and Wales*, British Archaeological Reports (British Series), **51**

McGrail, S 1981 *The Brigg 'Raft' and her prehistoric environment*, British Archaeological Reports (British Series), **89**

McGrail, S 1987 *Ancient boats in N. W. Europe*, London: Longman

Roberts, O 2004 'Reconstruction and Performance', in P Clark (ed), *The Dover Bronze Age boat,* English Heritage, 189–210

Switsur, R 1989 'Early English boats', *Radiocarbon*, **31**, 3, 1010–1018

Weerd, M de 1988 *Schepen voor Zwammerdam*, Haarlem

4. The legacy of Ted Wright

John Coates

This paper is offered in memory of Ted Wright (Fig 4.1) and in the spirit of his 1993 Festschrift (Coles *et al* 1993). Therefore, and with all acknowledgements to its editors, I quote from its very well expressed preface:

'Ted Wright's contribution to boat and wetland archaeology has been crucial to the development of new ideas and new projects over many years. Equally important is his enthusiasm for the subjects, infectious and always encouraging. Those who have been taken on a tour of the foreshore on the Humber at Ferriby are unlikely to forget that enthusiasm, nor their lost gumboots.'

I had the privilege of being so introduced by Ted to the mud of the Humber though I think I hung on to my boots.

Ted Wright's legacy extends over his wide interests which included geology, palaeontology, botany and archaeology, besides his wartime regiment, the East Riding Yeomanry, his company, Reckitt and Coleman, of which he was Overseas Director, the National Maritime Museum, of which he served as Trustee, and his family. He has been recognised as a pioneer of wetlands archaeology, particularly that of the Humber, but his main legacy which is of particular interest to this conference has sprung from his first discovery with his brother Claude, another amateur palaeontologist, of boat remains at North Ferriby as long ago as 1937. They were then relatively young lads (Ted was 19) but they had already been studying the shores of the Humber together for some years.

Fig. 4.1 Ted Wright, 1996.

In 1990 Ted published his book about these and later finds at Ferriby, entitled *The Ferriby Boats* (Wright 1990), now unfortunately out of print. The legacy of those finds is best described by him in its epilogue.

'The principal achievements of more than fifty years of work on the North Ferriby project are essentially three in number. Foremost is the discovery of a hitherto unknown school of boatbuilding practice, the possible ramifications of which in terms of origin, duration, and geographical distribution remain obscure. Second is the demonstration of a remarkable level of technical competence by people of the north-west European Bronze Age several centuries if not a millennium earlier than anything of the kind has been conceived as being within their capability. Third is the recognition of a realistic candidate in addition to hide boats or logboats for the carriage of cross-channel and coastal traffic from the Middle Bronze Age down to the prehistoric Iron Age before it can be presumed that any vessel of comparable capability became available.

While these gains may justly be claimed on the credit side, it must also be admitted that the programme has been dogged with misfortunes over the recovery and conservation of the remains of the boats themselves. Happily, as can be seen from this account, little of the essential information has been lost, the only real problem being to convey adequately the astonishing intricacy and craftsmanship revealed when the finds were first exposed. The difficulty is underlined by the fact that in the years since they were first published several authors have introduced deliberate crudity into copies of my earlier reconstructions, thus conveying a wrong impression of the skills of the boatbuilders of the period.

I trust that the contents of this book will counteract any such tendency. I also hope that its publication will lead on to the construction of a full-sized working replica and that theories can be tested in practice so as to reveal the true skills of the Bronze Age people of North Ferriby as shipwrights and seamen.'

That discovery was pioneering indeed, and it has not been without controversy as Ted politely indicated in his book. Controversy generated by his finds is not yet resolved, as may be clear from what Dr Gifford and I have yet to say here at Dover. Twelve years after the book and, regrettably, after Ted's death, there is something to report about reconstructing a Ferriby ship. Though so far called a boat, its dimensions, capability and provenance now known to be as early as in the third millennium BC should surely qualify it for that appellation, being as large as several of the Skuldelev 'ships' (Crumlin-Pedersen and Olsen 2002; Olsen and Crumlin-Pedersen 1958; 1967).

The first discovery at Ferriby (Fig 4.2) was made long before archaeology had, as it were, got its feet wet. University and then the Second World War interrupted Ted Wright's proper examination of the remains *in situ*. As a pioneer of archaeology below high water, he had for many years to be the keeper and guardian of his discovery with little support. In those circumstances of nascent understanding and some consequent indifference on the part of the archaeological and the nautical research establishment of the time, it is not perhaps surprising that he came to be regarded by some as being rather obsessive about Ferriby. Nautical and even estuarine archaeology were not to get going or attract much attention until modern diving gear became generally available. Also, in the absence of radiocarbon dating, there was no way of dating the remains which were consequently rather vaguely guessed to be Tudor, Roman or possibly Iron Age. Also absent then were any means of preserving waterlogged wood, so, after being extracted (Fig 4.3) from their stiff, glutinous, soon puddled, and regularly flooded beds, timbers soon dried and disintegrated. Some were even burnt in a wartime air-raid on Hull. It was all hard going but Ted did not give up and by his study during the rest of his life of the depositional structure of the site, of the tools needed to build the boats, and of parallels in known ancient boatbuilding elsewhere, he formed the considered but then generally disbelieved view that the Ferriby ships were fully developed well before the end of the third millennium BC. He has now been proved right.

His comprehensive book constitutes virtually the whole record of the boat finds at Ferriby after the loss by decay and war of the remains themselves. By 1990, radio-carbon dating of the Ferriby finds

Fig. 4.2 Simplified plan-view of Fs 1, 2, and 3 in their correct relative positions. Drawing: E V Wright.

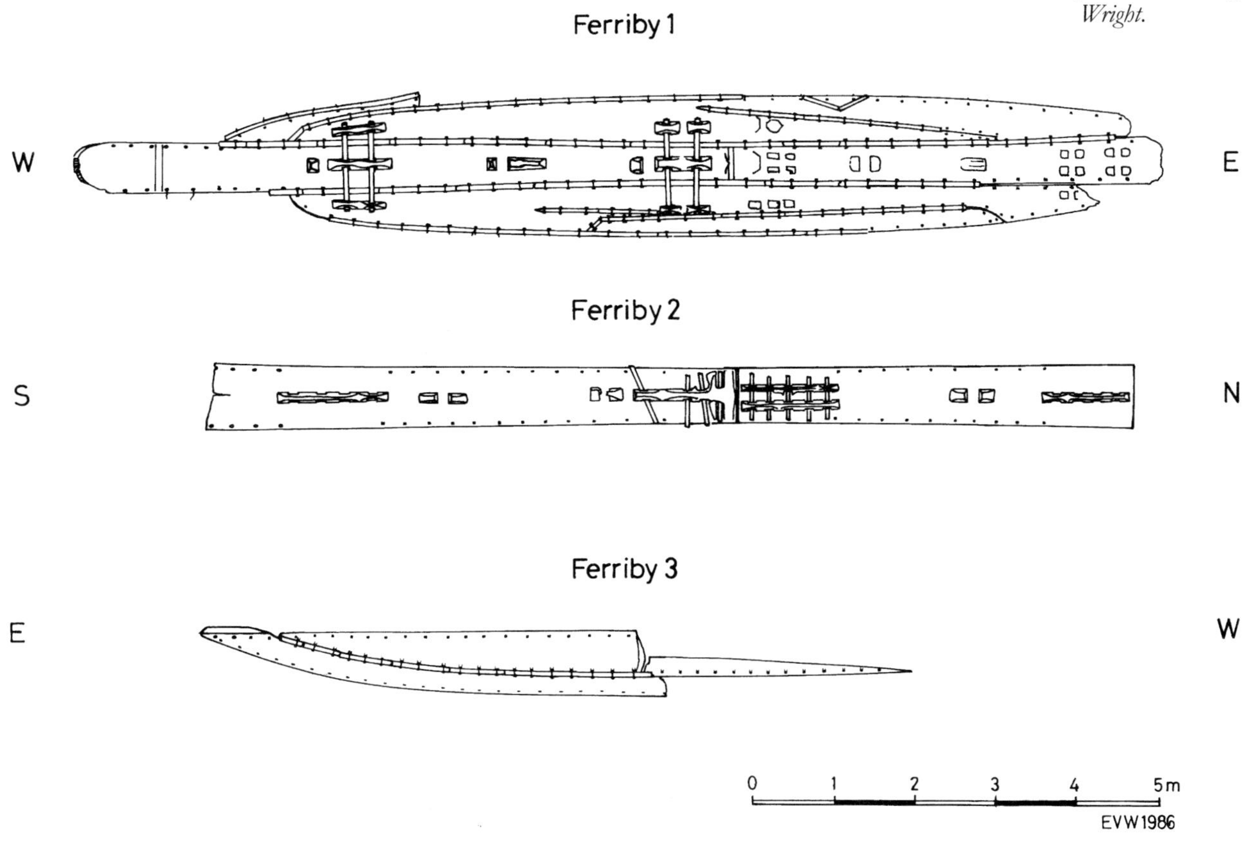

Fig. 4.3 Replica of western part of F1. Photo: NMM, Greenwich.

had yielded dates for the various remains ranging over nearly a millennium from about 1400 to about 600 cal BC, but more recent dating by accelerator mass spectrometry has put the earlier date back in the case of the second find to about 2000 cal BC, at present much the earliest date given to any sewn-plank boat remains yet found in Europe, increasing their importance the more. It was by a happy chance that that latest dating was known to Ted just before he died, justifying his opinion that (Wright 1990, 178):

They must however have been the product of an ancestry stretching back for many years before the date of F[erriby] 1 and F[erriby] 2 since by no stretch of the imagination could a design of such complexity have been reached by a single process of invention. Such an ancestry, of whatever duration and geographical spread, must therefore in the English context be related to 'Early' rather than 'Middle' Bronze Age cultures.

In his book, written just before the discoveries of sewn-plank fragments in the wetlands of the Severn and then of the boat here at Dover in 1992, the Ferriby finds had not been able to be connected at all securely with any other boat remains in north-west Europe, except possibly with the Brigg sewn-plank 'raft' dated to about 800 BC. As Valerie Fenwick has observed (Parfitt and Fenwick 1993, 78), the Ferriby and Brigg sewn-plank finds stood without archaeological context for decades but nevertheless they indicated 'that vessels more elaborate than dugouts or skin boats were used for water transport in the Bronze Age'. The question however as to whether the Ferriby finds were indicating sewn-plank ships of some useful seagoing capabilities or just boats for river traffic and ferrying has been much discussed. Ted Wright was delighted by the more recent finds at Dover and in Gwent from much the same period. These have provided some context for Ferriby and they raise the same questions about uses and capabilities.

In Chapter 5 of his book Ted Wright convincingly argues from his own careful records that the Ferriby finds were of seacraft though some essential points of his argument and therefore his conclusion have not been universally accepted (Wright 1990, 85–116). The question has wide implications for our understanding of the scope, limitations and character of Bronze Age sea-borne cultural influences and trading traffic between Britain and north-west Europe in that period.

The feature of two of the Ferriby finds which is central to this question is the rocker of the bottom. Ted Wright's records and his arguments based upon them show beyond reasonable doubt that the bottoms of both these vessels were originally rockered. It must therefore be disputed that, as one authority has stated (McGrail 2001, 186) 'it is not absolutely clear that a rockered bottom is compatible with the remains as excavated'. The remains are on the contrary only compatible with a rockered bottom. This is an important question and it calls for a rehearsal of Ted Wright's records and arguments.

He first found the eastern end of the keel plank of Ferriby 1 (F1) protruding from the plane of the mud surface (Fig 4.4) at a shallow angle, and then the western end which at that time appeared 'as a knob of dark wood protruding from the clay'. Probing down from the clay surface which photographs of the site show to have been virtually straight, he found that the depth of the plank increased for some 6 metres from the eastern end and then decreased towards the other end which turned upwards as shown in his drawings (Fig 4.5). Thus the keel and the whole bottom of Ferriby 1 was curved when discovered. Though he did not then measure those soundings, being concerned at that early stage to ascertain the extent of the buried

Fig. 4.4 (left) View from the ship site across to the Lincolnshire shore. Photo E V Wright.

Fig. 4.5 (below) F1: Pre-war and 1946 field records and reconstructed lengthwise sectional views of the pre-war excavations giving evidence of the in situ profile of F1. Drawing: E V Wright.

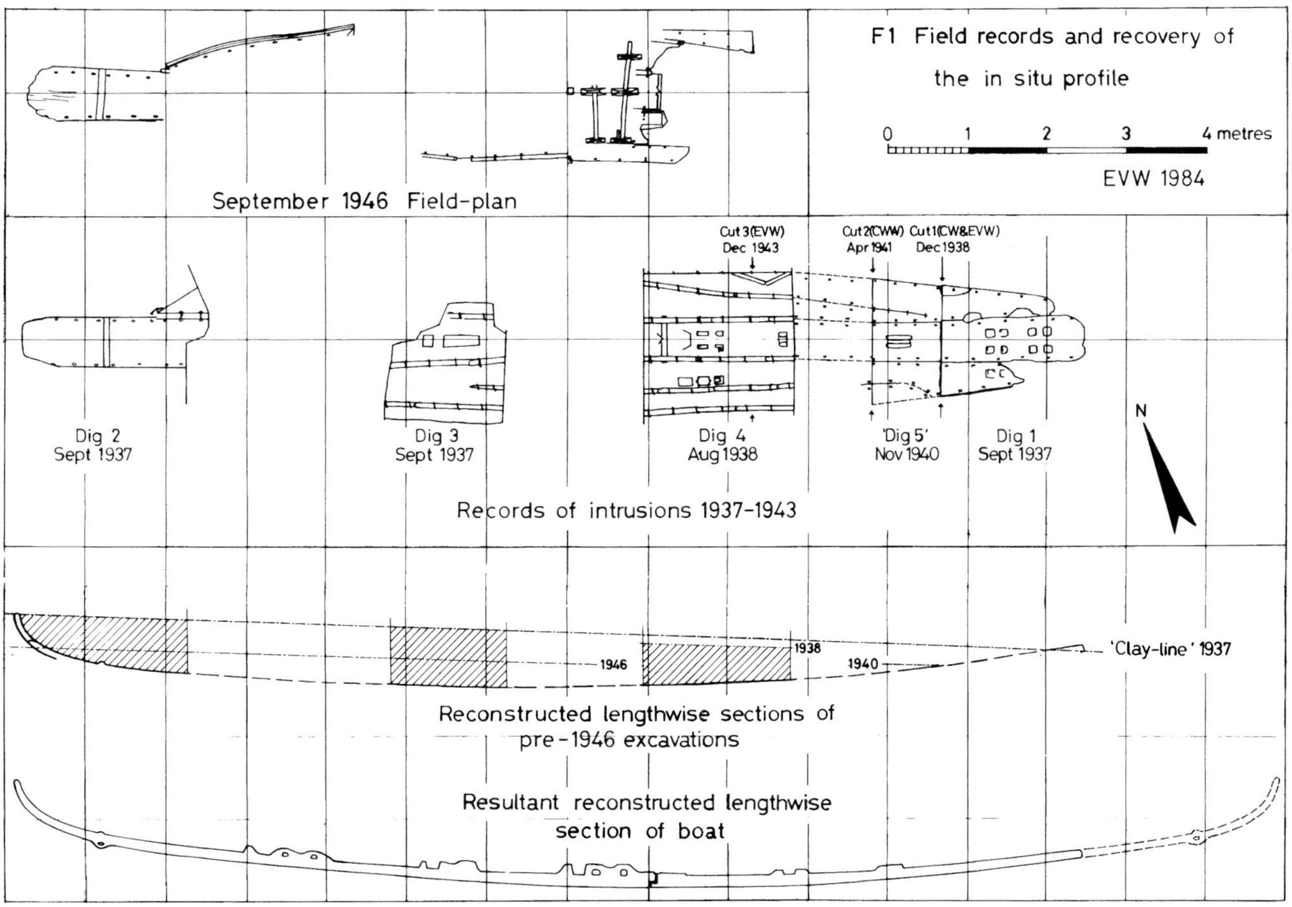

remains in plan, later excavations revealed intermediate lengths of keel and enabled him to reconstruct a consistent curve (Fig 4.5). He photographed the keel of F2, the second remains to be found, lying separated into its two planks (Fig 4.6) and that showed on examination that each plank as found had about the same curvature as the whole bottom of F1. While it is well known that timbers can deform after deposition, it is very unlikely indeed that these four keel planks, more than 100 mm thick, if they had been originally straight, would have been bent by post-depositional forces to the same curvature while lying in pairs about at right angles to each other and 50 metres apart. It would

Fig. 4.6 Drawing derived from E V Wright photograph from which measurements were made to recover the in situ profile of F2. Drawing: E V Wright.

Fig. 4.7 General arrangement drawings of Ted Wright's reconstruction of a complete hull. Drawing: J F Coates.

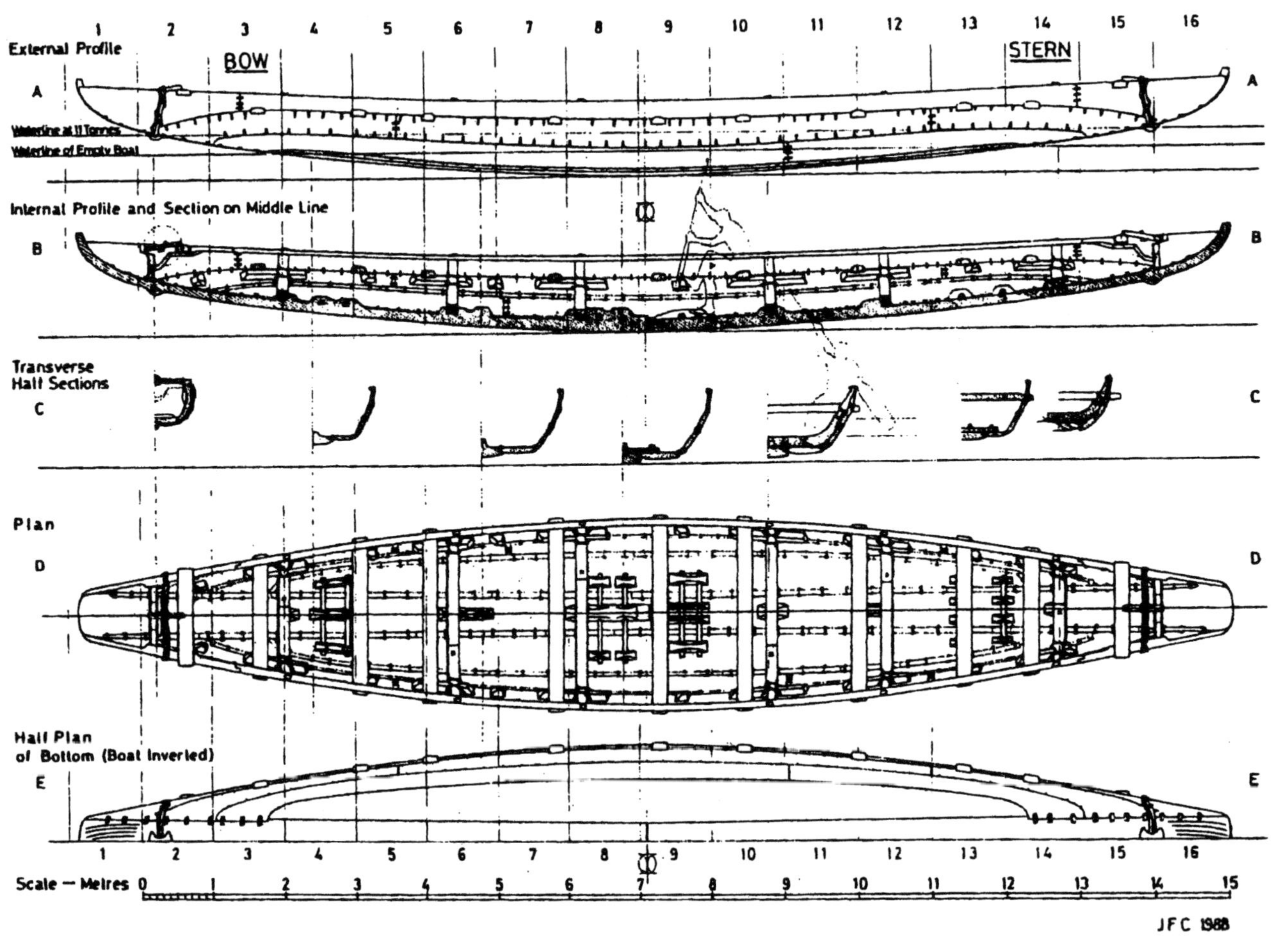

Table 4.1: L/B ratios for some slender latter-day types of seaboats

	No. of oars	*L (m)*	*B (m)*	*L/B*
Sutton Hoo (c. AD 600)	40 (2 oars to a thwart)	27	4.3	6.3
Skuldelev *2* (*c.* AD 1000)	60 (2 oars to a thwart)	29.5	3.8	7.8
Southwold Yawl	14 (2 oars to a thwart)	15	2.9	5.2
Cornish Pilot Gig	6 (2 oars to a thwart)	9.1	1.45	6.3

be more credible that they had been curved originally but had straightened post-deposition, but not the reverse. When one adds the fact that when found the keel planks of F1 were integral with nearly the full length of the rest of the bottom of the ship while F2 consisted of two separated keel planks only, very different loads in magnitude and distribution would have been required to bend the three to the same curvature as found. The probability that the post-depositional loadings on each were so different and also such as to give these two very different structures, if they had been flat originally, the same curvature as found must surely be virtually nil.

The presence of rocker (Fig 4.7) is certainly no mere embellishment as has been averred (McGrail 2001, 186) because it would very greatly improve not only manoeuvrability, but also stability and, not least, behaviour in waves. The difference in form and capability bestowed by rocker to a hull with cross-sections like those of F1 is between that of a craft only 0.7 metre deep without any sheer and fit for calm water riverine use only, and one about one metre deep amidships with a rather modest sheer rise of about 0.2 metre at each end of the hull and thus able to cope with moderate seagoing conditions to some useful degree even when carrying a load of nearly twice the weight of the bare hull with a freeboard amidships of 0.4 metre. For comparison, in large latter-day beach boats of about the same length, such as the Southwold yawls, sheer rise was nearer 0.5 metre, whereas a sheer of 0.2 metre was common in slender seaboats about 10 metres long. That comparison suggests that the rocker as found at Ferriby and derived by Ted Wright (Fig 4.5) may have been less than in the original hulls. Certainly the sheer achievable with the Ferriby construction is much dependent upon the rocker given to the bottom; the height of the upcurving ends of the keel planks themselves must be limited by the useable diameter of the tree bole from which they were fashioned and, in the absence of stitch holes in the curved top end, no hull-end planking to give additional height may be assumed. It is a pity that in his first reconstructions of these remains Ted Wright seems to have neglected the significance of his probings through the mud and of the slope of the eastern end of the keel. He and others assumed (Fig 4.8) that the keels were flat. For some time he tried various forms of minimalist reconstructions of that flat form such as would have had much use afloat. However he did eventually realise that in reviewing his own data that they showed beyond doubt that the bottoms were rockered, leading to the much more plausible reconstruction which he published in his book. It is most unfortunate that virtually all other publications show only a flat-keeled reconstruction or the remains of F1 in plan only (e.g. Cunliffe 2001, 68; McGrail 1987, 120; 2001, 185–6).

The Ferriby ships, judging from F1, were nearly 16 metres long (L) and yet only 2.5 metres in beam (B). That is a noticeably slender form of ratio L/B = 6 (Figs 4.7 and 4.9). This speaks strongly of the need in these vessels for a good performance by human propulsion or under sail, or both. That must have been wanted, for no one builds a long slender hull without good reason. The most likely reason would have been to accommodate enough paddlers or oarsmen. They each need about a metre of hull length in which to work and F1 could therefore accommodate up to about 18 paddlers or possibly 14 oarsmen, if two to a thwart, and in a manner consistent with the remains. Such crews would enable the ship to make headway if necessary against most commonly encountered currents and strengths of wind. For comparison here are presented some L/B ratios for some slender latter-day types of seaboats (Table 4.1).

A continuing point of controversy in reconstructing a Ferriby ship concerns the depth of hull and so the number of side strakes. It boils down to whether there were two or three strakes. If it was a river craft with a flat keel, a much-published type of reconstruction (as, for example, in Fig 4.8) with only the two side strakes for which there was direct evidence in F1, it would be at most 0.7 metre deep (D). The hull would in that case be 23 depths long (L), a very high L/D ratio indeed for a wooden structure, high but possibly not out of the question in a solely riverine craft, but certainly far too high for any seriously seagoing vessel (Sea trials of a reconstruction of the Hjortspring boat with a ratio of nearly 26 have, I understand, borne out the point).

If, in a two-strake Ferriby, the upper edge of the second strake was to reach near to the level of the

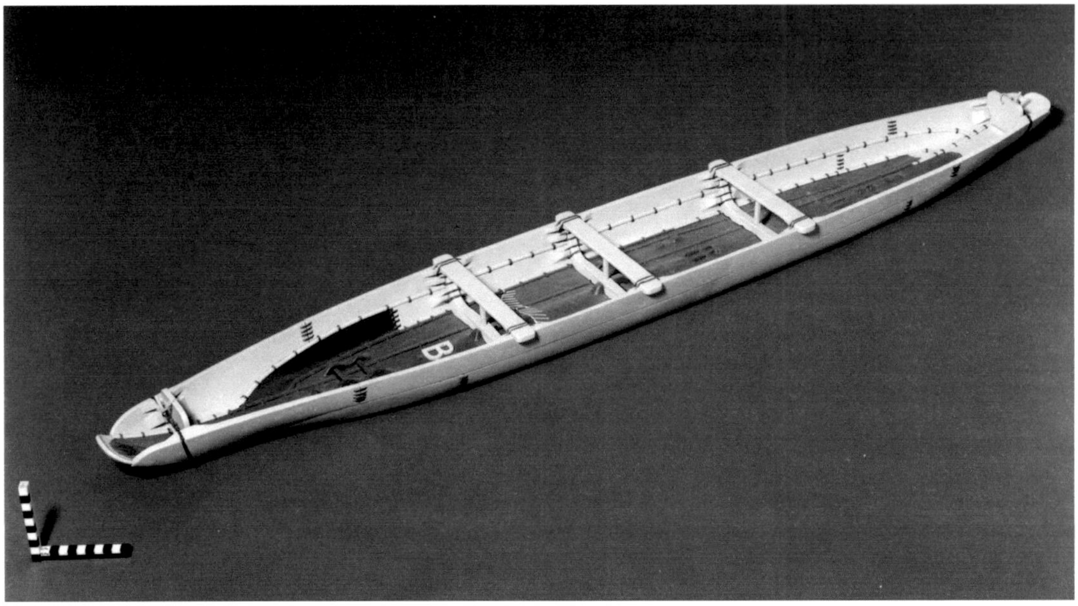

Fig. 4.8 Reconstruction model of F1 assuming a flat keel and bottom. The black part represents excavated elements; the white is conjectural. Photo: NMM, Greenwich.

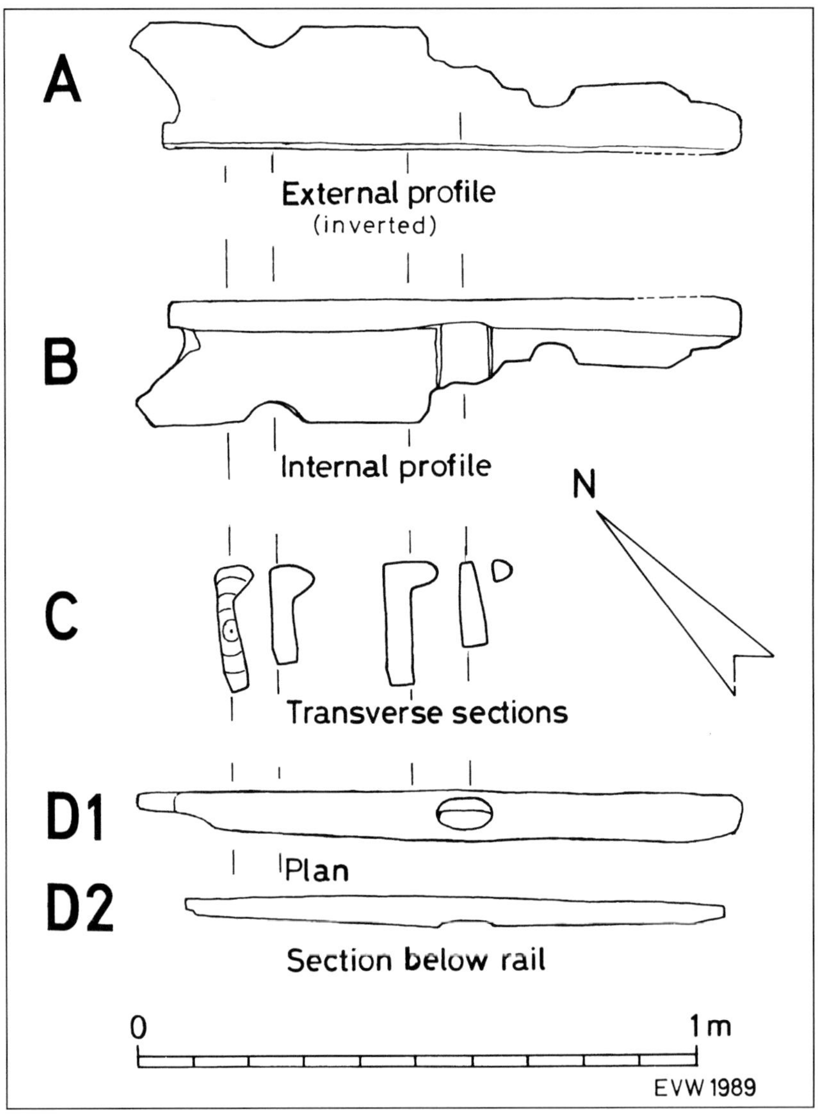

Fig. 4.9 F4 as recorded. Drawing: E V Wright.

	No. oars	*L*	*L/D*
Sutton Hoo	40	27	18 approx.
Skuldelev 2	60	29.5	16.3
Selsey galley	22	12 approx.	13
Southwold Yawl	16	15	13
Cornish Pilot Gig	6	9.1	13.5

Table 4.2: comparison values of L/D for some slender latter-day types of seaboats

top of the up-curving keel-ends, as most surely it must, its breadth at the ends of the first strake where it meets the keel plank would have to be at least 0.7 metre which is a tall order in itself, but shaping that strake in four places would be a task so demanding as to make such a hypothesis virtually unacceptable. Such wide and shaped timbers with double curvature would be prone to splitting in service and be laborious to replace. There would probably therefore have to be three strakes at the ends, one being a stealer (a short wedge-shaped length of planking used to fill empty spaces where the hull flares). But as it is beyond reasonable doubt that the bottom was rockered, and because any two-strake reconstruction would in any case be quite inconsistent with it, making nonsense of the rocker as found, it is most likely indeed that there would have been three side strakes in the Ferriby ships, as Ted Wright argued. The arrangement and number of surviving stitch holes between the ends of the first strake in F1 and the upturned end of the keel plank are consistent with two strakes ending on that length of keel plank and fastened with three stitches each, making a total of three strakes to form the sides of the hull (Fig 4.7).

Three side strakes could increase the hull depth amidships (D) to a metre or more, reducing the ratio L/D to 16 or less, an altogether more practical figure, though near the limit for a seacraft, particularly if wooden and heavily built as the Ferriby hulls certainly were. It follows that some seagoing capability should be contemplated and investigated. On this important point one can quote for comparison values of L/D in some of the same latter-day types of slender seaboats which were however clinker-built and much lighter relative to their sizes (Table 4.2).

Another important advantage of the rockered bottom is the flare of the side strakes which would naturally fit the chine and make the hull ship-shaped without requiring twist. Such flare greatly adds to stability, particularly when the ship is loaded. It seems reasonable therefore that because their bottoms were rockered the most likely form for Ferriby ships would be on the lines of that offered by Ted Wright in his book (Fig 4.7) and in a 1991 paper at the sixth International Symposium on Boat and Ship Archaeology (Wright 1994).

In 1996 a board publicly giving information about the Ferriby find and this reconstruction was set up by the North Ferriby Information Group and unveiled at the riverside walkway at North Ferriby. Here, Ted Wright can be seen holding his $^{1}/_{20}$th scale model of his reconstruction which is now in the Hull and East Riding Museum in Hull. A somewhat belated project is now underway to reconstruct F1 accordingly with the main object of testing its behaviour, both structural and operational, and its seagoing capability. This should go far towards fulfilling Ted Wright's hopes expressed in the epilogue of his book. It is good that it was possible to resolve upon this project with him and to his great pleasure just before he died.

On propulsion, in the absence of direct evidence, the project will not be able to do more than establish what would have been physically feasible. In the book, in deference to lack of other evidence for rowing in north-west Europe in the second millennium BC, the reconstruction is shown with paddlers, but the height of the gunwales above the thwarts would make oars easier to work; oars are, of course, much more effective than paddles at sea. Details of F4 (Fig 4.9), dated to the early half of the first millennium BC and believed by Ted Wright (in face of some dissent) to be part of a Ferriby type ship, do also show wear from what could be an absent thole and also holes in the right places for lashings for an oar or thole pad, so it is intended to explore the use of oars in the reconstruction. In the same vein, no one with any experience of relying on human propulsion over any appreciable distances at sea would not consider the possibility that these ships used sail (Fig 4.10), despite the apparent lack of convincing other evidence of sail in north-west Europe before the first century BC, though there is much earlier evidence of sail from other parts of the world. In F1 there is a saddle-shaped feature on the keel which suggests that it could have been a mast step. Ferriby type ships could certainly carry a useful sail which would very greatly extend their range of operation. Sailing will therefore be explored with the reconstruction afloat.

I appreciate that these hypotheses go beyond presently available supporting material evidence and can properly attract doubts. However it must never be forgotten, *pace* proper archaeological rigour, that

Fig. 4.10 Hypothetical sailing rig. Drawing: J F Coates.

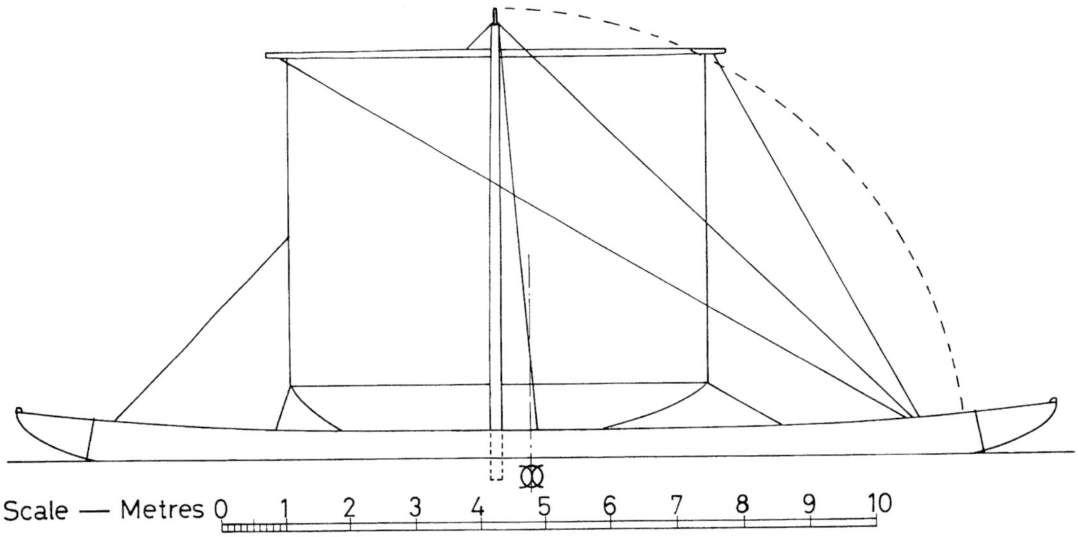

absence of evidence is not necessarily evidence of absence and few seamen would not be surprised, to say the least, if intricately-built and potentially capable Ferriby hulls, which represent large investments, were never taken to sea or if their propulsion was confined to paddles. Experiments, provided where there is evidence that they keep rigorously within, can do no harm and might reveal much.

The stitch holes of many ancient sewn planked ships are bored straight. They could have been and probably were made with bow drills and bits of bone, flint or obsidian. The stitches in a large part of the bottom of Ferriby, however, were found by Ted Wright to have been made in a cunning manner to protect them from grounding damage. That involved cutting curved holes which must surely have not been possible without chisels, probably bent and handled, which in turn could only have been of metal, which would have been bronze. The holes in question were also square in section. It would follow that these ships were intrinsically products of the early Bronze Age. Their leading date of before 2000 BC indicates that this detailed feature implies a rapid application of the new bronze technology.

The bottom stitches in Ferriby hulls as built are thus protected from grounding more securely than by methods used elsewhere: countersinking (Maori; Johnstone 1988, 208); wedging and removing the outside part (E. Africa; Chittick 1980); rebating the external edges of planks to lift stitches above the bottoms of planks (Brigg; McGrail 1981). Here we may glimpse one of the driving forces to overcome the fragility against grounding of much cheaper hide boats, short-lived, but otherwise fully seaworthy. The Ferriby remains are outstanding examples, rare to the point of uniqueness, of the high craftsmanship of that age (Fig 4.11), which may be labelled 'bronze', but timber was the commonest material for construction and, as Ted Wright understood so long ago, we have to look in wetland sites for evidence about this most important material aspect and achievement of the age, not to mention the social organisation and specialisation needed to make, use and maintain such complex artefacts as the Ferriby ships. There must still be much to be learnt in this field, probably beyond Dover and Gwent, to develop his pioneering work.

Faute de mieux, hide boats have hitherto been generally assumed to have been the main means of navigation at sea in that period and earlier. That idea may well have to be modified when we understand what the Ferriby and Dover types of ship can do. The extent of F1's seagoing capability and its robustness will, it is hoped, be demonstrated in the course of the reconstruction project. The project should also bring home to people today, as Ted Wright hoped, the astonishing intricacy, finish and craftsmanship of shipbuilders and, by extension all other woodworkers in north-west Europe 4000 years ago. That may well also transform our understanding of navigation and hence of the flow and distribution of goods, power and culture during that period.

Ted Wright's lifelong labours on his finds at

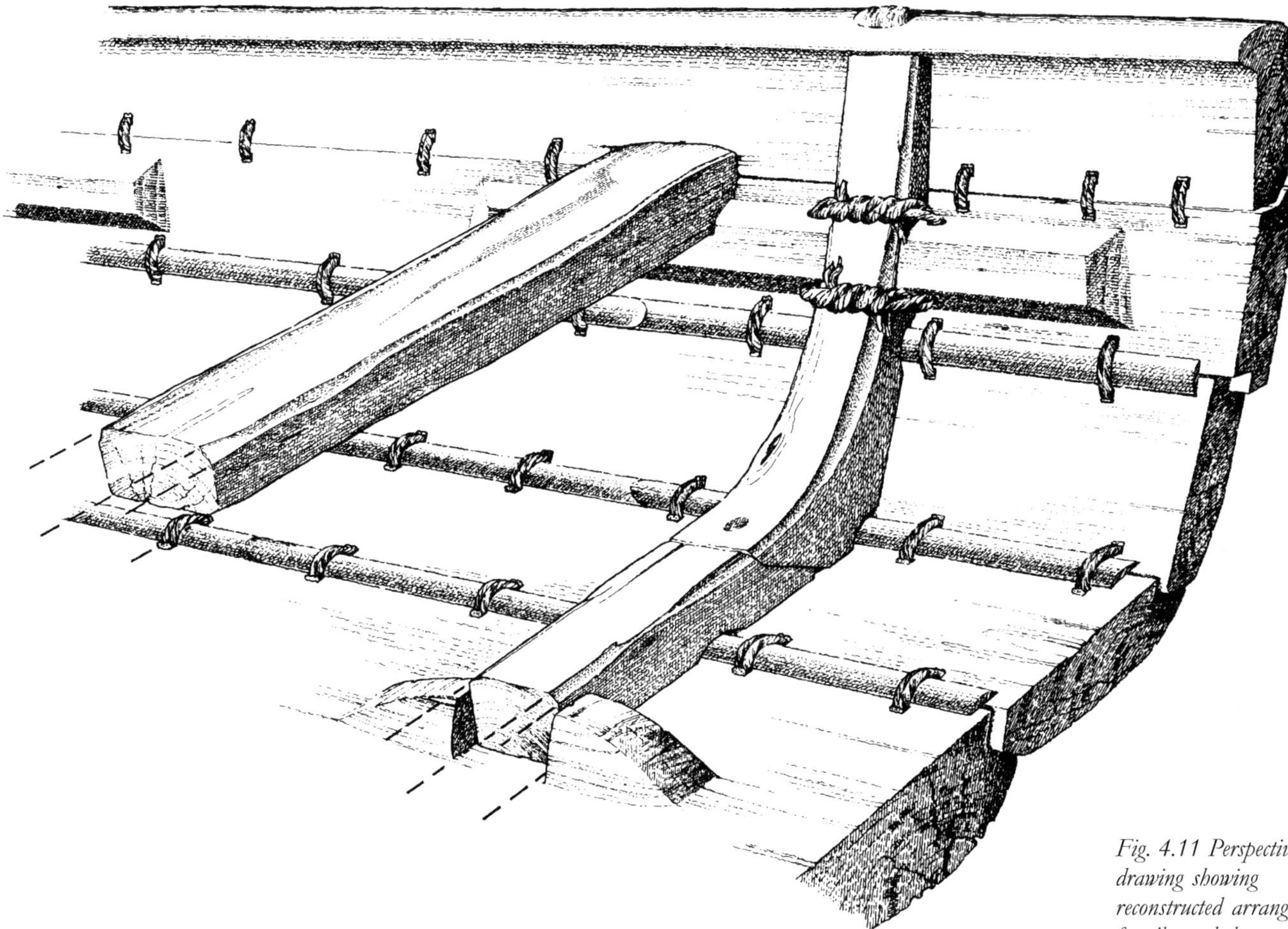

Fig. 4.11 Perspective drawing showing reconstructed arrangements for ribs and thwarts. Drawing: J Craig.

North Ferriby would then at last be nearer to a proper fruition. We owe it to Ted Wright to build upon his legacy in such a way to honour and preserve it for posterity.

Acknowledgements

I am grateful to John Coles, Valerie Fenwick and Gillian Hutchinson for allowing me to quote from Ted Wright's Festschrift, to the University of Hull for supplying me with his portrait, to the Hull and East Riding Museum for allowing me to quote and use material from *The Ferriby Boats.*

The Ferriby ship project could not have been established without the active help of Ted Wright's son, Roderick, the experience and enthusiasm of Edwin and Joyce Gifford, of Richard Darrah and Damien Goodburn and of chief shipwright, Jeff Bird, in building the preliminary half-scale model of the reconstruction, nor without the advice and support of David Miles of English Heritage and Malcolm Lillie of the University of Hull. I am also grateful to Edwin Gifford, Seán McGrail, Peter Marsden and Owain Roberts for their helpful comments made in the course of preparing this paper.

For permission to reproduce the figures given with this paper I am grateful to the following: for Fig 4.1, the University of Hull; for Figs 4.2, 4.4, 4.5, 4.6, 4.7, 4.9, 4.10 and 4.11, the National Maritime Museum, Greenwich, and John Craig for the use of his drawing, Fig 4.11.

List of references

Chittick, N 1980 'Sewn boats in the western Indian Ocean', *International Journal of Nautical Archaeology*, **9**, 297–309

Coles, J, Fenwick, V, and Hutchinson, G (eds) 1993 *A Spirit of Enquiry – Essays for Ted Wright*, Exeter

Crumlin-Pedersen, O and Olsen, O (eds) 2002 *Skuldelev Ships 1*, Roskilde: Viking Ship Museum, Ships and Boats of the North, **3**

Cunliffe, B 2001 *Facing the Ocean – The Atlantic and its Peoples*

8000 BC – AD 1500, Oxford: Oxford University Press

Johnstone, P 1988 *The Sea-craft of Prehistory*, 2nd edition, Routledge

McGrail, S 1981 *The Brigg 'raft' and her prehistoric environment*, National Maritime Museum Greenwich Archaeological Series, **6**, British Archaeological Reports (British Series), **89**, Oxford

McGrail, S 2001 *Boats of the World from the Stone Age to Medieval Times*, Oxford: Oxford University Press

McGrail, S, 1987 *Ancient boats in NW Europe: the archaeology of water transport to AD 1500*, London

Olsen, O and Crumlin-Pedersen, O 1958 'The Skuldelev Ships', *Acta Archaeologia*, **29**, 161–75

Olsen, O and Crumlin-Pedersen, O 1967 'The Skuldelev Ships II', *Acta Archaeologia*, **38**, 73–174

Parfitt, K, and Fenwick, V, 1993 'The rescue of Dover's Bronze Age Boat', in J Coles, V Fenwick and G Hutchinson (eds), *A Spirit of Enquiry – Essays for Ted Wright*, 77–80

Wright, E, 1990 *The Ferriby boats: Seacraft of the Bronze Age*, London

Wright, E, 1994 'The North Ferriby boats – A Final Report', in Crossroads in C Westerdahl (ed), *Ancient Shipbuilding: Proceedings of the Sixth International Symposium on Boat and Ship Archaeology Roskilde 1991*, Oxford; Oxbow Monograph, **40**, 29–34

5. Some thoughts on boats as Bronze Age artefacts

Francis Pryor

Introduction

It is with the greatest imaginable trepidation that a confirmed landlubber such as me ventures out into the choppy – I nearly said treacherous – waters of maritime archaeology. But having said that, it is maritime archaeology and not the practicalities of prehistoric seafaring that I wish to consider, so I won't allow myself to feel too intimidated. Incidentally I was delighted that this paper managed to stir up quite a hostile – although of course impeccably polite – response at the conference itself. It was intended to. The point I shall be making is that the archaeology of Bronze Age boats cannot be divorced from the Bronze Age itself. Boats are, when all is said and done, just artefacts, albeit very large and superbly crafted artefacts. The Bronze Age was the time and the context in which they were made, used, wrecked and disposed of.

Ritual and motivation

It is becoming increasingly apparent that Bronze Age people treated their possessions in ways that seem very strange to us today. Fundamental to this 'strangeness' is the frequent appearance of so-called 'ritual' in the way that so many artefacts were finally disposed of. The word 'ritual', however, has become like a red rag to many archaeologists and it doesn't need to be. The roots of this misperception lie in the way we try to understand prehistoric motives and behaviour. We tend to impose our own patterns of thought on the people we are attempting to study. It's natural to do so, but it can never lead to a rounded understanding of past behaviour. It's much better to try to understand what made people tick: what motivated them to do the things they did. Having tried to understand that, we can then attach labels to their actions, if we want to. Myself, I think such labels are often a mistake and are nearly always unnecessary. I should also add that it is fashionable in certain circles to discuss these new approaches in impenetrable language. I shall do my best to avoid this.

The first perceptual hurdle that we have to confront is the hard-and-fast distinction between what today we see as the distinctively different worlds of ritual and daily or domestic life. Nowadays those who believe in such things reserve ritual for church on Sunday. It's an aspect of life which is not allowed to impinge on other, more mundane things, such as relaxation or the necessary business of earning one's living. This separation is, I suppose, an aspect of Holiness, frequently honoured more in the breach than the observation. I can remember how we celebrated Grace before meals at school: heads were respectfully bowed for as short as possible; the words were said and we then dived like so many gannets into the food, thankful that the ritual had been so mercifully short. It may have been like that sometimes in prehistory, but I would suggest not often – and why? Because what Richard Bradley has termed 'ritualisation' gave pattern, structure and meaning to all aspects of prehistoric life (Bradley forthcoming). In other words ritual and practice were closely intertwined. One cannot be certain of course, but the levels of detailed ritual structure observed, for example, in even the smallest archaeologically visible action, such as the way that small pits were carefully back-filled in Neolithic and Bronze Age times. The care with which this was done suggests that ritual and belief pervaded everything that people did – in a way that seems senseless to modern perceptions. It must have been all-pervasive. Probably when you doled out a pan of porridge for the family you first set aside a portion for the ancestors and then the food was distributed strictly in the order of familial seniority. I would also suggest, from a wealth of circumstantial evidence, that the food would probably have circulated clockwise, as if mimicking the daily passage of the sun (Parker Pearson 1999a). So was this a ritual meal, or just breakfast? Both, in all probability, but it was also ritualised behaviour.

In order to grasp what might have motivated prehistoric actions we must briefly consider the concept of agency (Parker Pearson 1999b, 32–4). The idea of agency suggests that most human actions are considered, or thought about in advance. They don't just happen, unless of course one is involved in a traffic accident, but even then the actions that follow immediately after the accident are affected by agency. Agency – the thoughts lying behind what we do – is in turn affected by prevailing attitudes to the world we inhabit. The motivation lying behind the way modern western people do things is usually ultimately linked to work or money. This underlying motivation arises from modern (essentially capitalist and functionalist) attitudes to the world we inhabit. It is part of our cosmology or world view. Almost everything we do reflects the fact that we must go out to work and earn money. And when we stop working we want to relax. So we organise our workspace with efficiency in mind and we organise our play space with pleasure and relaxation in mind, because these are two of the main features of most modern peoples' cosmologies. These criteria affect the way we arrange our world, from the office to the kitchen at home – even to the gin palace ferries that take us on continental holidays. So what were the organising principles that gave structure to prehistoric cosmologies? Put another way, what might have motivated people to do things in the Bronze Age?

Prehistoric cosmologies

I've indicated the motivations that might lie behind modern agency. Had I been writing about the medieval period I would probably have suggested that the Christian Church was the dominant cosmology. But what about prehistory? There is now a wealth of evidence to suggest that people in the British Bronze Age were constantly trying to tie the man-made monuments of their landscapes into the natural order of things. In other words, they were giving the products of their own hands and minds a wider, deeper meaning and legitimacy that was thought to transcend the normal day-to-day world. That was why they were so concerned with such things as solar alignments, solstices and so forth. They also gave their structures other symbolic meaning. I found it hard, when excavating the Neolithic causewayed enclosure at Etton, near Peterborough, not to see it as a symbolic or ritualised expression of the landscape round about. Standing atop the great mound at Maes Howe, on Mainland Orkney, one is keenly aware that the ditch and bank that surround the tomb reflect and seem to miniaturize the hills on the skyline. Both sites are located within ritual landscapes and at both there is evidence that movement within the landscape was important. At Etton the causewayed enclosure forms the junction between two major cursuses and Maes Howe, of course, sits on a carefully marked-out processional way that ran along a narrow peninsula between two loughs, one salt, the other fresh.

From at least the Middle Bronze Age we see the appearance of a new category of site where the journey, often from some sort of 'mainland', to an island has become as important as the destination. Indeed, I sometimes think the two may even have been thought of as being part of the same thing. These new sites probably replaced the ritual landscapes of the Early Bronze Age. The great post alignment at Flag Fen, Peterborough is the best known British example of such a site, but many others are now known (Pryor, 2001, with refs). On the mainland of Europe, the Swiss site of La Tène is the most famous example (Vouga 1923). It is quite probable that these constructions were 'ordinary' causeways for most of the year, but at certain times the journeys across them assumed a rather different character: in effect the causeways and the people travelling over them became ritualised. These sites were not laid out haphazardly. At Flag Fen the posts closely follow the 'grain' of the Early Bronze Age and Neolithic landscapes that preceded them. At Fiskerton, in the Witham Valley, near Lincoln, the posts were replaced in years in which there was a total eclipse of the moon. Again, it would seem that this was an effort to tie the man-made site into the natural order of things (Field and Parker Pearson forthcoming).

Examples

At Fiskerton, Flag Fen and elsewhere, objects – some of them valuable – were dropped into the waters around the posts as offerings. As one might have expected from what was essentially a route-side ceremonial context, these items included harness fittings and at Flag Fen part of a wheel and two axles. The great road at Corlea in Ireland revealed parts of a cart or carriage which had been carefully disposed of (Raftery 1996, 251). If the symbolism of journeying on land was important – perhaps from this life to the Next – it is hardly surprising that boats, or pieces of boats are often found in these contexts. Indeed, I would be astonished if they were absent. Of course it's difficult to 'prove' that finds of boats in watery contexts are ritual or otherwise. My own feeling is that the sites themselves provide the contexts which are indeed overwhelmingly ritual, or as I have repeatedly said, ritualised. I also find it very persuasive that the relatively large numbers of British Bronze Age sewn and plank-built boats date from the Bronze Age, a time when the ritual deposition of a huge spectrum of artefacts was relatively commonplace.

One characteristic of Bronze and Iron Age offerings is that many of the objects had been broken or damaged in some way. At Flag Fen the wheel fragment (a complete third of a tripartite wheel) still had locating pins in position, suggesting perhaps that it had been snapped. It did not seem to have been carefully dismantled. Leaf-shaped swords had their cutting edges deliberately smashed, pins and brooches were bent or bashed and shale bracelets were shattered. Of course one must be careful not to discount post-depositional damage, but the Ferriby boats were incomplete, as were the fragments found at Caldicot in South Wales – another Flag Fen-style post alignment site, complete with closely comparable offerings (Nayling and Caseldine 1997).

Another way to ritually destroy a boat is to sink it. I visited the extraordinary logboat in the gravel quarry at Shardlow, Nottinghamshire, which had been jam-packed with massive boulders (Fig 5.1). Near to it was a post alignment and finds of Bronze Age metalwork (Denison, 2003). I cannot imagine how the grossly over-laden boat could ever have floated. Besides, it makes more sense to transport such heavy loads using a catamaran-style arrangement of two logboats lashed to a load-bearing deck of some sort. To my eyes that vessel had been deliberately sunk. One of the three Iron Age logboats found recently at Fiskerton, one had been pegged into position in a manner which suggested to the excavator that the vessel could not have been used. Whether or not one accepts his judgement (and I do) the fact remains that the tool marks on the underside of the best preserved boat were almost as crisp, clear and fresh as the day they were hewn (Fig 5.2). It could only have been used for a very short time indeed, like some of the bronze offerings found at Flag Fen, which had actually broken along casting flaws. In other words it is entirely possible that some items were actually made to be offered up in this way.

This discussion of damage leads me to the Dover boat, but first we must briefly divert towards Hasholme in north Lincolnshire (Millett and McGrail 1988). The Hasholme Iron Age boat is the largest logboat known from Britain and I believe it to be the exception – or one of the exceptions – that proves the rule I am arguing for. It was substantially complete and the director of the excavation, Professor Martin Millett, is still convinced that it was a genuine wreck or accidental loss (*pers. comm.*, October 2002). This view was disputed at the conference, but I still prefer the excavator's opinion that the ground conditions were so treacherous – soft, silty-clay muds – that recovery would have been impossible. Besides, if the Iron Age sailors had wanted to remove it – and were capable of so doing – they would have done so. If they didn't, we must regard it as yet another ritual deposition, which was something that the objectors to Martin Millett's explanation were otherwise so keen to dispute. One cannot have it both ways.

The most interesting aspect of the Hasholme boat was undoubtedly the decorated transom board. We can never know what that U-shaped decoration was meant to symbolise, but it seems likely that it was an expression of the boat's name or identity; or

Fig. 5.1 The logboat from Shardlow gravel quarry, Derbyshire, in situ, lying on her side. Note the cargo of large sandstone blocks that fill the boat.

Fig. 5.2 A view of the underside of the logboat from Fiskerton, showing the fresh state of the tool marks of hewing.

maybe that of her owner or owners. The end board of the Dover boat had been deliberately removed and I wonder whether this had been done deliberately – maybe to pass the name or tradition on to another vessel. One cannot tell. But it is quite clear from the experimental work carried out by Richard Darrah and Damian Goodburn that it would have been impossible to have re-used the Dover end board (Clark 2004). I have always found it extremely difficult to work well-seasoned oak with a bronze axe, and I suspect this would have applied in the Bronze Age too. This leads me to suspect that the deliberate removal of the side planks was a ritualised act of destruction, as well. Also, for what it's worth, there was plenty of life still left in the vessel which was by no means worn-out. She was well-used, but far from decrepit. In other words, her deposition or disposal was not a practical necessity, as she still appears to have been seaworthy.

Finally, the situation of the Dover boat on the edge of a coastal creek, at the junction between the maritime and the inland environment, is interesting. Very often Neolithic and Bronze Age ritual sites and finds are located in such liminal or boundary zones (Edmonds 1999, 80–108). I take the Dover boat to be no exception.

List of references

Bradley, R J forthcoming 'In the Dutch mountains: the ritualisation of domestic life in Neolithic society'

Clark, P (ed) 2004 *The Bronze Age Dover boat*, English Heritage

Denison, S (ed) 'Tale of the Bronze Age barge sunk in the Trent', *British Archaeology*, **4**, March 2003

Edmonds, M 1999 *Ancestral Geographies of the Neolithic: Landscapes, Monuments and Memory*, London: Routledge

Field, N and Parker Pearson, M 2004 *Fiskerton – an Iron Age timber causeway with Iron Age and Roman votive offerings: Volume 1: the 1981 excavations*, Oxford: Oxbow Books

Millett, M and McGrail, S 1988 'The Archaeology of the Hasholme Logboat', *Archaeological Journal*, **144**, 69–155

Nayling, N and Caseldine, A 1997 *Excavations at Caldicot, Gwent: Bronze Age palaeochannels in the lower Nedern Valley*, Council for British Archaeology Research Report, **108**, York

Parker Pearson, M 1999a *The Archaeology of Death and Burial*, Stroud: Sutton

Parker Pearson, M 1999b 'Food, Sex and Death: Cosmologies in the British Iron Age with Particular Reference to East Yorkshire', *Cambridge Archaeological Journal*, **9**, 43–69

Pryor, F M 2001 *The Flag Fen Basin: archaeology and environment of a Fenland landscape*, English Heritage Archaeological Report, London

Raftery, B 1996 'Trackway Excavations in the Mountdillon Bogs, Co. Longford, 1985–1991', *Transactions of the Irish Archaeological Wetland Unit*, **3**, University College Dublin, 291–342

Vouga, P 1923 *La Tène: monographie de la station publiée au nom de la Commission des fouilles de La Tène*, (Leipzig)

6. Round the headland or over the horizon? An examination of evidence for British prehistoric efforts to construct a seaworthy boat

Owain Roberts

Only the largest Bronze and Iron Age boats discovered in the British Isles would have been capable of completing day-long coastal passages. Such voyages could be as arduous as any crossing of the English Channel or the Irish Sea. Since length in a shallow, fairly narrow hull governs the average boat speed available for voyaging it is possible that the complexities of sewn or stitched-plank boat-building, other than log-boats, were restricted to the largest sizes possible within the limits of prehistoric technology (Fig 6.1).

The concluding remarks in my reconstruction and assessment of the Dover Boat for the Canterbury Archaeological Trust (Roberts 2004) included 'that one needed to be an optimist to go to sea' and this applies more so in prehistoric times when boat structures, navigation, weather and tides are considered, yet evidently many sea-crossings and coastal passages were undertaken. So to encourage such optimistic attitudes it is clear that the odds were in favour of survival and were good odds too!

A prehistoric seaman was a successful boat builder with a tradition and awareness of coasts beyond the horizon and of lands extending for ever. Certainly, pioneering voyages of discovery were completed by many earlier generations long before any of the known British prehistoric boats were realised by their builders. We have no difficulty in accepting that even until the second half of the nineteenth century, some short-seas coasting was still undertaken without charts and relied fairly successfully on rote learning of coast-line features, a knowledge of soundings, handed-down wisdom and weather lore. Apart from the steering compass which had evolved by the thirteenth century into a satisfactory instrument, the methods employed had their origins in that 'mysterious haven-finding art' codified in prehistoric times.

To paraphrase Wilfred Thesiger's account of his desert travels, *The Life of My Choice* (1987), when describing the Tuaregs' methods of route-finding, he said they were

'…travelling as men had travelled for untold generations across the seas [deserts], dependent for their survival on the endurance of their boats [camels] and their own inherited skills…'.

In contrast with the first millennium AD, the last historic thousand years is crammed with evidence of an exponential growth in the use of boats and ships, changes in size, materials, construction, propulsion and the essential development of the intricate art and science of ship design. The prehistoric period being considered is the previous two millennia BC. In the British Isles it is singularly lacking in evidence. How prehistoric boats may have been used over that period is based on the discovery

Fig. 6.1 Perspective view of the Dover reconstruction.

of very few boats having substantial remains. These are the Ferriby group from 2000 BC and later (Wright 1990), Dover from 1550 BC (Clark forthcoming), and a re-interpretation from 1992 of the Brigg 'raft' as a seagoing craft from 800 BC (Roberts 1992). After this we have a centuries-long 'black hole' in our knowledge of boats in the British Isles. In addition to this tiny group are a few major sized log-boats whose origins are almost as incredibly distant and nearly as continuous as the history of the curragh. The curragh has been a brilliantly successful method of boat building and its origins disappear probably into the nautical beginnings of the prehistoric period. Though successful, it has been a dead-end in design terms since it has been impossible to develop it from its origins. The very qualities which make it successful in many important respects are the same which create its limitations as will be considered later.

In these different methods of construction we have clues to the differing styles of seamanship that would have been possible or necessary in prehistoric times. Structurally the boats are grouped as:

1. hide-covered, woven-and-lashed framework of impressively little weight;
2. hollowed logs with slight end modifications having a displacement measurable in tonnes but of shallow draft;
3. stitched or sewn assemblies of thick carved planks showing an awareness of the need for framing, again displacing tonnes and of shallow draft.

During the 'black hole' period, iron nails and planking of regular size had appeared as shown by ships of the Veneti (Caesar 50 BC), and a little later following our period but surely a development out of it, the Blackfriars I (Marsden 1994) and Barland's Farm boat (McGrail and Roberts 1999).

One might suspect that all British wooden prehistoric craft are variants of developed log-boats. Having discovered only three variations should not blind us to the possibility of a range of other differing styles, depending on other trends and on inspiration gained by hundreds if not thousands of years of nautical interaction with the Continent. Variants might include wooden derivations of the curragh form, if not its construction, as perhaps illustrated by the Brigg Craft (Fig 6.2) and even the Broighter Boat model, (to be seen in the National Museum, Dublin), both perhaps an attempt to combine the curragh's seaworthy form with the wooden boat's structural stiffness.

The risks inherent in passage-making

Coastal and short-sea passage-making is governed by tides and winds where average boat speeds are low and dependent for the most part on the strength of the crew or the wind. Coastal passages would be undertaken with fair tides. River estuaries may be dependent on flood tides for access. Tides may produce dangerous overfalls at headlands or off river mouths. The timing of tides coupled with the frequency of springs and neaps and the phases of

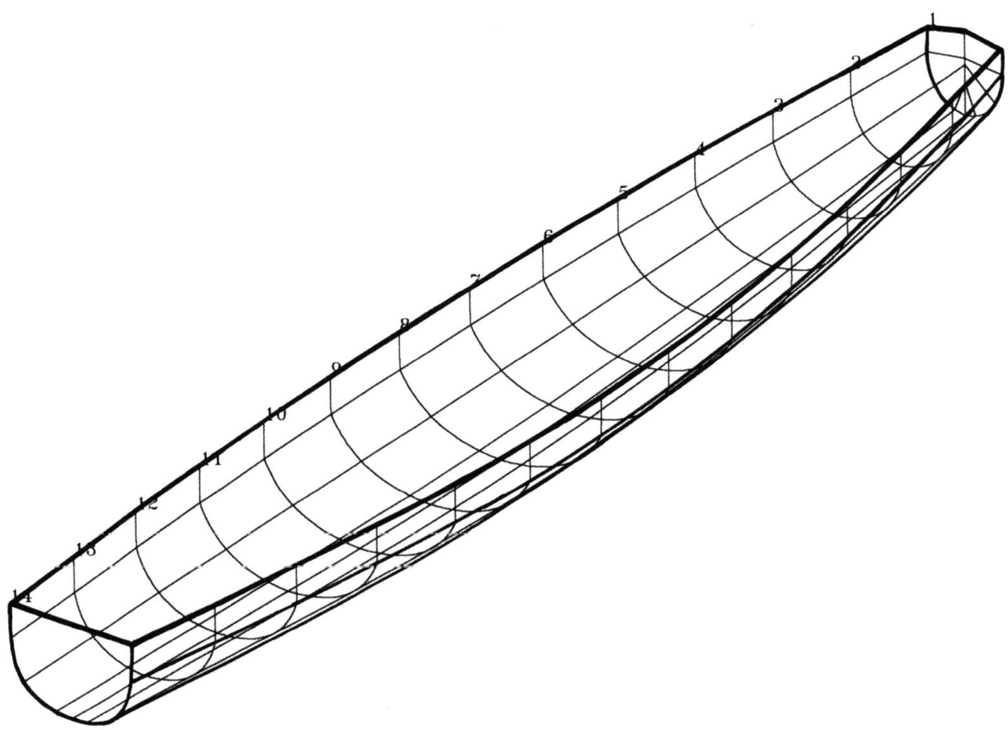

Fig. 6.2 The Brigg Craft as wire frame perspective.

the Moon meant that the prehistoric seaman knew some essential basic astronomy. One wonders if astronomy in general had its origins in the maritime observations. Strand walking also relies on such tidal knowledge.

Coasting would be in daylight since at night, except under an exceptional full moon, the coast has a Stygian blackness, especially if a cliff coast. Distance off the land is difficult to estimate. Yet the use of a lead-line to stay in a constant depth of water and hence a course parallel to an uncertain coast-line is a possible prehistoric ploy. Familiarity with a coast would surely imply a rough knowledge of the adjacent sea bottom depths and its tell-tale variations. Those seamen of the nineteenth century undertook similar coastal pilotage using a lead-line to identify soundings and a compass, all backed by immense local knowledge. The alternative was to make an offing until dawn.

Sea crossings would take prehistoric seaman over the horizon in the certain knowledge that a destination existed; it may be said that the communities of the Atlantic fringe of Europe formed a single cultural zone, linked by the sea, (Cunliffe 1997). Crossing to the Continent by the Dover Straits is no less of an undertaking than crossing from Wales to Ireland or from Pembroke to Land's End or from the Cumbrian coast to the Isle of Man, not just because of the distances involved but because of the exposure to poor landfalls and changes in weather. To arrive in daylight could mean an overnight passage. A landfall some miles up or down of the destination would have been frequent, as in the nineteenth century and even to the middle of the twentieth century.

Coastal passages in shallow-drafted boats always had the safety margin of a nearby coast should bad weather, nightfall or a sinking condition make a landing desirable. Beaches tend to be friendly whereas cliff coastlines need a careful approach.

Offshore passages would always be liable to threatening changes in weather, but often there are long weather-windows of calm. Observations of the latter would allow settled weather to be selected. Prehistoric seaman would have been a meteorologist out of necessity. Out-running a change in the weather to find shelter may be just possible. Eventually, survival in such open, narrow boats would mean lying head to wind and waves. Was the sea anchor or drogue a prehistoric invention, essential for survival, holding the boat, hove-to, in its most stable position to the waves? It would be nearly as important as each crewman's personal bailer. It would rest the crew, allowing more to bail while the boat was rearing and plunging over breaking crests (Fig 6.3). Bailing would be needed continuously. Spray would be blowing aboard and the boat would be flexing continuously as stitched seams worked, (stretched and flexed), and leaked.

Time on passage would depend mainly on boat length. Smoothness of the hull and a reduction in the bluffness of the ends would assist. The number of paddlers or oarsmen would be that best able to sustain a suitable power output with some reserve crew for resting. In rough seas and headwinds a large hull mass would maintain momentum between strokes. High freeboard and very low mass equate to a windage problem and a loss of tween-strokes momentum; one thinks particularly of curraghs.

Archaeological evidence for coastal and short-seas passage-making

There is sparse evidence of the sea-going capabilities of the known prehistoric boats, but we should remember the solid support for such activity from land archaeology. This is by inference, where similar cultures have been studied in areas separated by considerable expanses of sea.

None of the sea areas around the British Isles qualify for 'park-lake' status, when the dangers are considered of a crossing between say Cumbria and the Isle of Man, or a passage from Dover round Dungeness to Rye. Yet the archaeological evidence is for a continuous dependency on suitable seaworthy boats handled by competent seamen during the last millennia BC (Fig 6.4).

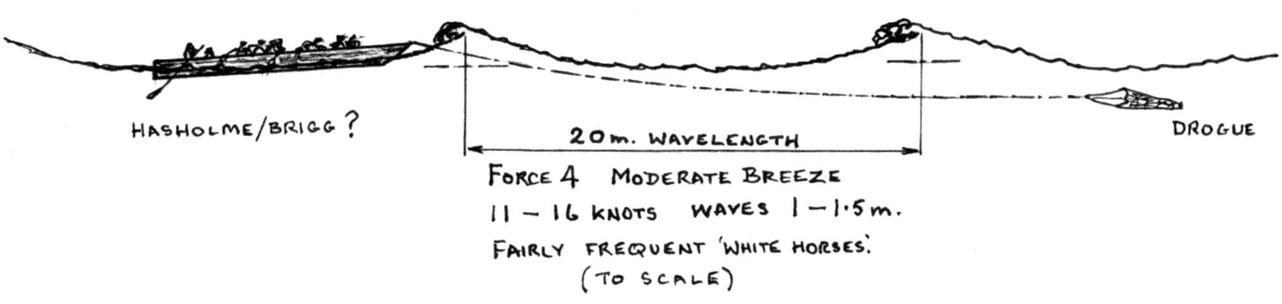

Fig. 6.3 Hove-to from a sea-anchor

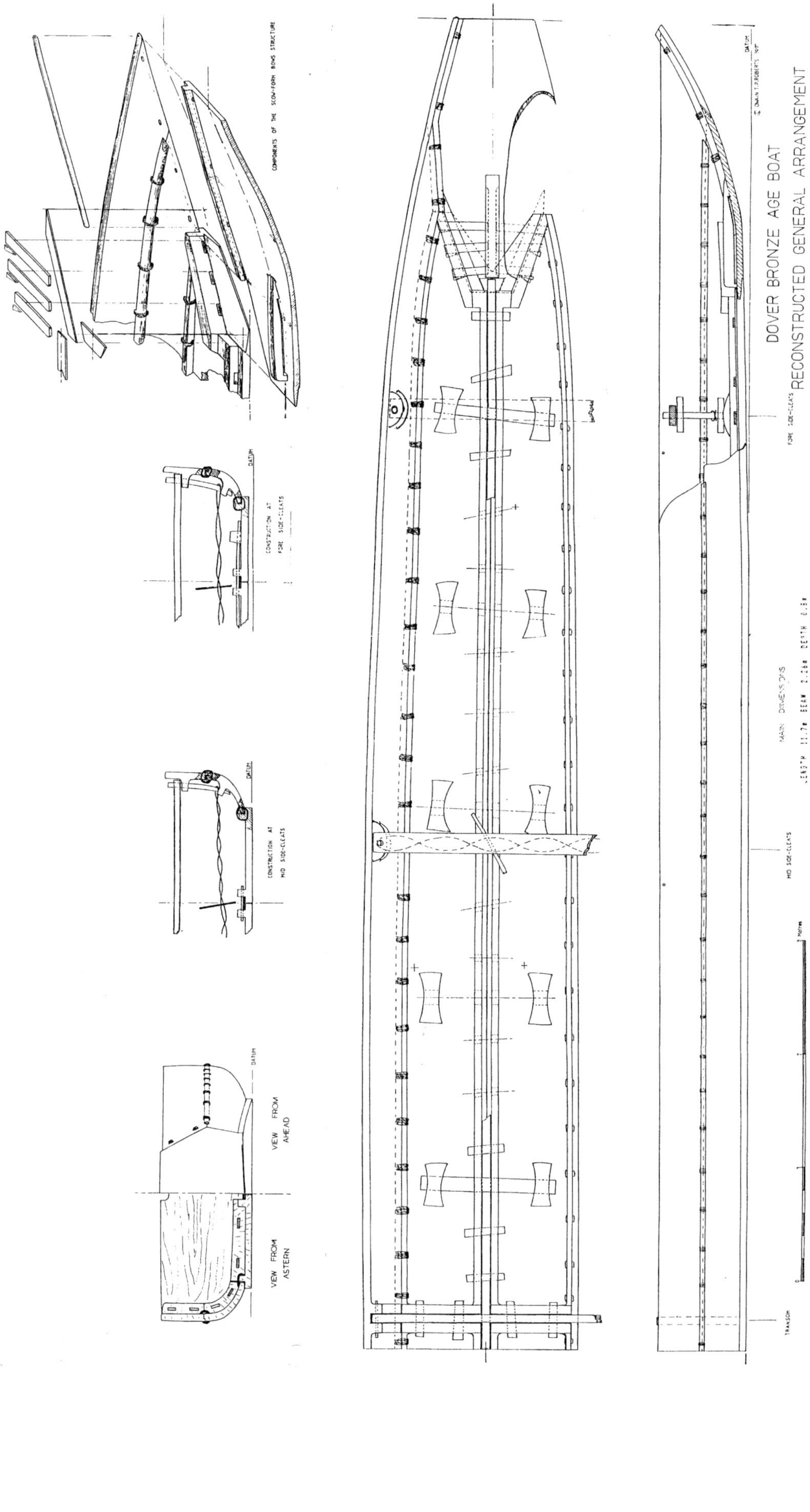

Fig. 6.4 A reconstructed plan of the Dover boat.

As Professor Cunliffe writes (1997):
'There is sufficient to show that, for at least 3 millennia, the communities of the Atlantic had maintained a degree of contact such that many aspects of culture, especially belief systems and technological skills, were held in common.'

Structure – advantages, drawbacks and observations

Those prehistoric boats which have survived are just that, boats. They have shallow draft and a modest displacement to maintain a safe freeboard for seawork, yet without a depth of hull which would interfere with propulsion. Shallow draft is essential in paddled or rowed craft since there is less drag and less weight (Fig 6.5). It is possible to maintain a satisfactory speed over long distance and to manoeuvre inshore and land on a beach without the need for deep-water harbours and anchoring. The down-side is that such forms tend to be affected by winds since shallow-drafted hulls show little resistance to wind pressure. A side wind may cause excessive leeway, or from ahead it may slow a boat's progress. In contrary winds the wooden craft might be superior to a curragh over a lengthy voyage, the greater mass enabling easier maintenance of forward momentum between strokes.

My calculations for Dover, Brigg Craft, Hasholme and Brigg log-boat indicate no more than 3 to 4 knots boat speed for long endurance. Above a certain speed, as in all craft, wave-making becomes marked and absorbs much of the energy put into trying to go faster at a rate far in excess of the extra speed gained. Paddlers may go very fast but for only a few minutes. Figure 6.6 shows this effect very clearly as the paddling ducks accelerate for some crumbs.

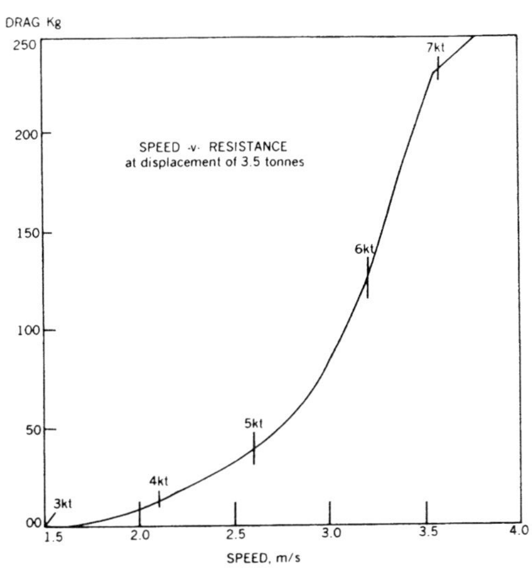

Fig. 6.5 Speed-Resistance Graph for the Dover boat.

Fig. 6.6 Ducks at speed.

Logboats

Logboats should hardly leak, at least when new, though constructed ends and inevitable drying out might cause problems. This is a great advantage when compared with a stitched or sewn boat which starts life with perhaps 400 or more plugged stitch-holes and four or more full-length, immersed seams constantly oozing water. There is no need to make laborious arrangements for stitch protection in the construction of a logboat which is to be dragged up a beach.

These advantages may have assured the sea-going logboat a long period of use despite being an anachronism. They were used for sea-crossings as late as the sixth century AD since Adamnan describes very large logboats in use between Iona and the mainland for carrying timber (Hornell 1973).

The lengths at 14m and nearly 13m respectively of the Brigg logboat of 800 BC (McGrail 1978) and the Hasholme logboat of 300 BC (Millett and McGrail 1987) together with the locations of their discovery, suggest they were intended for the estuaries rather than their rivers. Their dimensions would make them unhandy in many British rivers where even turning could be fraught with the possibility of capsize, as any experienced river canoeist would understand.

Estuaries may be as wild as the open sea in some conditions of wind and tide, so a Brigg or Hasholme crew having the skill to negotiate such waters would regard coastal passage making within their capabilities in moderate conditions. Logboats such as those from Poole or Clifton, having shallower hulls though not necessarily narrower beam than Brigg or Hasholme, would be unsuitable for sea work because of insufficient freeboard (Table 6.1).

Freeboard is a prerequisite for seawork where a Force 4 wind, a quite common moderate breeze, will create waves of about a metre height and with occasional breaking crests. The related Force 4 wavelength of about 20 m. is the right form for inducing a large logboat to 'plunge', sometimes into the face of an approaching wave. The square section of the largest logboats, as in Brigg and Hasholme, provides adequate freeboard which when coupled with a scow or sloping bows, ensures sufficient buoyant lift to avoid scooping waves aboard under such conditions.

In Force 4 beam-winds, both log-boats would have suitable freeboard, but even with a dense cargo stowed low, their modest stability would encourage their crews to look for a suitable shore, or change course, putting the waves more on the bows or on the stern. Beam on to a wave of 20m wave-length, there is the possibility of synchronism with the narrow but shallow-drafted logboat's natural rolling period, resulting in capsize. These limits make me wonder if logboats were ever used for open water crossings and my instinct says 'No' – but a long, prehistoric tradition of seamanship and their intense knowledge of the behaviour of such boats make me incline to the view that open water crossings would have been considered an acceptable risk in the opinion of these prehistoric seamen. To be an acceptable risk implies careful planning and a normally high success rate for open water passage-making, despite the inevitable losses that must have occurred. An intimate understanding of their craft's behaviour would counter many of her theoretical deficiencies. As an extreme case, consider the Inuit's kayak of slight stability and his ability to roll-up after a capsize.

Curraghs

Curraghs, presumably having proportions in prehistoric times similar to those still active in western Ireland, were the most remarkable of nautical inventions. They solved all the problems of stability up to extreme angles of heel. They offered survivability under the most extreme weather conditions because of the highly buoyant form, coupled with a lightness unattainable from other methods of construction. They were fast rowing machines, easily driven over wide sea-crossings which, because of the curragh's other attributes, could be faced with equanimity. They could be beached and carried above high-water with little effort.

The curragh's origins must lie in the earliest times of a hunting society when tools for converting large trees were yet to be developed. Large scale basket-work using young trees then a covering of skins would have been the route. The curragh suggested

Table 6.1 Part of the Beaufort Wind Scale (from Reed's Nautical Almanac 1981, 811)

Beaufort number	*mean wind speed in knots*	*open sea criterion*	*probable wave height (m)*	*probable maximum height (m)*
Force 2	4–6	light breeze small wavelets, still short but more pronounced crests have glassy appearance but do not break	0.15	0.3
Force 3	7–10	gentle breeze large wavelets crests begin to break foam of glassy appearance possibly scattered white horses	0.6	1.0
Force 4	11–16	moderate breeze small waves becoming longer fairly frequent white horses	1.0	1.5

for the first time the concept of pre-erecting a frame to a pre-determined shape before covering it with a homogenous, watertight layer. All would be developed within an ancient, empirical design theory which gave guidance to decisions about hull proportions and strength of structure. In the meantime in the British Isles and for many thousands of years, until lighter clinker and carvel building methods were adopted, prehistoric man continued to hack away at large pieces of timber in a vain attempt to build a boat capable of similar performance.

The curragh's skin takes the shape of the framework easily in three dimensions and is watertight, with sewn edges making good seams. However, this is not a stressed-skin construction, being only as tight as it can be pulled over the framework. It has no resistance to altering shape. Only part of the skin is tight at any one time as the hull flexes in a hogging and sagging cycle. Battens evenly spaced over the ribs counter some of this, as does a space-frame gunwale. Modern curraghs built at Purteen on the west coast of Ireland actually have smooth, carvel planking over the ribs but it is thin, lath-like and clearly intended to stiffen-up the skin covering or canvas as it is now. I believe this could be a solution derived from the earliest days of pit-sawing which would allow the easy production of such laths with a regular thinness, perhaps originally as waste. Some curraghs have external flat keels and bilge rubbers where they work off stony beaches.

Earlier it was suggested that the wonderful curragh has been a dead-end in design terms being impossible to develop further. The skin is one problem. However, if the curraghs were built much bigger, then the scantlings of the whole framed structure would need increasing, so that the advantages of light weight would be lost. Indeed the stiffness imparted by the planking in a wooden boat of similar size would never be matched in an enlarged curragh.

I would suggest that the late 17th century drawing held in the Pepys Library, Cambridge, purportedly of a very large curragh belonging to the 'Wild Irish', shows a complete lack of understanding of curragh construction by the artist, so might be the result of a vaguely recollected scene drawn much later.

Involvement in 2001 on the periphery of an attempt to move a new Preseli blue stone from Milford Haven to the River Avon allowed me to analyse the lines of the curraghs being used. These were 10m in length, to the proportions of Dingle curraghs and with excellent buoyancy and stability values. I understand that they were good pulling boats. Though built with the traditional structure, my concern about the scantlings was justified on examination of the hulls after a failed attempt to transport one stone. The buckling of the hull surface between the sheer and the bilge showed the need for a much stronger and hence heavier framing for curraghs built over-large for the usual scantlings.

The Wellington bomber's geodetic construction applied to Tim Severin's curragh built for the 'Brendan Voyage' adventure is a modern solution to the problem of flexibility, neither consistent with traditional methods, nor presumably with prehistoric ones (Mudie 1986). J M Synge describes 'the frame of slender laths which bent and quivered as the waves passed under them' while on passage in an Aran Island curragh (Synge 1907, 1979).

Despite the limits on size, probably about 10m, the curraghs would have been of outstanding importance from prehistoric through to recent times in maintaining sea connections among the British Isles and with the Continent. The inspiration for their building method and the consideration of their proportions as a design process pointed the way to the future for all wooden boat and ship construction.

The change from carving log-boats to that of carving planked boats is demonstrated by the four prehistoric boats found in Britain. The Ferribies, Caldicot and Dover are examples of a cultural mind-set that attempted to build wider log-boats by carving extra, massive pieces to enclose the new, desirable shape.

A log-boat is dependent for the integrity of its shape almost entirely on the thickness of the bottom and sides (Fig 6.7). Those frames carved on the inner surface seen in a few log-boats are not part of the construction process, but a reinforcement of the weak angle between the bottom and sides. The carved-to-shape, multi-part derivatives of log-boats from Ferriby, Caldicot and Dover need the invention of very clever, interlocking seam joints, stitching and gap-filling techniques. The paucity of framing shows the dependence still placed on the self-supporting properties of a massive monocoque structure of edge-joined and jointed, carved slabs of timber, with some justification. After all, the method worked for at least five boats found at Ferriby and others.

On the other hand, the Brigg Craft from 800 BC shows that techniques and thinking had moved on, or been introduced from elsewhere. In her we have a five-planked boat, edge-joined by the sewing of five similar pre-shaped, tapering strakes, thinner than the previous boats and without an interlocking edge-seam (Fig 6.8).

To each side is sewn an extra strake, effectively a wash-strake to improve freeboard. Support for the five strakes is provided by a regular, light bent framing system passing through up-standing carved cleats similar to those found a thousand years earlier but with a use which is echoed in Scandinavian boats over a thousand years later (Crumlin-Pedersen 1997). A central-strake of a limited number of strakes is also a concept found later in the

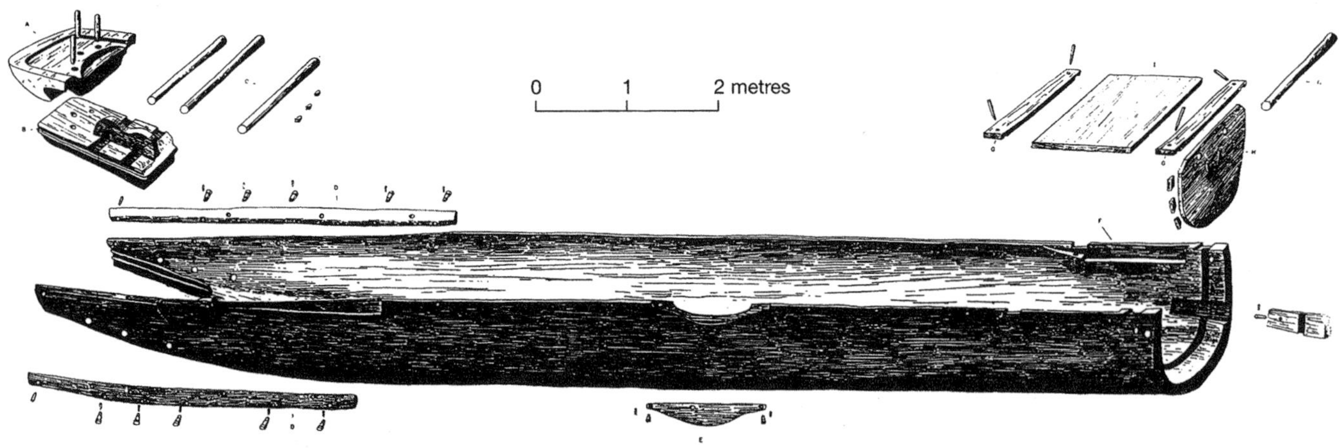

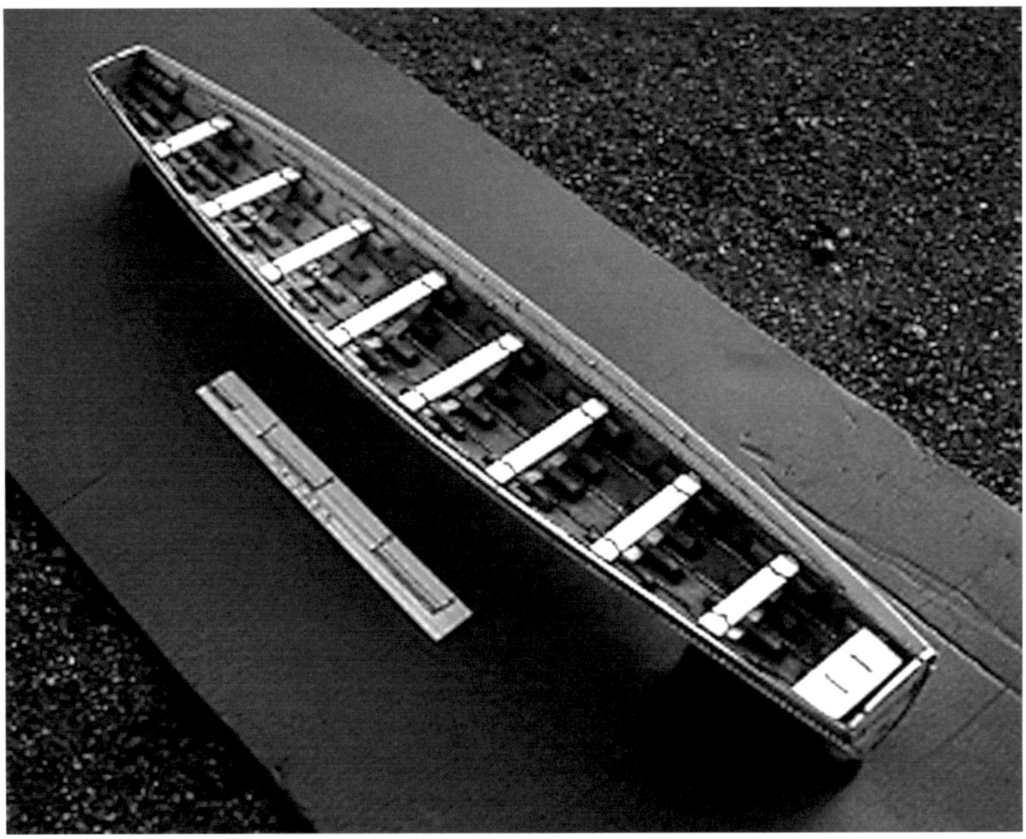

Fig. 6.7 (above) The Hasholme log-boat.

Fig. 6.8 (right) A model of the Brigg Craft.

Hjörtspring Boat (Greenhill 1976), the boat from Årby (Cederlund 1993) and others.

Seaworthy proportion

All of the known prehistoric boats gain dramatically improved sea-going capabilities in comparison with large log-boats, simply by doubling the beam (Fig 6.9). Neither length nor depth-of-hull of both types seem to have been increased significantly if at all, the average for length being 13.7m and for depth-of-hull 0.92m.

Beam combined with a rectangular (rather than a nearly-square) section produces a useful range of stability essential for seawork. The prehistoric boats have a beam to depth ratio ranging from 2:7 to 2:8 whereas the large log-boats are 1:2 and 1:7. The length of a log-boat is limited by the size of tree, as is the hull cross-section. Tree length seems to have been the limitation on the Brigg Craft too, since her strakes are in one piece.

In the Ferribies, and presumably the Caldicot, creating longer boards by butt-jointing is a feature. In the Dover, full-length boards based on available

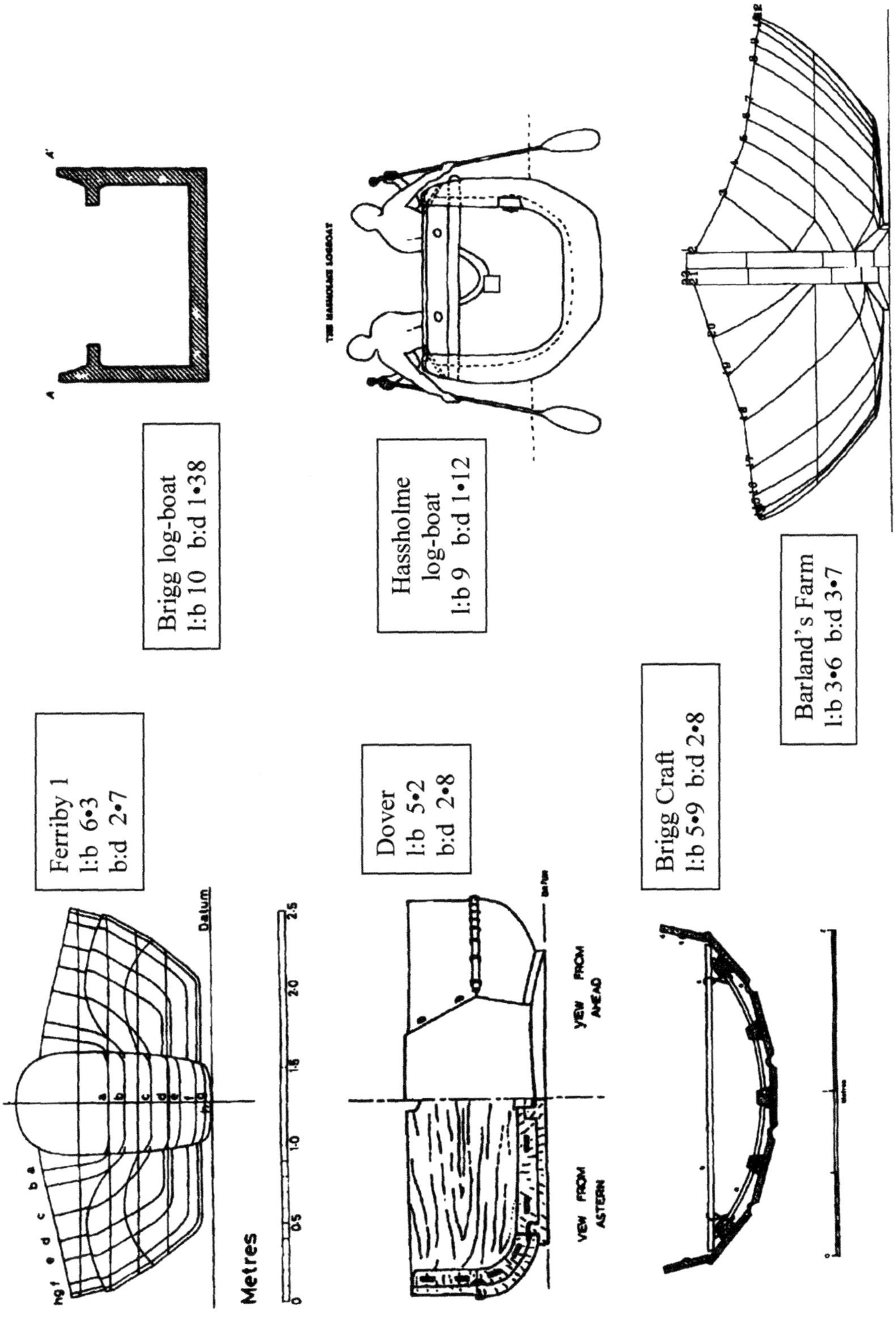

Fig. 6.9 Proportions of some Prehistoric boats.

tree length are used. Despite this there is a difference of only four metres in length between them. One might have expected even longer boats being built using these methods. However, the limitation on length is not that of the available timber, or how much it may be extended, but the limitations imposed by the stitching joining the strakes.

When re-constructing the Dover Boat it was necessary, as part of the analysis, to consider longer versions despite the likely length-to-depth ratios being quite unsuitable for sea-work, due to their being too flexible (Fig 6.10).

Calculations showed hogging and sagging strains to be comfortably resisted by the original stitching, but only up to a length of about 12 metres for serious seagoing. The evidence for freeboard was limited, but clearly one upper strake was missing, which by reconstruction of the bows and a reference to the widths of other parts of the boat was supported by a reasonable Beam to Depth ratio of 1:2. This was the minimal realistic solution, the maximum length being limited by the strength of the stitching which was obtained by calculation and matched the diameter of the original recorded withy stitches (Table 6.2).

Fig. 6.10 Dover; three versions.

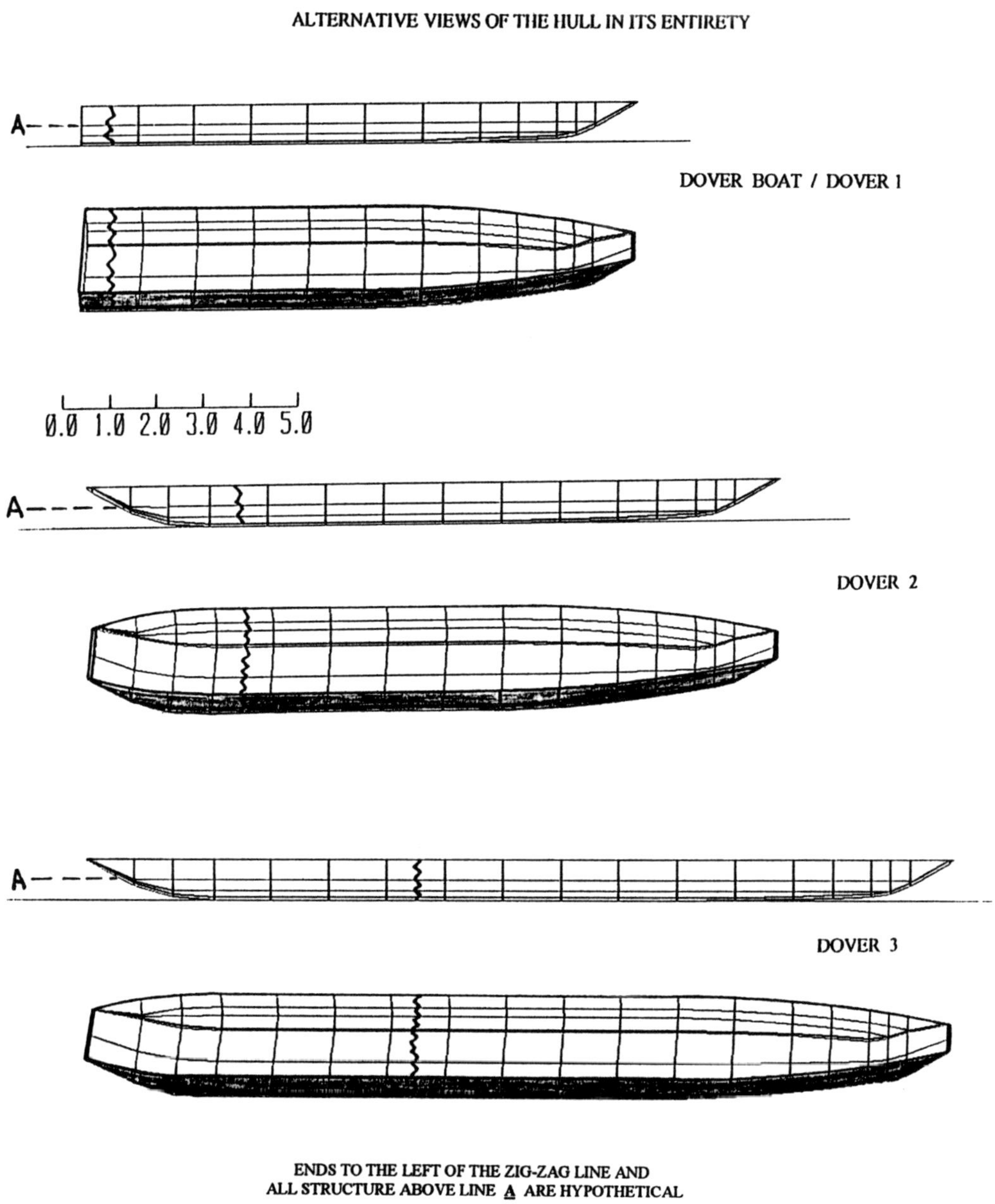

Structural needs in prehistoric boats

From a careful estimation of the volume of the structures I consider that, despite the monocoque forms of the prehistoric log-boats and their developments as seen in Ferribies, Dover and Caldicot, the amount of timber that went into their construction is about the same as would be in eighteenth or nineteenth century undecked work-boats of similar length, though having more beam and a different distribution of the timber. Any heavier and they would not have had sufficient seaworthy freeboard when loaded.

Length, as proposed above, was restricted by the inability of the stitching method to withstand flexing from hogging and sagging strains. This includes passage-making even in calm weather, since the application of the paddlers' or rowers' power to the hull would cause some distortion and seam movement. Log-boats would not suffer this way but sagging and hogging between waves could cause the sides to buckle slightly outwards and inwards frequently in time with the reversing forces. This could eventually destroy the integrity of the bottom-to-side area. Perhaps those many holes each side of the Hasholme's sheer line were intended for the insertion of athwartships 'preventer- lashings' against sagging and for beams in compression when wracking, as when a boat is crossing waves obliquely. It is possible that hogging was less of a problem than sagging because of the buoyant full ends.

In the Ferribies and the Dover, apart from thwarts, resistance to flexing is obtained from the shaping of parts of the hull as 3-D carvings having form stiffness. In the Dover particularly there is the first evidence of a boat being assembled around a notional centre-line, as opposed to each side of a central piece of timber resembling the denuded bottom of a log-boat. To resist bending, the two massive bottom slabs have been carved back from their logs to leave deep, up-standing rails down the centre and at both edges, clearly in the prehistoric knowledge that depth in a section of a girder induces resistance to bending. The chine-girders provide further stiffness, besides being an elegant solution to the problem of joining the bottom of the hull to its sides. In the Ferribies, bottom stiffness is obtained by arching the bottom profile; that is giving it rocker, which also closes off the ends. The carved side planking is then better able to withstand the tension and compression arising from hogging and sagging (Fig 6.11).

Rocker is an important stiffening feature of the curragh's flexible framing, combined with the space-frame gunwale mentioned earlier. Rocker is an essential feature in the Brigg Craft, combined with all the strakes fixed in tension by being bent and sewn to hold their curved form. Rocker improves manoeuvrability but may affect straight running.

Version	*average diameter of single withy for 3 strand stitch*
Dover 1	12-18mm
Dover 2	14-21mm
Dover 3	20-28mm

Table 6.2 Stitch diameters (average diameter in the archaeological record was 14.6mm)

In both sewn and stitched boats, hogging and sagging destroys stitches and the water-proofing material within the seams. Their destruction leads to slackness between planking and uncontrollable leaking and the need to re-stitch. As suggested earlier, the stitched boat is limited not by length of tree but by the inevitable flexibility of each individual stitch, which permits greater hog and sag as hull length increases. Based on calculations for the Dover boat, it is believed that the total flexibility rises even faster than the length increases.

Stitch spacing, and the number of stitches, is limited by the need to retain plank strength between each stitch slot. However, the Brigg Craft is sewn with a continuous 'thread' which requires a line of paired 'holes' matching the smaller diameter of the thread material. Consequently the holes are able to be closely spaced along the edges of adjoining strakes, the thread enclosing a seam batten over luting material pressed onto the seam (Fig 6.12).

This continuous method is similar in principle to that employed successfully in the building of Balam boats in the Bay of Bengal or Masula surf-boats on the east coast of India. This is similar in principal to the Nin Boat of 2nd century AD and the Ljubljana boat of about the 5th century BC. The close-up sewing patterns counter seam flexibility better than individual well-spaced, individual stitches of thick withy material.

Instability and the need to bail

Only a little bilge water in a flat-bottom hull will cause instability – the 'Ro-Ro effect'. Log-boats are particularly susceptible to this free-surface effect, arising from unrestricted bilge water movement because of their square cross-section and narrowness. Stitched boats probably made more water continuously. Bailing would reach a fine art. In the iron-fastened Barland's Farm boat, a deeply worn area upon the keel plank has been made by long and regular bailing, perhaps needed in old age.

In Dover, the parallel fore-and-aft ridges would slow down the surge of water. Dunnage of reeds and twigs would reduce this in other boats. For dunnage to work, the boat must be rolling from side to side, as she would on the sea. Dampening of the rhythm of the water swilling from side to side would

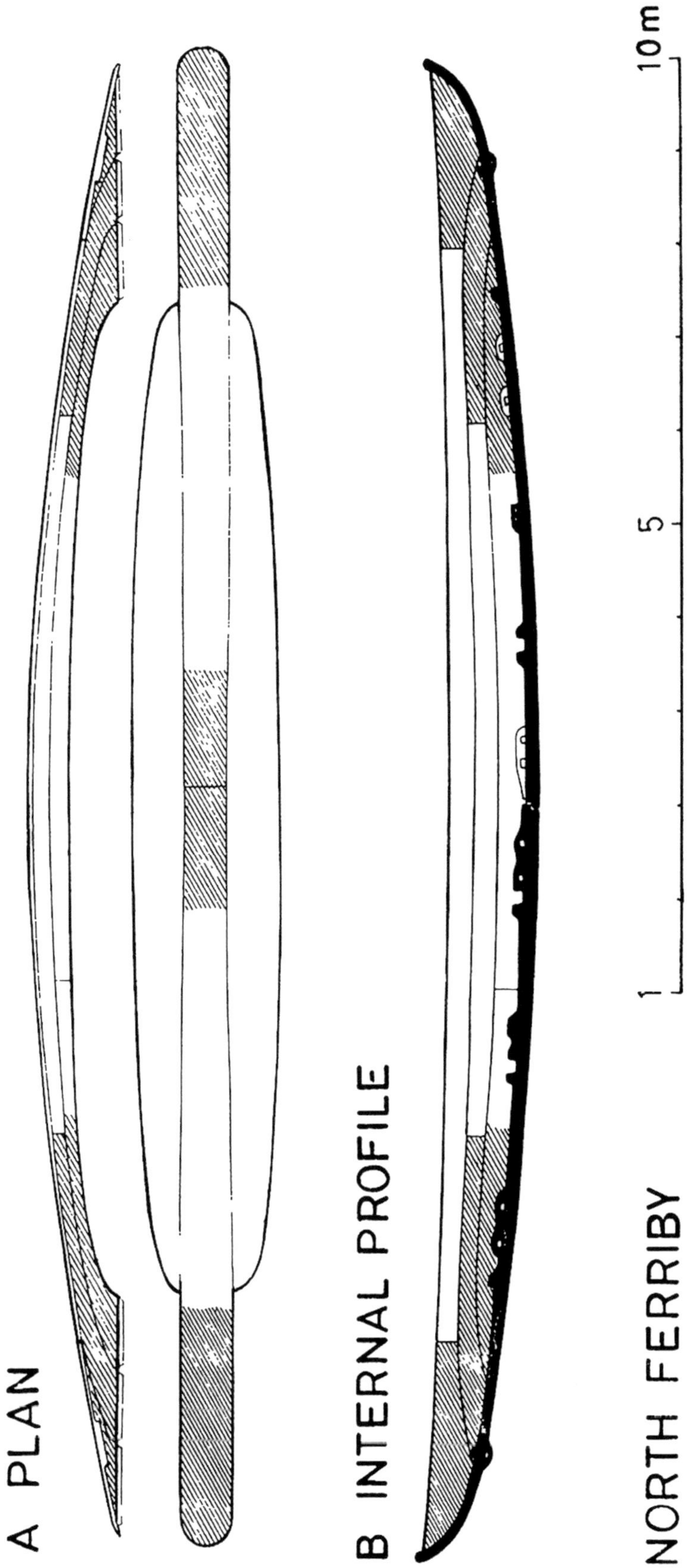

Fig. 6.11 Ferriby 1.

Fig. 6.12 Sewing within the Brigg Craft.

Fig. 6.13 The Dover boat: paddling and rowing positions.

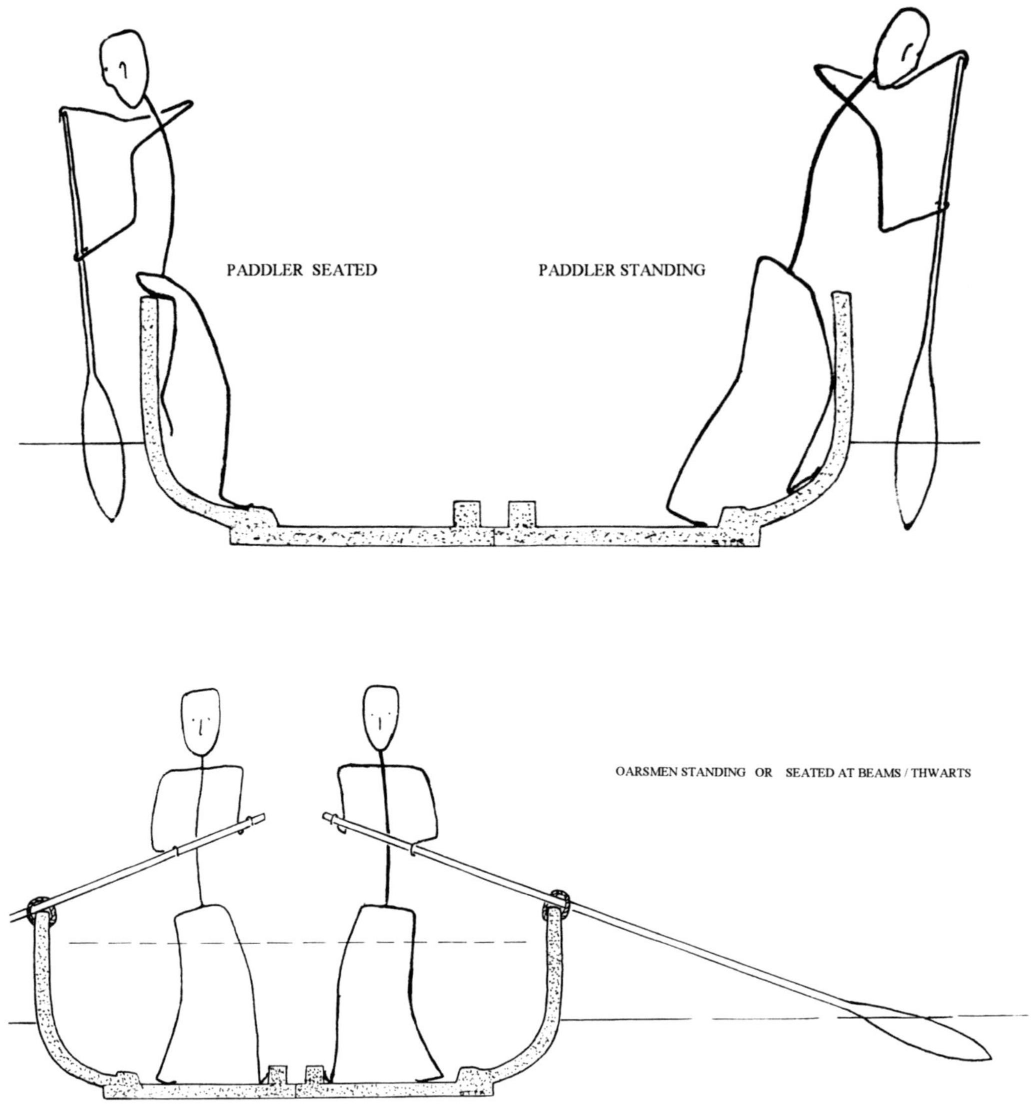

occur, making it less likely that the leeward bilge would also be the deadly recipient of all the bilge water. Inland usefulness for dunnage therefore is limited to padding under rough cargoes.

Propulsion – paddles, oars or sail?

Average speed must be sufficient to enable open-water crossings to be completed before exhausting the crew, to avoid bad weather, or to maintain a vector course in cross-tide passages. Narrow log-boats being paddled must not be deeper than a standing paddlers' hips. This restriction would also apply to stitched boats, which would be a governing factor when deciding depth of hull, unless oars were used. However, other factors limit hull depth too, as discussed earlier. The Ferribies, the Dover and the Brigg Craft must be regarded as using paddles or perhaps oars for their voyaging, though the evidence for oars comes later (Fig 6.13).

Sculling, that is the use of one long sweep or oar in a notch or yoke over the stern is not to be discounted, since in capable hands and in a directionally stable hull such as a logboat or a Dover type, it produces impressive propulsive power. A long stern sweep is not necessarily limited to steering.

Curraghs are pulling boats capable of rowing in any direction despite the weather, but are subject to much leeway in side winds because of shallow draft and very light weight. Rowing vector courses in such conditions, that is courses allowing for sideways drift or leeway, would be normal for their expert oarsmen.

During a course made down wind, a small sail could have been set in those earliest British prehistoric boats, but only for sailing before the wind (Fig 6.14). Shallow draft restricts sailing to downwind courses. No prehistoric evidence exists for dagger-boards, leeboards or deep rudders, which are essential for cross-wind courses in such boats (Roberts 1984). This is true of all the known prehistoric boats, which in any case are narrow, having Length-to-Beam ratios between 5 and 6, compared with the Barland's much healthier 3:6. A small sail set before a following wind is possible, (as is suggested here for Dover), but stepped in the first third of the hull since any further aft would easily induce a broach in a following sea, leading to capsize in such narrow boats.

Hornell's photograph of an Aran curragh under sail illustrates this, as do his records of Dingle curraghs showing holes in the for'ard thwarts for temporary down-wind rigs. Curraghs, as Synge describe, are in any case too flexible and unsuited to the tensions of a useful sailing rig and the compressive force of a mast, again another reason why the Broighter model is unlikely to be an Iron Age curragh but a boat of wooden construction.

Conclusion

From the evidence one might conclude that most voyaging around headlands depended on muscle power alone well into the last 1000 years BC. Cross-Channel and cross-Irish Sea voyaging can, by interpreting weather patterns, be a broad reach or a following-wind passage. Considering the distances involved, it is likely that rowed or paddled passages were linked to suitable winds until comparatively deep-hulled ships were developed, resulting in the Veneti ships, Barland's Farm coasters, Blackfriars short-sea traders and St. Peter's Port deep sea traders (Rule 1990).

The late Iron Age fisherman's type anchor and chain from Bulbury (Cunliffe 1972) would have belonged to a deep drafted vessel obliged to anchor in foul tides and light winds, rather than attempting to row any distance. The Veneti became so adept at sailing with finesse that they indulged in what really was a protection racket, collecting dues on shipping rounding Ushant between Biscayan and Channel ports. We have Caesar's description of this. It is the

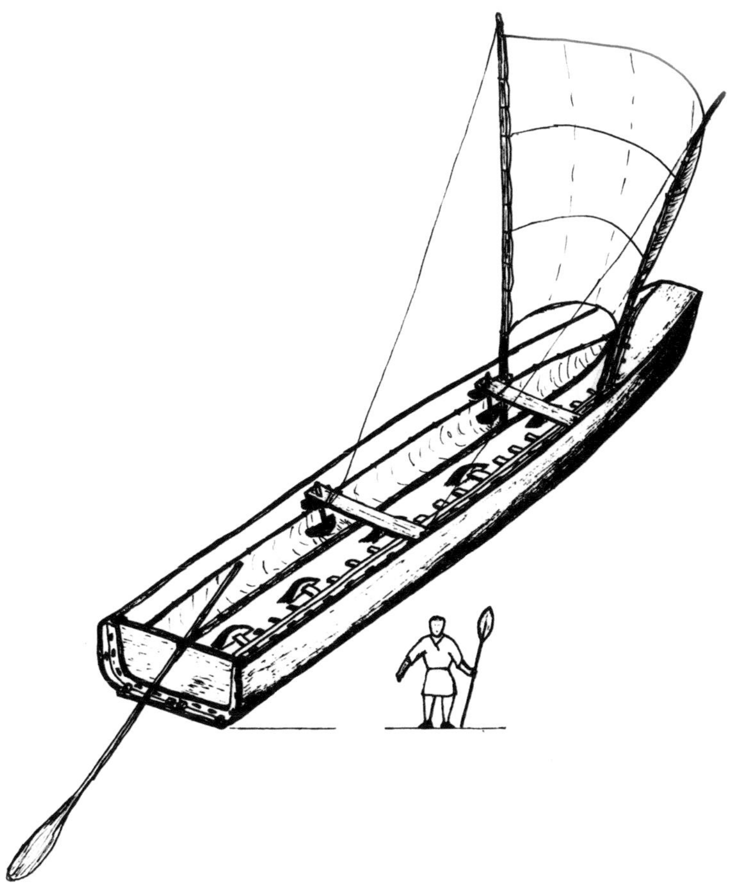

Fig. 6.14 The Dover boat under sail?

density of commercial traffic in the final century BC that made such activity worthwhile that should make one wonder, apart from the fleetness of the Veneti ships.

Did improvements in boats of the British Isles arrive with waves of Iron Age Celts? Sharpening of stems and the shaping of sterns are important concepts. Clearly trade contacts with the Mediterranean would have made Ancient Britons aware of nail-fastened ships, so when was metal fastening adopted?

The change to iron nails in the British Isles would have had the same impact on stitched-plank boat building as did the aluminium pop-rivet on early 'sticks and string' aeroplane construction. Nails overcome the dimensional constraints arising from sewing or stitching. Increased dimensions lead to greater displacement and a dependency on sails rather than oars (and certainly not paddles).

Evidence for a reliance mainly on sail is not available for the British Isles (except for the Broighter model) until The Gallic Wars III and descriptions of the Veneti. However, Professor Cunliffe's description of Pytheas' crossing to the British Isles, voyaging as far north as Iceland and beyond can only imply a general use and widespread knowledge of sail for many centuries prior to the 4th century BC (Cunliffe 2001).

Yet again, such voyaging would be based on the experience gained during the second millennium and earlier, in boats like the Ferribies, Dover, Brigg Craft, an assortment of large log-boats – and curraghs everywhere, which had been rounding headlands with regularity and venturing with confidence over the horizon to countries as well known to themselves as their own.

List of references

Caesar, J 50 BC, *The Conquest of Gaul III*, trans. S A Handford, London 1951

Cederlund, C O (ed), Arbman, H, Greenhill, B, Roberts, O T P 1993 *The Årby Boat*, Museum of National Antiquities Monograph, **2**, Stockholm

Crumlin-Pedersen, O 1997 *Viking-Age Ships and Shipbuilding*, Ships and Boats of the North, **2**, Schleswig and Roskilde

Cunliffe, B 1972 'Late Iron Age metal work from Bulbury, Dorset', *Antiquaries Journal*, **53,** 293–308

Cunliffe, B 1997 *The Ancient Celts*, Oxford: Oxford University Press

Cunliffe, B 2001, *Pytheas the Greek*, London

Greenhill, B 1976, *Archaeology of the Boat*, London

Hornell, J 1973 *The Curraghs of Ireland*, Society for Nautical Research Monograph, Greenwich

Marsden, P 1994 *Ships of the Port of London, Part 1*, English Heritage Archaeological Report, **3**

McGrail, S 1978 *Logboats of England and Wales, Parts 1 and 2*, National Maritime Museum Greenwich Archaeological Series, **2**, British Archaeological Reports (British Series), **51**

McGrail, S and Roberts, O T P 1999 'A Romano-British Boat from the shores of the Severn Estuary', *Mariner's Mirror*, **85:2**, 133–146

Millet, M and McGrail, S 1987 'The Archaeology of the Hasholme Logboat', *Archaeological Journal*, **144**, 69–155

Mudie, C 1986 'Designing Replica Boats', in O Crumlin-Pedersen and M Viner (eds), *Sailing into the Past*, Roskilde

Roberts, O T P 1984 'Viking Sailing Performance', in S McGrail (ed), *Aspects of Maritime Archaeology and Ethnography,* National Maritime Museum

Roberts, O T P 1992 'The Brigg 'raft' reassessed as a round bilge Bronze Age boat', *International Journal of Nautical Archaeology*, **21:3**, 245–258.

Roberts, O T P 2004 'Reconstruction and performance', in P Clark (ed), *The Dover Bronze Age boat*, English Heritage, 189–210

Rule, M 1990 'The Romano-Celtic ship excavated at St. Peter Port, Guernsey', in McGrail, S (ed), *Maritime Celts, Frisians and Saxons*, Council for British Archaeology Research Report, **71**, 49–56

Synge, J M 1907 *The Aran Islands*, reprinted OUP 1979

Thesiger, W 1987 *The life of my choice*, Harper Collins

Wright, E 1990 *The Ferriby Boats*, London

7. North-west European seagoing boats before AD 400

Seán McGrail

The British and Irish archipelago began to take shape towards the end of the last Ice Age as sea levels rapidly rose. In the Mesolithic period around 6,500 BC, with sea levels still rising, Britain became an island as inundated lowlands became the southern North Sea and the eastern Channel. From this time, if not earlier, seagoing vessels would have been needed, not only for two-way contacts between the European mainland and Britain, but also for exploration and settlement of islands within the archipelago (Cunliffe 1994, 45, 82; 2001, 111–142). Theoretically there are three sorts of boat that might have been used for these overseas voyages: hide boats, logboats and plank boats (McGrail 2001, 10–12, table 1.2), and we may ask: is there excavated evidence for these?

Logboats are known in this region from *c.* 7,500 BC (McGrail 2001, 172–4), the oldest one being that from Pesse in the Netherlands. Plank boats, however, are unknown until the Bronze Age *c.* 2000 BC (McGrail 2001, 184–190; Wright *et al* 2001), and there is no firm excavated evidence for hide boats, although there are documentary references to their use from the mid-1st millennium BC onwards (McGrail 2001, 181–3). What then could have been the early seagoing craft in these waters?

Seagoing capability

First let us consider how to decide whether an excavated boat was seagoing or not. Early boats are generally excavated in far from ideal conditions. Some are represented only by a single fragment. Those that have the recognisable form of a boat are usually in a non-floating attitude, their remains are fragmented, fragmentary, distorted and compressed, and parts have been displaced. Upperworks seldom survive, and it is rare for both bow and stern to be found. Furthermore, there is seldom any evidence for propulsion or steering. For our present purposes the question to be asked is: would the vessel such remains represent have best suited use at sea, or within estuaries and archipelagos, or on inland waters – to use three broad environmental categories.

Seagoing voyages may be coastal or open sea passages; these can differ in the severity of weather experienced and in the availability of havens. Although stressful conditions can be experienced within estuaries and archipelagos (and, indeed, on large lakes), these are generally protected from the worst effects of adverse weather and have the further advantage over seagoing passages that, in the event of trouble, the crew can more readily put into some haven or run their boat ashore. Open archipelagos and the outer reaches of estuaries can be more challenging than inner estuaries and compact archipelagos.

There are three main types of evidence which may help us to decide whether an excavated vessel would have been seagoing. First, evidence concerning the environment in which the vessel was found; second, finds directly associated with the vessel; and third, the vessel itself.

The environment

At first sight this might appear promising. But boats were not necessarily used in the environment from which they are excavated: river craft can be swept out to sea (a plausible explanation for the Kilnsea sewn plank boat fragment (van de Noort *et al* 1999) being found on the coast beyond the present bounds of the Humber estuary) and seagoing ships can be abandoned up-river (see, for example, the early-15th century royal warship *Grace Dieu* in the River Hamble near Bursledon; Friel 1993).

Furthermore, vessels may be re-used in other roles away from their operational environment: as pontoons, as river bank or sea wall reinforcements, underwater blockages, hards or causeways; or they may be broken-up and used as fill on reclaimed sites. They can also become coffins, or used in other ritual ways as has been suggested for the Dover boat by both Champion (Champion forthcoming) and Pryor (Pryor and Taylor 1993; Pryor this volume).

Cargo, ballast, and personal possessions

These have very rarely been found with prehistoric boats in NW Europe. In any case, they are ambiguous as indicators of overseas voyages. A particular type of cargo, ballast or possessions may suggest at least one overseas voyage, but exotic cargo may be transferred from seagoing vessel to lighter for carriage ashore or up-river. Ballast of overseas origin may have been embarked from a mound dumped by another vessel, whilst exotic possessions may be used by the crew of river craft and/or may have been traded through several hands (McGrail 1991, 83–6).

The hull

The presence of barnacles and other salt water creatures on an excavated hull may indicate recent seagoing. On the other hand, exotic types of hull timber (identified by species recognition or by dendrochronological comparisons) may have been imported in another vessel.

A more direct way of determining seagoing abilities is to assess potential performance. But before that can be done, the contemporary environment and the form and structure of the original vessel must both be reconstructed. Although great progress is being made, at present environmental reconstructions are usually very 'broad brush' in both time and space, lacking the detail needed. Whilst, even when excavated remains can be reconstructed authentically (and this is not always possible – see below), theoretical assessment of seagoing potential may not be easy since a number of interacting factors have to be considered: the strength, durability and watertight integrity of the hull; its stability, and its operational freeboard. Manoeuvrability, controllability, seakindliness and dryness have also to be evaluated. An open boat below a certain size is unlikely to have been seagoing, but a decked vessel, *ceteris paribus*, could have been. Shape is also important: a rockered bottom, a 'boat-shaped' underwater hull, and a sheerline rising towards the ends suggest a seagoing vessel; a rectangular box shaped vessel is likely to have been used on river and lake.

A seagoing vessel

Most of these characteristics contribute towards the safety of vessel and crew, and it is impossible to know now what the approach to risk assessment in earlier times was. In recent centuries adventurers have crossed the Channel, and even the Atlantic, in the most unlikely vessels, and it may be that, on specific occasions, prehistoric mavericks also put to sea in what would be regarded as unsuitable craft. Nevertheless, it is important to remember that, as prehistoric archaeologists, we are looking for patterns and regularities. As Coles (2001, 21) has argued in the context of Wetlands Studies:

> *'The freakish acts of the past, one-off ... [events] ... can add little to our understanding of the interactions and relationships ... between people and their environments'.*

It seems wise, therefore, to assume that the ancient mariner was a 'prudent' mariner who would make good use of his boat's capabilities but not act recklessly. In other words, when evaluating whether a vessel would have been seagoing or not, we have to consider normal, rather than abnormal use. A 20th century analogy would be that, in the most unusual (unique?) circumstances of the Dunkirk evacuation in 1940, some of the vessels used were river and harbour craft that otherwise would never have been considered for such cross-Channel passages. This definition of 'seagoing' is therefore proposed:

> *'An excavated prehistoric raft or boat may be considered seagoing in a specified environment if it can be shown that, in the hands of a prudent mariner, it could have been relied upon to carry a reasonable load on a sea passage of some duration, in the weather and sea conditions generally prevailing in antiquity at the particular time and place.'*

It could be argued that this definition is too restrictive. Prehistoric seamen may have waited for a period of settled summer weather – even the one perfect day – before undertaking an overseas voyage. Furthermore, it may be claimed that all the artefacts known to have been carried overseas within this region could have been transported in a handful of voyages each century, and from this, if a rough and ready allowance is made for missing data, one might conclude that only a handful of voyages each year would have been needed. Such hypotheses could lead to the proposition that, in prehistoric times, almost any type of water transport would have been 'seagoing'. But such reasoning ignores Coles' argument that normal use should be considered, rather than abnormal, or even freakish, possibilities. Investigations based on that mode of reasoning would add little, if anything, to our knowledge of ancient technology or the prehistoric maritime way of life. Whilst acknowledging that prehistoric seamen could well have taken advantage of favourable weather, it is necessary to investigate whether less-than-perfect weather and sea conditions could also have been used so that a rounded picture of prehistoric achievements may be obtained.

Re-appraisal of excavated evidence

How then do we assess whether or not the boat that excavated remains represent would have satisfied the definition of seagoing given above? There are three stages in such an investigation (McGrail 1997, 313–374):

1. Determine precisely what was excavated.
2. Reconstruct the original form and structure of the hull, the propulsion outfit and the steering arrangements.
3. Evaluate the reconstruction(s).

Experiments in the natural sciences can be repeated, thereby permitting verification or modification of the original experimenter's findings. Historians may similarly investigate a colleague's deductions by going back to the original documents or illustrations. Unlike these, an archaeologist's 'experiment' cannot be repeated: an excavation, such as that of the Romano-Celtic boat at Barland's Farm in Gwent (Fig 7.1), now exists only as recovered remains and site records (McGrail and Roberts 1999; Nayling and McGrail 2004). The nearest we can get to repeating an excavation 'experiment' is to re-assess the remains and the documentation, and then combine the information from these sources into an 'as found' scale drawing or model. The term 'as found' is used here in a special way. It does not mean the boat as depicted in site plans and sections, nor the post-excavation scale drawings of individual elements. It means:

'the boat as excavated, but with displaced members re-instated, fragmented members made whole, distorted and compressed parts restored to their original shape, and the hull rotated to the presumed attitude when afloat'.

This re-arrangement of the excavated evidence is best presented as a scale model (Fig 7.2) or as plans and sections (Fig 7.3). Making models and compiling plans both require intellectual rigour and clearly presented arguments if they are to provide a firm, unchallengeable base for the subsequent reconstruction process of 'filling in the missing pieces'.

Instead of the phrase 'as-found', Ole Crumlin-Pedersen uses the term 'torso', by analogy with ancient statues which are displayed in museums without noses, heads or arms. He has, for example, used the 'torso' presentation to describe the re-assembled remains of the five medieval Skuldelev ships (Crumlin-Pedersen and Olsen 2002, 120–5, 168–175, 225–6, 264–6, 292–4). The 'torso' concept has also been used at Roskilde to describe drawings and models of the Hedeby wrecks (Crumlin-Pedersen 1997, 88–9, 100, 306–7) and the Ladby medieval burial ship (Sørensen 2001, 183–194).

The Ladby ship of *c.* 900 AD was excavated by the National Museum of Denmark in 1934–7 (Thorvildsen 1957), and Roskilde's recent re-appraisal of the remains and the archival documentation has set standards for others to follow (Sørensen 2001). The excavated remains – mainly lines of nails and a shaped impression in the natural matrix (Fig 7.4) – were similar to those of the *c.* AD 600 ship from burial mound 1 at Sutton Hoo, both vessels being early examples of the Nordic building tradition. Early attempts to reconstruct the Ladby ship's original form and structure were not convincing, again like Sutton Hoo. The recent Roskilde research on the Ladby material involved (*inter alia*) the use of an ingenious method of displaying the recorded nail positions in a three-dimensional model (Fig 7.5), which allowed distortions to be investigated, so that the original lines of the vessel could be determined (Sørensen 2001, 185–234) as a step towards full reconstruction.

The Science Museum's 'provisional plan' of the Sutton Hoo ship, compiled in 1939 and published in Dr Bruce-Mitford's great work (1975, 259, fig 185), is generally considered unsatisfactory. The British Museum's 'archaeological reconstruction' and 'lines' (Bruce-Mitford 1975, 434, figs 324–325) were evidently based on a review of the 1939 data and on evidence from the 1963–5 re-excavation (presumably including that from a fibre-glass cast of the ship impression; Bruce-Mitford 1975, 280–8, fig 209), but precisely how these two drawings were compiled has never been fully explained. The Sutton Hoo ship must be a prime candidate for the use of the Roskilde re-assessment method to establish an 'as found / torso' datum before any further attempts are made to reconstruct this vessel.

Similar re-appraisals need to be undertaken on several other excavated boats and ships about which there are widely differing views. These include the Brigg 'raft' (McGrail 1981), as well as the Ferriby boats (Wright 1976; 1990; 1994), those vessels thought to be Romano-Celtic, and many of those thought to be Cogs (McGrail 2001, 433). Should it be no longer possible for the excavator of these vessels to undertake this re-assessment, it will have to be undertaken by others.

Even when the excavator could take on this task, an independent, inter-disciplinary group could well be preferable from the discipline's point of view. An archaeologist alone would be inadequate, as would a naval architect, a boatbuilder, or a model builder. People with these skills are needed within the group, and an historian when the vessel is of Roman or medieval date. Furthermore, at least one of the group must have seafaring experience. It may prove difficult to identify people with the necessary knowledge and time to become members of such a team, but this is a challenge to which Maritime Archaeology must respond if it is to retain credibility as a scholarly sub-discipline. It may be that the informal group known as the International Symposia on Boat and Ship Archaeology (ISBSA) could select appropriate specialists (McGrail 2000).

Such a rigorous audit should first seek to establish precisely what had been excavated. Without this, our perception of early water transport could be very misleading. Furthermore, without such a re-appraisal, 'replica' building is wasted effort.

Reconstruction

The aim of the second phase of the three-phase assessment of performance is to produce a reconstruction drawing (Fig 7.6) based directly on

Fig. 7.1 The Romano-Celtic boat from Barland's Farm, during excavation in Dec. 1993. Photo: Glamorgan-Gwent Archaeological Trust.

Fig. 7.2 (left) A 1:10 'as-found/torso' model of the Barland's Farm boat. Photo: Newport Museum.

Fig. 7.3 (below)An 'as-found/torso' measured drawing of the Barland's Farm boat. Plans: Glamorgan-Gwent Archaeological Trust.

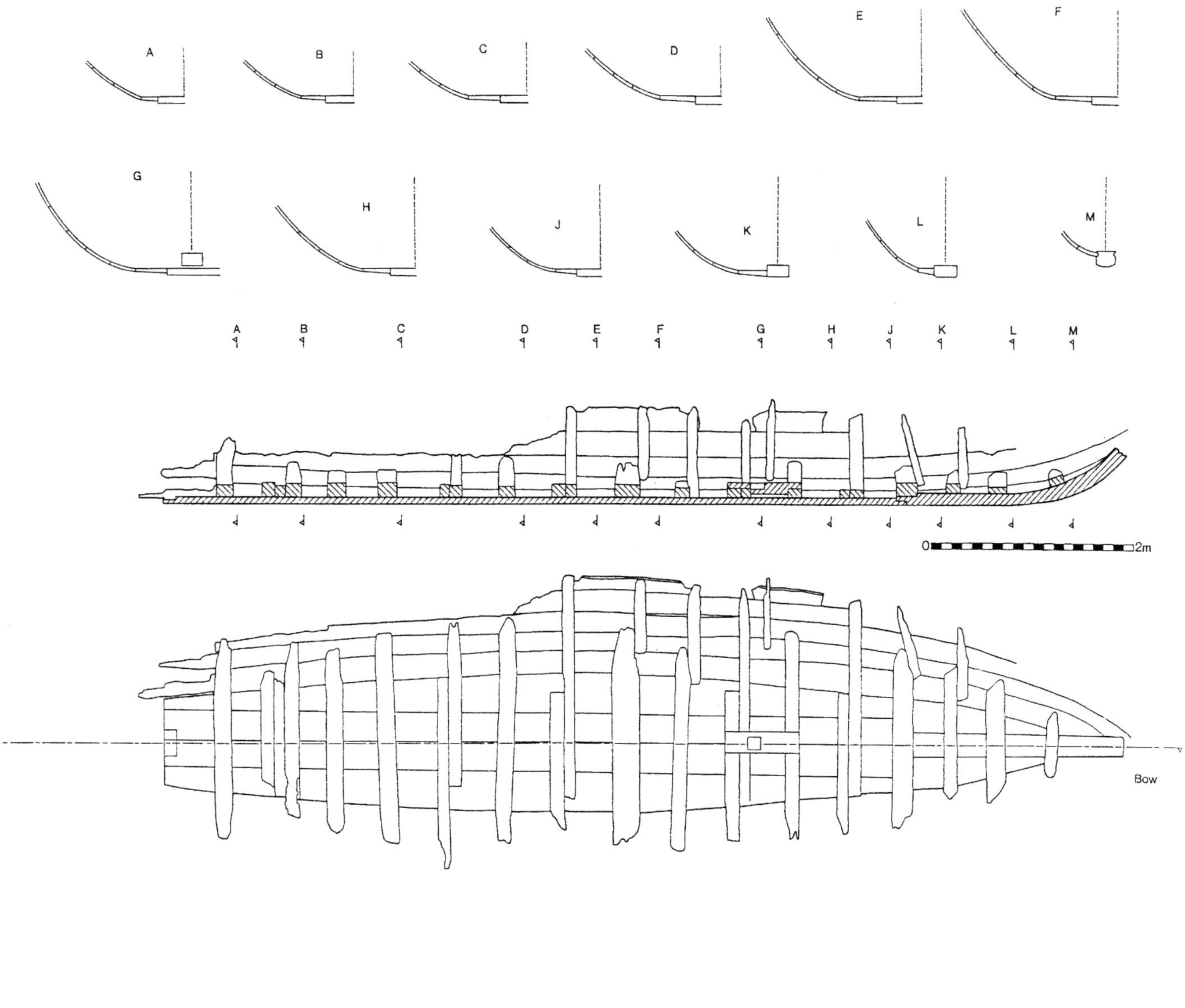

Fig. 7.4 The Ladby ship during excavation in 1935. Photo: The National Museum of Denamrk.

the first phase 'as-found/ torso' model or drawing (Figs 7.2 and 7.3): this is not always possible. Once again, teamwork and scholarly presentation of arguments are essential. Evidence from fastenings and from shadows of missing timbers may be used to fill in missing parts, as may the extension of existing planking runs.

Arguments of symmetry and the recognition of patterns in the layout of the framing can also help to fill in gaps. If rules of proportion can be demonstrated, they may also be used, as may comparative evidence from contemporary or earlier vessels from the same tradition. Elements added to what was excavated (and the tools and techniques needed to produce them) must be from the same 'technological environment' as the excavated vessel.

Suggestions that timbers should be added solely because they appear to be structurally or operationally necessary to 21st century eyes should be treated with great caution. If innovations from later times (for example, in the light of present knowledge, sail in NW Europe before the late-1st millennium BC) are incorporated, detailed arguments for such anachronisms must be given. The inclusion of elements (anachronistic or not) merely because they would improve performance cannot be justified. It is also most important to avoid confused arguments such as: this vessel is likely to have been seagoing, therefore she would have had extra freeboard and/or rocker; thus, since she has been reconstructed with this/these feature(s), she must have been seagoing.

In some instances (for example, when only sparse or very puzzling remains survive), the archaeological discipline will be best served by the admission that no reconstruction is possible, rather than 'filling in' the missing elements merely for the sake of reaching a conclusion. Even where more substantial remains survive and reconstruction can be attempted, there will inevitably be an element of uncertainty, if only in the detailed shape and structure of the hull (especially the ends), and in the means of propulsion and steering. Where differences between possible solutions to such ambiguity are not fundamental (for example: with or without figurehead; rudder or steering oar; or different types of sail), alternative reconstructions of such details may be proposed.

Where radically different reconstructions are envisaged (for example: with sail or without sail; flat-bottomed, rockered, or round-bilged) it has been suggested that minimum and maximum reconstructions be compiled (McGrail 1997, 313–4; 1998, 192–3). The minimum reconstruction should be in accordance with Occam's razor criteria (as advocated by Peter Marsden in this volume): the reconstructor must make minimum additions to the 'as found / torso' drawing and each addition must be fully justified. The maximum reconstruction is more difficult to specify since individual perceptions will inevitably determine how far beyond the minimum solution the maximum reconstruction can 'reasonably' be taken. The over-enthusiastic use of computer-aided design methods will also increase the likelihood of reconstruction being taken beyond what others would consider valid.

Taking all things into consideration, the archaeological discipline will be best served if reconstructors stick to minimum solutions. In the event that maximum reconstructions (or any reconstruction beyond the minimum) are attempted, drawings of both minimum and maximum solutions, together with supporting arguments, should be published and subjected to informed criticism. It may be that a consensus would then emerge as to how far (if at all) the reconstructor would be justified in departing from the minimum version.

Assessment of performance

The reconstructed drawing (Fig 7.6) is used in this third phase to estimate the performance of the vessel by eye, or by calculation as done by Owain Roberts for the Dover boat (Roberts forthcoming). Performance assessments can be derived from the reconstruction drawing using displacement curves and form coefficients, calculations of stability and rowing geometry, and estimates of sailing potential; these then lead to consideration of seagoing abilities. This may be as far as many projects need go. Alternatively, a reconstruction (colloquially, 'replica') may be built, followed by trials and full and timely publication (Coates *et al* 1995).

These three methods of performance evaluation are in ascending order of complexity and cost; they are also in ascending order of the impact they will make on the reader or spectator. The built reconstruction (a 'three-dimensional floating hypothesis'; McGrail 1992) will thus be correspondingly more misleading if errors have been made in compiling the 'as-found / torso' drawing, and/or in deducing the full reconstruction.

Because of financial and other constraints it is unlikely that the building and testing of a reconstruction of a particular vessel will be repeated (at least, in the short term). It is therefore essential that, before such an experiment is undertaken the chosen reconstruction should have the unqualified approval of that undefined, inter-disciplinary group that constitutes the scientific academic constituency for the history of nautical technology.

To achieve this, the 'as-found / torso' drawings, the reconstruction drawings and the supporting arguments have to be published widely and then subjected to criticism in specialist seminars and in a more broadly-based forum.

Excavated boats

We may now examine the evidence for prehistoric boats in the light of the preceding discussion, and seek to identify which could have been seagoing.

Logboats

Many prehistoric logboats have been found in north-west Europe (Arnold 1995–6; McGrail 2001, 172); a number have been recorded and published to acceptable standards. Boats built from a single log are necessarily narrow in proportion to their length. Furthermore, they have little freeboard, and their limited breadth at the waterline means poor transverse stability. Such characteristics are acceptable

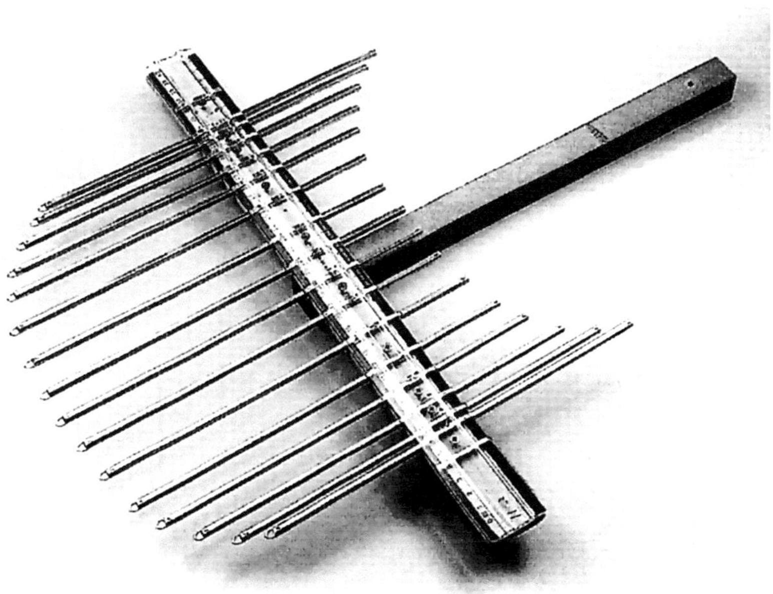

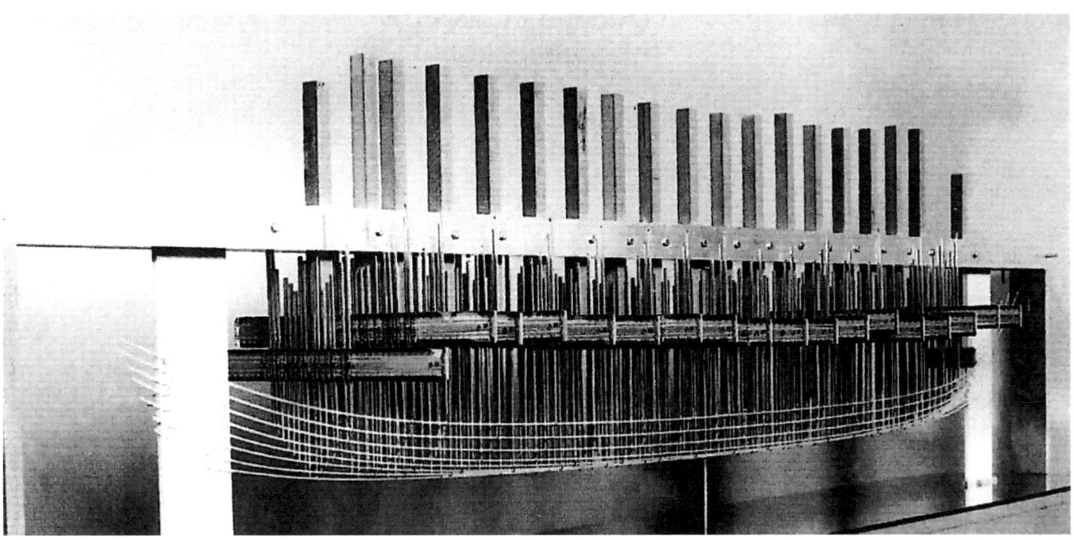

Fig. 7.5 (above) A template with adjustable rods used to check the lines of nails on a model of the Ladby ship impression; (left) templates were used to adjust the fibreglass battens of the Ladby model to give fair lines. Photos: Viking Ship Museum, Roskilde.

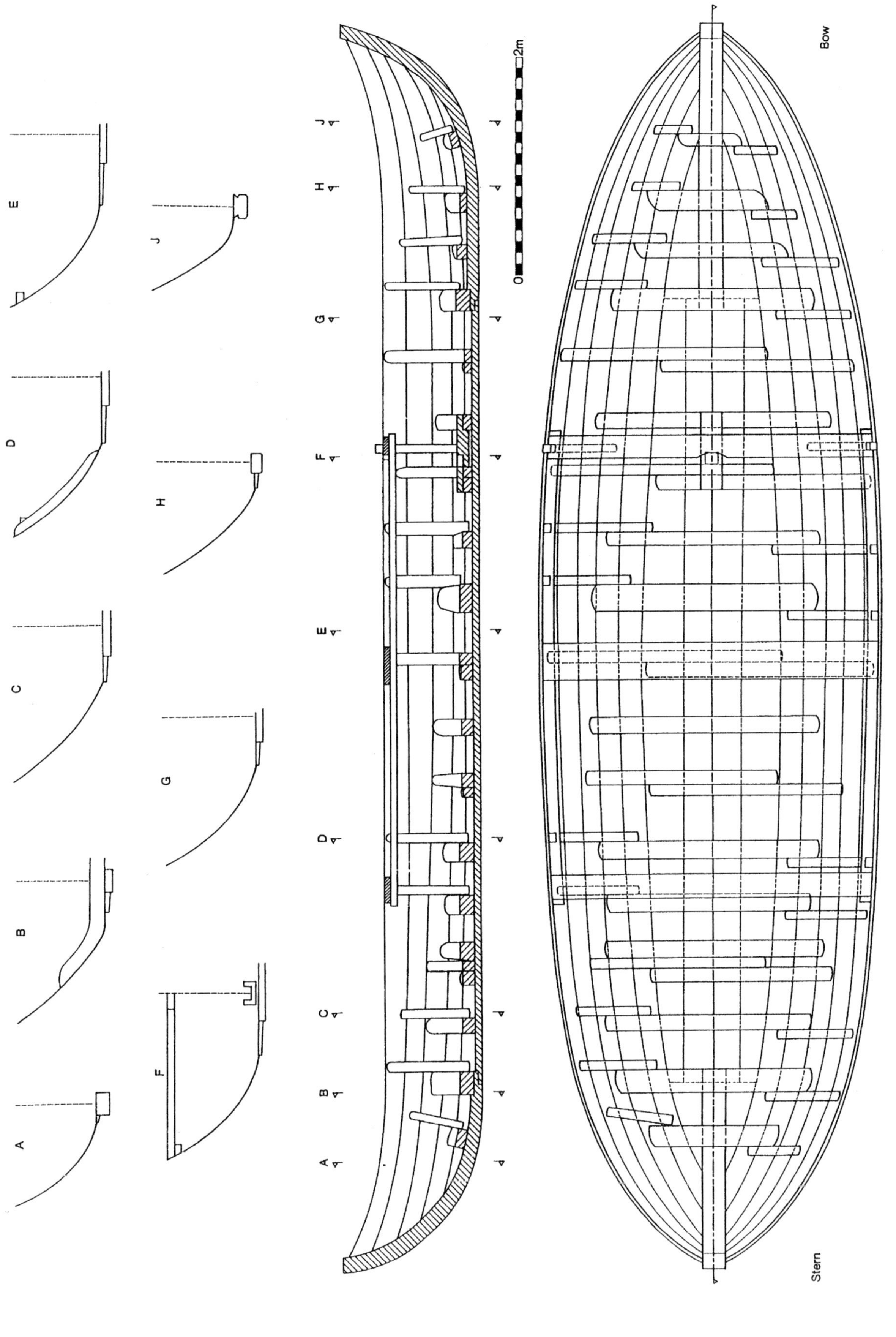

Fig. 7.6 Reconstruction drawing of the hull of the Barland's Farm boat. Plans: Glamorgan-Gwent Archaeological Trust.

on rivers and lakes but not in more testing conditions. However, logboats may be modified in several ways to give them seagoing potential (McGrail 2001, 178–9):

Freeboard can be improved by adding strakes to increase the height of sides.

Stability may be improved by: fitting stabilisers at the waterline; pairing two boats; expanding a single hull.

The evidence indicates that washstrakes may have been fitted to logboats from the Neolithic onwards. On the other hand, the evidence for stabilisers and pairing is inconclusive, and, at present, there is only anecdotal evidence for the expansion of prehistoric logboats. The north-west European logboat scene thus seems to be an increase in logboat freeboard, but not in stability. On present evidence, the conclusion must be that early logboats are unlikely to have been regularly used at sea, in open archipelagos, or in the outer reaches of estuaries.

Plank boats

There is a sewn-plank boat from Hjortspring in Denmark of 350 to 300 BC (McGrail 2001, 191–2). This boat has undergone a theoretical and practical re-appraisal during the past decade. It therefore seems best to postpone discussion of her until the Roskilde report is published.

British prehistoric sewn plank boats have been excavated in four regions:

Humber Estuary

The Ferriby boats of *c.* 2000 to 1700 BC (Wright 1990; 1994; Wright and Switsur 1993; Wright *et al* 2001).

The Kilnsea fragment of *c.* 1800 BC (van de Noort *et al* 1999).

The Brigg 'raft' of *c.* 800 BC (McGrail 1981; 1985).

Severn Estuary

The Caldicot fragments of *c.* 1750 and 1100 BC (Nayling and Caseldine 1997, 210–217).

The Goldcliffe fragments of about 1000 BC (Bell *et al* 2001, 74–82).

Test Estuary

A fragment from Testwood near Southampton dated to *c.* 1100 BC (Wessex Archaeology 1996).

Dover

The Dover boat of *c.* 1550 BC (Clark forthcoming).

These boats may provisionally be divided into two groups by reference to their date and to their plank fastenings.

Group A: Ferriby 1, 2 and 3, Dover, Caldicot 1 and Kilnsea

These boats from *c.* 2000 to 1500 BC have interlocking, edge-to-edge or half-lap planking fastened together by individual lashings through large holes (25–35mm across). They were early, and ropes of some size were used as lashings.

Group B: Brigg 'raft', Caldicot 2, Goldcliffe, Ferriby 5 and Testwood

These are from *c.* 1100 to 500 BC, and they have edge-to-edge and bevel-lap planking fastened together by running stitching through small holes (10mm across). They were generally later than Group A, and light cord was used to sew the planks together.

Of these vessels, only Ferriby 1, the Brigg 'raft' and the Dover boat have been reconstructed. The Dover boat was not published at the time of writing, but in papers and discussion at the Dover conference in November, 2002 (this volume) differing views were expressed on the performance and function of this boat, and arguments for and against seagoing potential were presented. Furthermore, different reconstructions were outlined of the environment in which the Dover boat would have been used, in one of which this boat's role could have been that of a ferry across a river or a lagoon. When the publication is available, the data presented there may help clarify the boat's role.

The present author's assessment of Ferriby 1 and the Brigg 'raft', by eye and by simple calculation, is that seagoing was not their usual role. These boats did not have the shape or the structure to match the stability, the freeboard or the seakindliness required by a boat regularly used at sea. The Ferriby boat's primary role was probably as a cross-estuary ferry on a stretch of the Humber where there have been ferries since at least Roman times, the last being three British Rail coal-fired, paddle-wheel ferries which survived until the Humber Bridge was built in the 1980s. In medieval and earlier times such cross-Humber passages connected south-north routes along the Lincolnshire Wolds and the Lincoln Edge to similar routes on the Yorkshire Wolds. Before large-scale drainage of the Humber's lower catchment area was undertaken in the 18th century AD, these passages were even more important than in recent times since the nearest alternative route then lay many miles to the west.

The Brigg 'raft' would have been used as an east-west ferry across what is now the River Ancholme, then a tidal creek of the Humber, at a nodal point in this valley where the two upland regions, the limestone Lincoln Edge to the west and the chalk Lincolnshire Wolds to the east, were closest (McGrail 1981, 248–9).

These assessments are based on Wright's minimum reconstruction of Ferriby 1 (Fig 7.7), and the present author's reconstruction of the Brigg 'raft' (Fig 7.8). However, others have published different reconstructions of both these boats: (Ferriby: Wright 1990, fig 5.17. Brigg: McGrail 1994; Roberts 1992), and these appear to be more seaworthy than the reconstructions used in this paper. How then can we decide between alternative reconstructions?

The answer to this question is to follow the three-phase procedure described above. A team of specialists should examine the timbers and the documentation of Ferriby 1 and the Brigg 'raft' so that securely based 'as-found / torso' drawings may be compiled, and a small-scale model built of each one. Only after these drawings and models have been subjected to wide criticism should thought be given to reconstruction. In turn, any reconstruction should be criticised by peer review and revised where necessary. Not until then should the possibility of building three-dimensional 'floating hypotheses' be considered (Coates *et al* 1995).

Over the past decade or so, Professor Crumlin-Pedersen has re-assessed his earlier work on the five Skuldelev ships, and has established precisely what was excavated 45 years ago from the 11th century blockage in Roskilde fjord. He is currently re-assessing the prehistoric Hjortspring boat (excavated in 1921–2) in a similar manner, and will shortly publish definitive reconstructions and performance assessments of this boat and the five Skuldelev ships. This three-phase approach to reconstruction and performance assessment of earlier finds should now be followed in Britain.

A different type of plank boat?

Although logboats continued in use from prehistoric times until the medieval period and later, evidence for plank boats in this region fades away from the eighth century BC until the early centuries AD, the only find of note being the Hjortspring sewn plank boat of the later-4th century BC. There are, however, hints in the British archaeological record that there may have been plank boats which differed significantly from the known sewn boats, and which might have been used during the Bronze and Iron Ages. A boat-shaped, Early Bronze Age, log coffin from Loose Howe in north-east England has both keel and stem worked in the solid oak (Elgee 1949; McGrail 2001, fig 5.25); and two oak logboats, Poole (*c.* 300 BC) and Holme Pierrepont 3 (*c.* 200 BC), also have 'false' stems (McGrail 1978, catalogue 59, 112) (Fig 7.9). Such representations contribute little if anything to the structure or form of a logboat, and they may have been copied from a contemporary (possibly seagoing) plank boat (McGrail 2001, 192–3).

Plank boats of the first to fourth centuries AD

During the early centuries AD, after the so-called plank boat 'Dark Age', evidence for three different traditions of plank-built vessel has been excavated in north-west Europe. Remains of vessels from London, eastern Ireland and the lower Rhinelands have flush-laid planking fastened together by

Fig. 7.7 A scale model of the minimum reconstruction of Ferriby boat 1. Elements coloured black were excavated, the remainder is conjectural. Photo: National Maritime Museum, Greenwich.

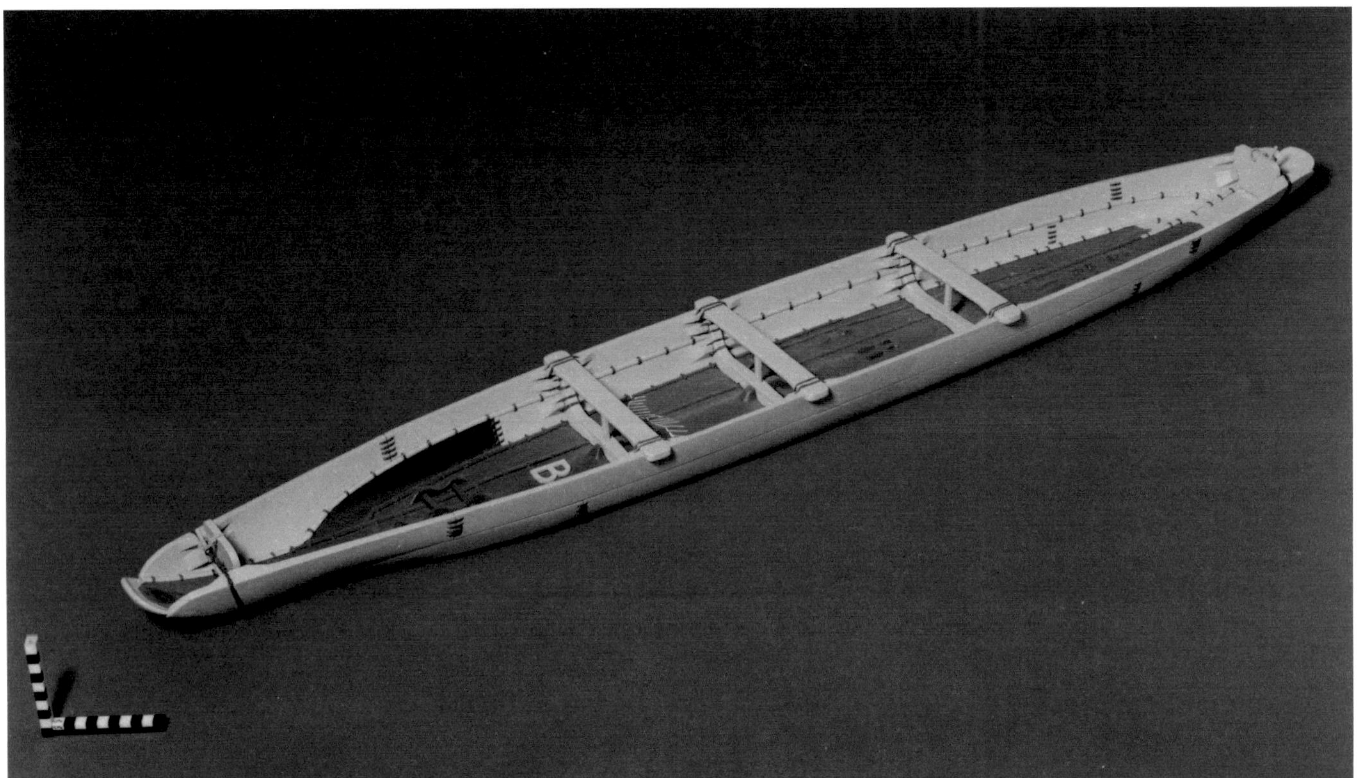

Fig. 7.8 (left) A scale model of the minimum reconstruction of the Brigg 'raft'. Elements within the white outline were excavated, the remainder is conjectural. Photo: National Maritime Museum, Greenwich.

Fig. 7.9 (below) The bows of the Poole logboat, showing the 'false' stem. Photo: Poole Museums.

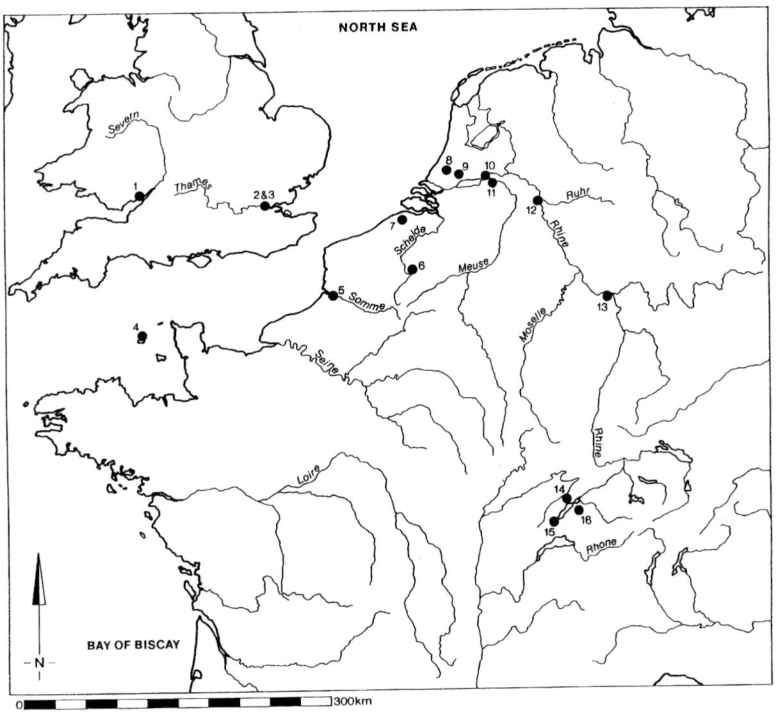

Fig. 7.10 Distribution map of Romano-Celtic boats. 1. Barland's Farm; 2. Blackfriars; 3. New Guy's House; 4. St Peter Port; 5. Abbeville; 6. Pommerroeul; 7. Bruges; 8. Zwammerdam; 9. Woerden; 10. Kapel Avezaath; 11. Druten; 12. Xanten; 13. Mainz; 14. Bevaix; 15. Yverdon; 16. Avenaches. Map: Glamorgan-Gwent Archaeological Trust.

wooden mortise and tenon joints, a diagnostic feature of the Classical Mediterranean tradition (McGrail 2001, 194–5). In Scandinavia, boats from Valderoy and Halsnøy have overlapping planking fastened together by sewing, whilst the Bjorke extended logboat has nail-fastened, clinker planking similar to that which was to become a defining characteristic of the medieval Nordic tradition (McGrail 2001, 192, 208–9).

The third of these traditions is known as 'Romano-Celtic': 'Romano' primarily because the boats and ships excavated are dated to the 1st to 4th centuries AD; and 'Celtic' because these excavations were in regions formerly occupied by Celtic-speaking peoples (McGrail 2001, 196–207). The distribution extends from Switzerland in the south-east, along the Rhine to the Low Countries and the Channel Islands, and on to the Thames and Severn estuaries in the north west Fig 7.10). Most of these vessels were canal and river 'barges', but three of them were seagoing: the mid-2nd century Blackfriars 1 ship from the River Thames in London (Marsden 1994, 33–95); the late-3rd century St Peter Port ship from the main harbour of Guernsey (Rule and Monaghan 1993); and the *c.* AD 300 boat from Barland's Farm on the northern shores of the Severn Estuary (McGrail and Roberts 1999; Nayling and McGrail 2004).

There is a fundamental difference between these seagoing Romano-Celtic vessels and the Bronze Age and Iron Age sewn plank boats. In prehistoric times, a builder of sewn plank boats thought of his boat in

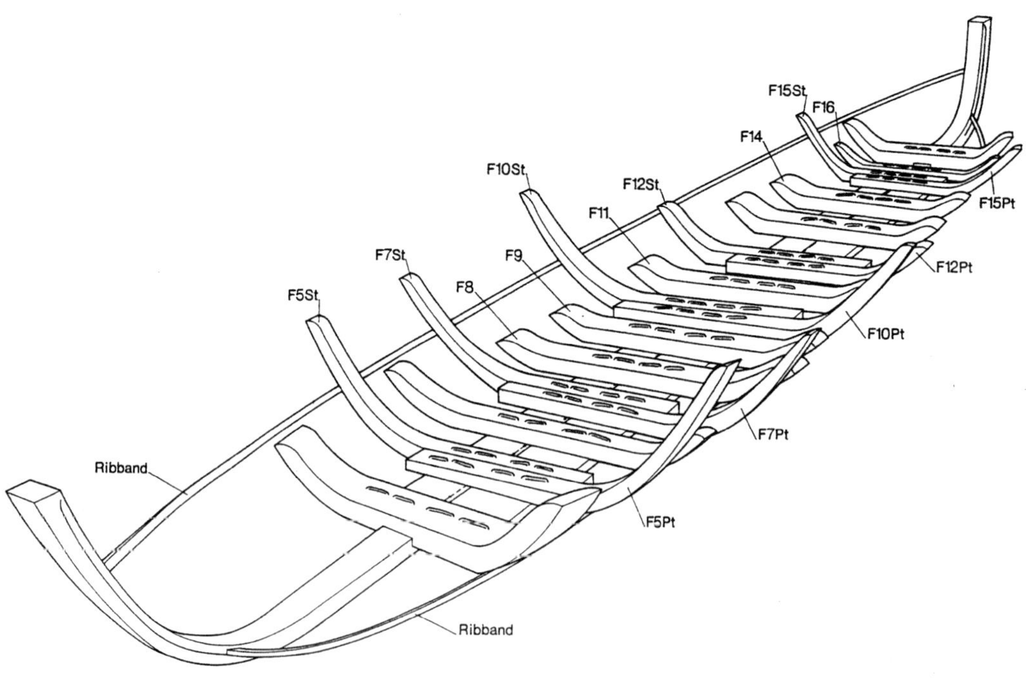

Fig. 7.11 Building the Barland's Farm boat – stage 4: most of the framing has been hewn to shape, fastened to the plank-keel and posts, and faired to give the form of the hull. Drawing: Glamorgan-Gwent Archaeological Trust.

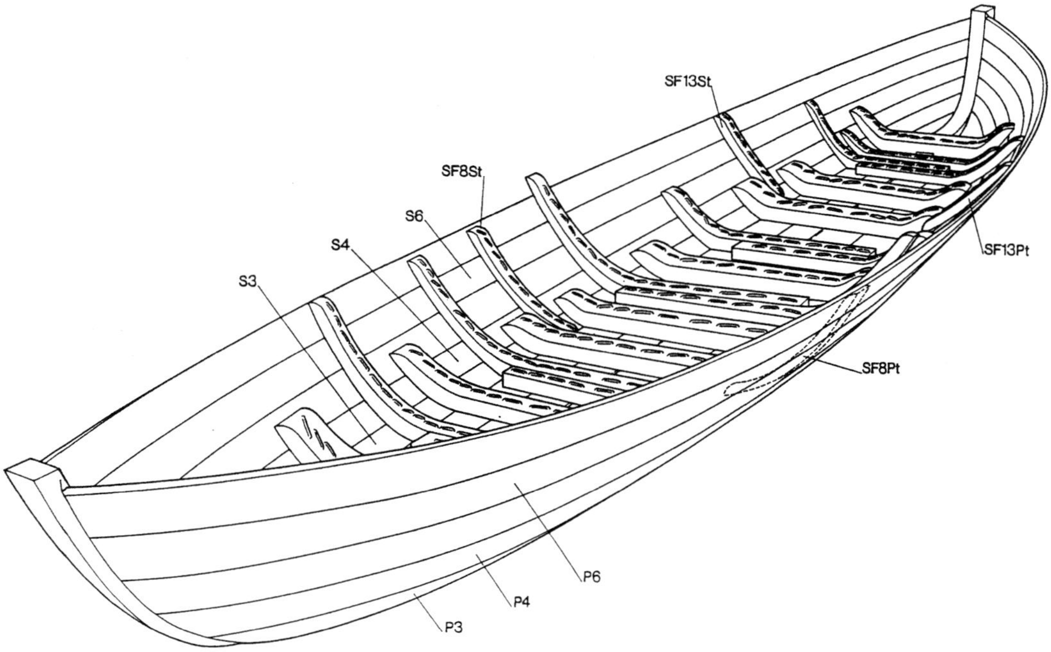

Fig. 7.12 Building the Barland's Farm boat – stage 6: the planking has been fastened to the framing. Drawing: Glamorgan-Gwent Archaeological Trust.

terms of the planking: his planking was hewn to shape and fastened together by lashings or by sewing to create the shape of hull he wanted. In contrast, the Celtic builder of 100 to 400 AD thought of his plank boat in terms of the framing: his planking was not fastened together; rather it was fastened to framing which had already been erected (Figs 7.11 and 7.12). This distinction can also be made between the Romano-Celtic style of ship and boat-building and the contemporary Classical Mediterranean and proto-Nordic traditions.

Romano-Celtic seagoing planked vessels were designed and built framing-first: this was evidently an innovative technique, the origins of which are not clear. There are some resemblances between Romano-Celtic building techniques and those of the prehistoric sewn boats: for example, both Ferriby and Celtic boats had plank-keels. Furthermore vessels of both traditions are heavily built – there is none of the thin planking and elegant lightweight timbers of the Nordic tradition in either of these groups (McGrail 2001, 220–1; McKee 1976, fig 4). The fundamentally different Celtic building sequence cannot, however, have originated with the prehistoric sewn plank boat builders. Again, although the use of sawn planking in these Celtic seagoing vessels probably reflects Roman influence, all other techniques appear to be indigenous, and the framing-first sequence cannot have originated in the Classical Mediterranean tradition. Nor can it have come from the Nordic tradition which was also clearly planking first; nor, for that matter, could it have been derived from logboat builders.

Hide boats

Consider, however, hide boats (Fig 7.13; McGrail 2001, 181–3). These are built framing-first: the framing is first designed and built; then a hide cover is fastened to that framing (McGrail 1998, 173–182, fig 10.1). Could the Celts have taken the framing-first sequence they used to build their hide boats and used it to design and build plank boats?

There are claims that hide boats have been excavated (Bishop and Dore 1988, 7; Ellmers 1984; Sheppard 1926; Watkins 1980), but none of these is convincing, and such flimsy remains may continue to be elusive. However, seagoing hide boats are known from documentary sources to have been used in these waters from the 5th century BC onwards (McGrail 2001, 182–3), and may well have been used earlier.

In general, hide boats are more seaworthy and more seakindly than the equivalent plank boat, and they have greater transverse stability, and can carry a bigger load. A hide boat could match the specification for an early seagoing boat. An assessment of construction techniques[1] suggests that hide boats could have been built well before the tools and techniques for building logboats had been evolved (McGrail 2001, 11, table 1.2). In other words, there could have been hide boats as early as the Mesolithic.

Seagoing hide boats of recent times were keelless and had a framework of laths fastened together by lashings, treenails or iron nails. However, there is evidence from the 17th century and from Classical times which suggests that early seagoing hide boats

Fig. 7.13 An oared Kerry navog or curach under way off the west coast of Ireland in the 1960s. Photo: Paul Johnstone.

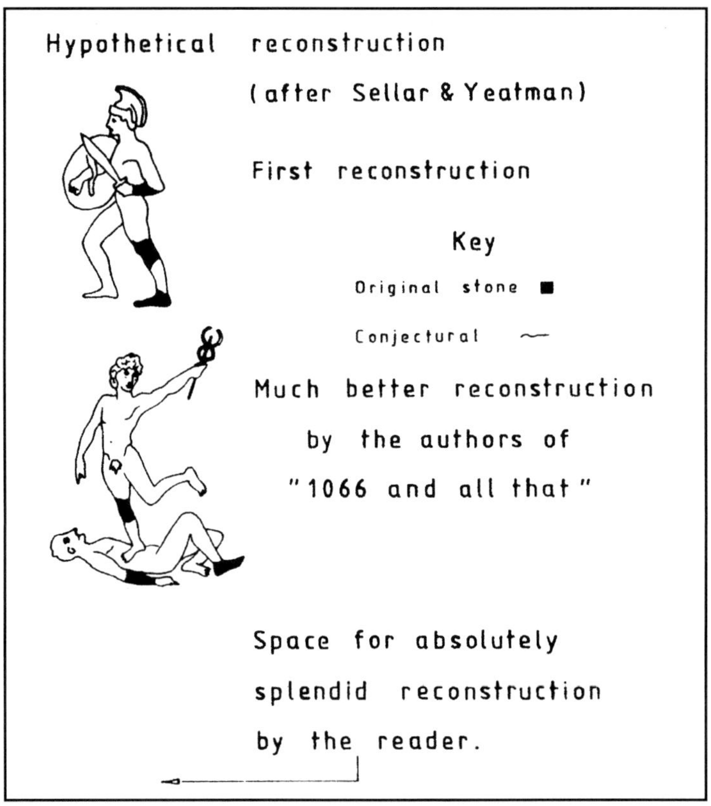

Fig. 7.14 Hypothetical reconstructions. Adapted from a drawing by J. Reynolds on p.91 of 'And Now All This' by W. C. Sellar and R. J. Yeatman (1944). London: Methuen.

had keels and a woven wicker or osier framework which would have been stronger yet more resilient than the present-day counterpart (McGrail 2001, 182).

It is conceivable, therefore, that not only might the hide boat have been the forerunner of the framing-first sequence of the Romano-Celtic boats and ships, but also that it might have been the workhorse seaboat of prehistoric north-west Europe. For the present, however, these possibilities must remain conjectural for lack of excavated evidence.

Should the remains of an early hide boat be found, its performance should be assessed using the three-phase process described earlier in this paper. This must be pursued with scholarly rigour since, without that, unwarranted and misleading reconstructions can readily be produced (Fig 7.14) leading to invalid conclusions about seagoing capabilities.

Acknowledgment

I am most grateful for criticism of an earlier draft of this paper by Dr Basil Greenhill, Professor Ole Crumlin-Pedersen, Professor Barry Cunliffe and Dr Jon Adams.

Note

[1] In the theoretical assessment of the materials and techniques used to build simple forms of water transport, much of the dating evidence was taken from Grahame Clark's incomparable *Prehistoric Europe: the Economic Basis* (1952) and his *World Prehistory*. (1977). Although the main trends identified by Professor Clark probably still hold good, much early material has been excavated in the past 50 years and dating methods are now significantly more accurate. An up-dated 'Economic Basis' is badly needed.

List of references

Arnold, B 1995–6 *Pirogues monoxyles d'Europe centrale*, Archéologie Neuchateloise. **20/21**, 2 volumes

Bell, M, Caseldine, A and Neumann, H 2000 *Prehistoric Inter-tidal Archaeology in the Welsh Severn Estuary*, Council for British Archaeology Research Report, **120**

Bishop, M C and Dore, J N 1988 *Corbridge: Excavations of the Roman fort and town, 1947–1980*, English Heritage Archaeological Reports, **8**, London: English Heritage

Bruce-Mitford, R 1975 *Sutton Hoo Ship Burial: Volume 1*, London: British Museum

Champion, T forthcoming 'Deposition of the boat', in P Clark (ed), *The Dover Bronze Age boat*, English Heritage

Clark, P (ed) forthcoming *The Dover Bronze Age boat*, English Heritage

Coates, J, McGrail, S, Brown, D, Gifford, E, Grainge, G, Greenhill, B, Marsden, P, Rankov, B, Tipping, C and Wright, E 1995 'Experimental Boat and Ship Archaeology: Principles and Methods', *International Journal of Nautical Archaeology*, **24**, 293–301

Coles, J 2001 'Energetic activities of commoners', *Proceedings of the Prehistoric Society*, **67**, 19–48

Crumlin-Pedersen, O 1997 *Viking Age Ships and Seafaring in Hedeby/Haithabu and Schleswig*, Roskilde: Viking Ship Museum, Ships and Boats of the North, **2**

Crumlin-Pedersen, O and Olsen, O (eds) 2002 *Skuldelev Ships 1*, Roskilde: Viking Ship Museum, Ships and Boats of the North, **3**

Cunliffe, B (ed) 1994 *Prehistory of Europe*, Oxford: Oxford University Press

Cunliffe, B 2001 *Facing the Ocean*, Oxford: Oxford University Press

Elgee, H W and F 1949 'EBA burial in a boat-shaped coffin from N.E. Yorkshire', *Proceedings of the Prehistoric Society,* **15**, 87–106

Ellmers, D 1984 'Earliest evidence for skin boats', in S McGrail (ed), *Aspects of Maritime Archaeology and Ethnography*, Greenwich: National Maritime Museum, 41–85

Friel, I 1993 'Henry V's Grace Dieu and the wreck in the R. Hamble near Bursledon, Hampshire', *International Journal of Nautical Archaeology*, **22**, 3–19

Marsden, P 1994 *Ships of the Port of London: 1*, London: English Heritage

McGrail, S 1978 *Logboats of England and Wales*, Oxford: British Archaeological Reports (British Series), **51**, (2 volumes)

McGrail, S 1981 *The Brigg 'Raft' and her Prehistoric Environment*, Oxford: British Archaeological Reports (British Series), **89**

McGrail, S 1985 'The Brigg 'raft': problems in reconstruction and in the assessment of performance', in S McGrail and E Kentley (eds), *Sewn Plank Boats*, Oxford: British Archaeological Reports (International Series), **276**, 165–194

McGrail, S 1991 'Bronze Age seafaring', in N H Gale (ed), *Bronze Age Trade in the Mediterranean*, Studies in Mediterranean Archaeology, **110**, Jonsered: Paul Astroms Forlag, 83–91

McGrail, S 1992 'Replicas, reconstructions and floating hypotheses', *International Journal of Nautical Archaeology*, **21**, 353–5

McGrail, S 1994 'The Brigg 'raft': a flat-bottomed boat', *International Journal of Nautical Archaeology*, **23**, 283–8

McGrail, S 1997 *Studies in Maritime Archaeology*, Oxford: British Archaeological Reports (British Series), **256**

McGrail, S 1998 *Ancient Boats in N. W. Europe*, Harlow: Longman

McGrail, S 2000 'ISBSA: past, present and future', in J Liwin (ed), *Down the River to the Sea*, Gdansk: Centralne Muzeum Morskie, 269–272

McGrail, S 2001 *Boats of the World*, Oxford: Oxford University Press

McGrail, S and Roberts, O 1999 'Romano-British boat from the shores of the Severn Estuary', *Mariner's Mirror*, **85**, 133–146

McKee, E 1976 'Identification of timbers from old ships of NW European origins', *International Journal of Nautical Archaeology*, **5**, 3–12

Nayling, N and Caseldine, A 1997 *Excavations at Caldicot, Gwent*, York: Council for British Archaeology Research Report, **108**

Nayling, N and McGrail, S 2004 *The Barland's Farm Romano-Celtic boat, Gwent,* York: Council for British Archaeology Research Report **138**

Pryor, F and Taylor, M 1993 'Use, re-use or pre-use? Aspects of the interpretation of ancient wood', in J Coles, V Fenwick and G Hutchinson (eds), *A Spirit of Enquiry: Essays for Ted Wright*, WARP Occasional Paper, **7**, 81–84

Roberts, O T P 1992 Brigg 'raft' re-assessed as a round bilge Bronze Age boat, *International Journal of Nautical Archaeology*, **21**, 245–258

Roberts, O T P forthcoming 'Reconstruction and performance', in P Clark (ed), *The Dover Bronze Age boat*, English Heritage

Rule, M and Monaghan, J 1993 *A Gallo-Roman Trading Vessel from Guernsey*, Guernsey Museum Monograph, **5**, St. Peter Port

Sheppard, T 1926 'Roman remains in North Lincolnshire', *Transactions of the East Riding Antiquarian Society*, **25**, 170–4

Sørensen, A C 2001 *Ladby*, Ships and Boats of the North, **3**, Roskilde: Viking Ship Museum

Thorvildsen, K 1957 *Ladby-Skibet*, Copenhagen: National Museum

Van de Noort, R, Middleton, R, Foxton, A and Bayliss, A 1999 'The 'Kilnsea boat' and some implications from the discovery of England's oldest plank boat remains', *Antiquity*, **73**, 131–135

Watkins, T 1980 'A Prehistoric coracle in Fife', *International Journal of Nautical Archaeology*, **9**, 277–286

Wessex Archaeology 1996 *Testwood Lakes, Netley Marsh, Hampshire: Meadow Lake Excavations: Assessment Report*, unpublished report, Trust for Wessex Archaeology

Wright, E V 1976 *The North Ferriby Boats: a guide book*, Greenwich: National Maritime Museum Monograph, **23**

Wright, E V 1990 *The Ferriby Boats: Seacraft of the Bronze Age*, London: Routledge

Wright, E V 1994 'The North Ferriby boats: a final report', in C Westerdahl (ed), *Crossroads in Ancient Shipbuilding*, 29–34

Wright, E V and Switsur, V R 1993 'Ferriby boat 5 fragment', *Archaeological Journal*, **150**, 46–56

Wright, E V, Hedges, R E M, Bayliss, A and Van de Noort, R 2001 'New AMS radiocarbon dates for the North Ferriby Boats', *Antiquity*, **75**, 726–734

Note added at proof stage:

The re-assessment of the Hjortspring boat (discussed on pages 59 and 60) has been published:

Crumlin-Pedersen, O and Trakadas, A (eds) 2003 *Hjortspring: a pre-Roman Iron-Age Warship in Context,* Ships and Boats of the North **5,** Roskilde: Viking Ship Museum

8. The use of half-scale model ships in archaeological research with particular reference to the Graveney, Sutton Hoo and Ferriby ships

Edwin Gifford and Joyce Gifford

Introduction

Although small-scale models have a long history of use by civil engineers to analyse the strength of complex bridges and buildings, and by naval architects to predict the performance and seaworthiness of ships, they have been little used or appreciated by those outside these two professions. This short paper is an attempt to clarify the apparently complex relationships between the model and the full-size ship in a spirit of constructive helpfulness to archaeologists and historians as they view our half-scale model of Ferriby I.

Choice of scale

The most usual scale of models for use in towing tanks is in the order of one-tenth but this is too small for studying details of construction and rigging which can be better done at half-scale. At this size the model can be crewed, albeit with full-size humans, and construction methods and rigging details replicated.

Cost

The main advantage of building a half-scale model rather than a full-size ship is that the cost of building, storage, maintenance and crewing of the model is approximately one-tenth that of the ship. The vessel can be conveniently transported by road. Its main disadvantage is that it will not make the true visual impact on the spectator, which only a full-size replica can do.

The relationships between the full-size and the model – the scale effect

These relationships are not widely understood, partly because they are rarely explained and partly because they vary from one characteristic to another – displacement, sail area, speed, strength and seaworthiness. A consequence has been some misplaced scepticism about the value of models to indicate the performance of originals, for which precise accuracy of details is often not necessary.

Displacement

This varies as length (L) × breadth (B) × depth (D) so the displacement of a half-scale model will be $\frac{L}{2} x \frac{B}{2} x \frac{D}{2}$ or one-eighth that of the ship.

Speed

Froude's Law of 1876 states that 'when two different vessels of the same shape are propelled by forces in the ratio of their displacements then their speed will be approximately in the ratio of the square roots of their waterline lengths' (Barnaby 1967, 167–169).

In the case of the half-scale model the waterline length will be half that of the ship, so the model speed will be the ship speed divided by $\sqrt{2}$.

Propulsive force

Following Froude's Law, at model speeds, propulsive force will be roughly proportional to displacement so for a paddled or rowed ship, a half-scale model would require one-eighth the number of crew.

Again following Froude's Law, if a ship is propelled by sail then, in a half-scale model, the area of the sail will be one-eighth that of the full size vessel.

Strength

This relationship causes most confusion as the strength of the half-scale hull structure will be one-eighth that of the ship, but the bending moments from the displacement will be one-sixteenth those of the ship, so the model hull structure will have an equivalent strength of twice that of the ship. Which is why model aircraft bounce!

If the model is to be used to determine the

strength of the full-size ship, then the strength of the relevant structural members must be halved.

Seaworthiness

This is relatively simple to understand but not to measure. The reaction of a vessel to waves is in direct relationship to its linear dimensions, so a half-scale model requires a half-scale wave. If the ship is to survive a two metre sea, then the model must ride a one metre wave.

The application of these relationships will be illustrated by the results of the trials of our half-scale model of the Graveney ship built in 1987, Sutton Hoo ship built in 1993, and the model of Ferriby I, completed this year. This was built primarily to validate the hypothetical reconstruction as drawn by Ted Wright and John Coates, to examine methods and costs of building and to test the speed and seaworthiness of the ship.

Fig. 8.1 (above) Ottor sailing.

Fig. 8.2 (right) Ottor's mast step.

Model building

We started our experimental building of half-scale models of ancient ships in 1987 because we could not accept the generally held view that Anglo Saxons were unable to sail until the Vikings came. This belief seemed to be based solely on the lack of archaeological evidence for mast steps and projecting keels, disregarding hull shapes.

We began with the 14 metre Graveney ship partly because of its relatively small size and partly because of the excellent contribution by Eric McKee in the Graveney report which gives drawings for a suggested reconstruction (Fenwick 1978). This we built with our own hands in order to explore the methods of Saxon shipbuilding.

The original vessel was built with massive oak timbers but as we were primarily concerned with building a hull of the correct shape, we economised by using pine instead of oak planking and a much reduced number of frames. The keel plank in the original was flush with the bottom planks and surprisingly unworn, hinting that at one time the vessel had a false keel. For our purposes a mast was stepped directly on the mid-ship frame and the sail area was designed to suit the stability of the model hull. The mast and rigging were of one-eighth the strength required for the full-size ship.

Even without any keel projection the model Ottor sailed very well (Fig 8.1), but not surprisingly made some 30° leeway when close-hauled. When fitted with a 40mm projecting keel the leeway was reduced to about 15°. By a remarkable coincidence, a Saxon keel of comparable dimensions was discovered in London during our sailing trials, fully justifying our experiments (Goodburn 1994). Speeds of five knots were obtained in a moderate breeze, equivalent to seven knots in the ship. Windward performance was further improved by fitting bowlines. The model steered well and could tack easily. We had no doubt that the ship would have been capable of sailing in the Thames Estuary and of crossing the English Channel in moderate weather (Gifford and Gifford 1996). A further advantage of the half-scale model was that we could readily experiment with modifications to the rudder and mast-step when new discoveries were made (Fig 8.2; Goodburn 1993).

Encouraged by the sailing behaviour of our first vessel we built a half-scale version of the 28 metre Sutton Hoo ship which had also been described as a rowing vessel because of the apparent lack of a mast-step and a projecting keel. This was despite the evidence of the hull shape and the provision of three close-set frames at the stern. These were to carry a more powerful rudder than would have been needed under oars alone (Fig 8.3).

Although structural analysis showed that the ship was capable of carrying sail, we built the model

Fig. 8.3 Sutton Hoo ship 1939.

Fig. 8.4 (left) Sae Wylfing hull.

Fig. 8.5 (above) Sae Wylfing sailing on the River Deben.

lightly to avoid over-strength. We halved the number of frames and, apart from the two oak top strakes, the planking was in pine. This also saved money. Once again we were interested primarily in hull shape as the best indication of whether or not it was built to be sailed. Experience with the Graveney model made the shaping of planks and the building of the hull more straightforward (Fig 8.4).

As expected, this Sutton Hoo model, Sae Wylfing, sailed very well indeed, with no problems even when sailing at the top of Force 5, with only one reef and a crew of eight (64 in the full-size ship) and a one metre sea running (Fig 8.5). Speeds in excess of 7 knots were measured on a broad reach, equivalent to 10 knots in the full-size ship. Windward performance was also good, especially when trimmed level by the crew, when leeway as little as 10° could be achieved (Fig 8.5).

During these trials, various depths of keel were fitted, finally settling on a projection of 40mm. Regrettably there was no evidence of keel or mast-step available from the excavations. Two different mid-ship mast steps were tested, a longitudinal one resting on three frames and one in a single transverse frame, in the manner of the third century Blackfriars ship, suggested by Katherine Their *(pers. comm.)*. We have learned that Basil Brown, described by Seamus Heaney as 'the shipwright of the earth ship', was banished from the central part of the ship by the excavators of the treasure. Consequently details of the ship's structure in this area appear not to have been recorded.

We now believe, as a result of our model tests, that the ship was fast and weatherly. Easy landing and launching was facilitated by shallow draught, small keel projection and the easily-raised side rudder (Fig 8.6). We may even conjecture that ships such as this were the instruments of the Wuffingas' power and wealth.

The half-scale model of the 16 metre Ferriby I, dated to 1800 BC

In May 2001 Ted Wright, just before his death, bequeathed his research to John Coates and to us with the request that we should build and test a half-scale model, primarily to examine the validity of his and John Coates' published plans for a reconstruction (Figs 8.7 and 8.8). We were also to explore Bronze Age methods of shipbuilding and to test the ship's speed and seaworthiness.

The building of a Bronze Age plank boat was a completely different challenge from building the Saxon ship models as it involved the bending and carving of green oak and sewing the parts together with yew withies. The latter are not readily available in quantity and the use of half-scale withies presented such difficulty that we tested some at Southampton University for strength and elasticity and sought an alternative material of comparable qualities. Future research will be undertaken when funds permit. Meanwhile, a recently developed pre-stretched polyester halliard rope was used and a mastic compound for caulking instead of moss.

Fortunately Richard Darrah was able to select and obtain an oak tree that had been felled the previous year and was of a suitable size and shape for the main planks. A part model was built by Jeff Bird in softwood (Figs 8.9 and 8.10) to prepare patterns and templates for the Darrah team to work from, alongside the Wright/Coates' plans. Planks were prepared and given their first shaping in Shropshire before being delivered to Hampshire to be stored in a tank of water until needed. One imagines that Bronze Age shipbuilders would have used the nearest available oak and prepared planks *in-situ*.

The broad keel plank projects below the two bottom side planks and is in two parts, each end of the ship being formed by an upswept shape reflecting that of the base of the tree. To achieve the 'rocker', or slight curve, required by the fitting of the first side strake (Fig 8.11), a certain amount of bending was necessary. This caused much debate. Some heat was needed, but there was no evidence of charring on the ship's bottom so hot water rather than direct fire must have been used. Did Bronze Age man immerse the planks in long wooden or clay troughs with water heated by hot stones?

Such treatment was not possible in our workshop so we enclosed the planks in a PVC sleeve and fed in steam from a wallpaper stripper (Fig 8.12). The planks were supported at their ends and weights placed on top until the required curvature was obtained. After four hours of steaming, with a temperature of about 70°C within the sleeve, the 60mm planks were bent to shape. Twice that time would probably be needed for the full-size.

The system of longitudinal carved cleats and transverse timbers worked well in aligning the bottom planks during assembly and stitching (Fig 8.13). We doubled the spacing of the stitches so that the shear strength of the stitching would be to scale. The ingenuity and quality of workmanship in the original is most impressive, so we were puzzled by the absence of stitches at the boxed butt joint in the keel plank amidships. Then John Coates suggested that because of the long end overhangs and the fine lines fore and aft, the vessel would almost always be in a hogging mode, that is with the ends tending to droop, putting the bottom planks in compression and the top strakes in tension. The ship thus acts as

Fig. 8.6 Sae Wylfing landing in a fresh breeze on the Solent.

Fig. 8.7 (right) Ted Wright's perspective of Ferriby I.

Fig. 8.8 (below) General arrangement drawings of Ted Wright's reconstruction of a complete hull. Drawing: J F Coates.

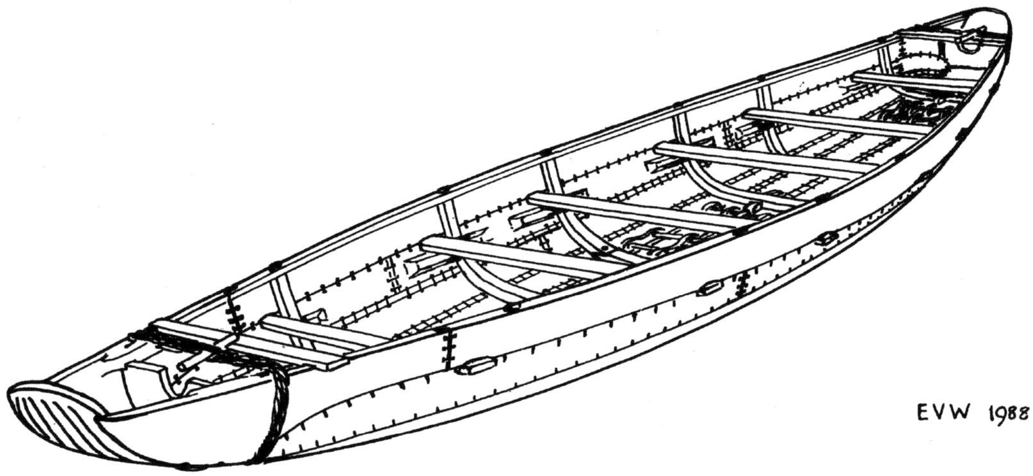

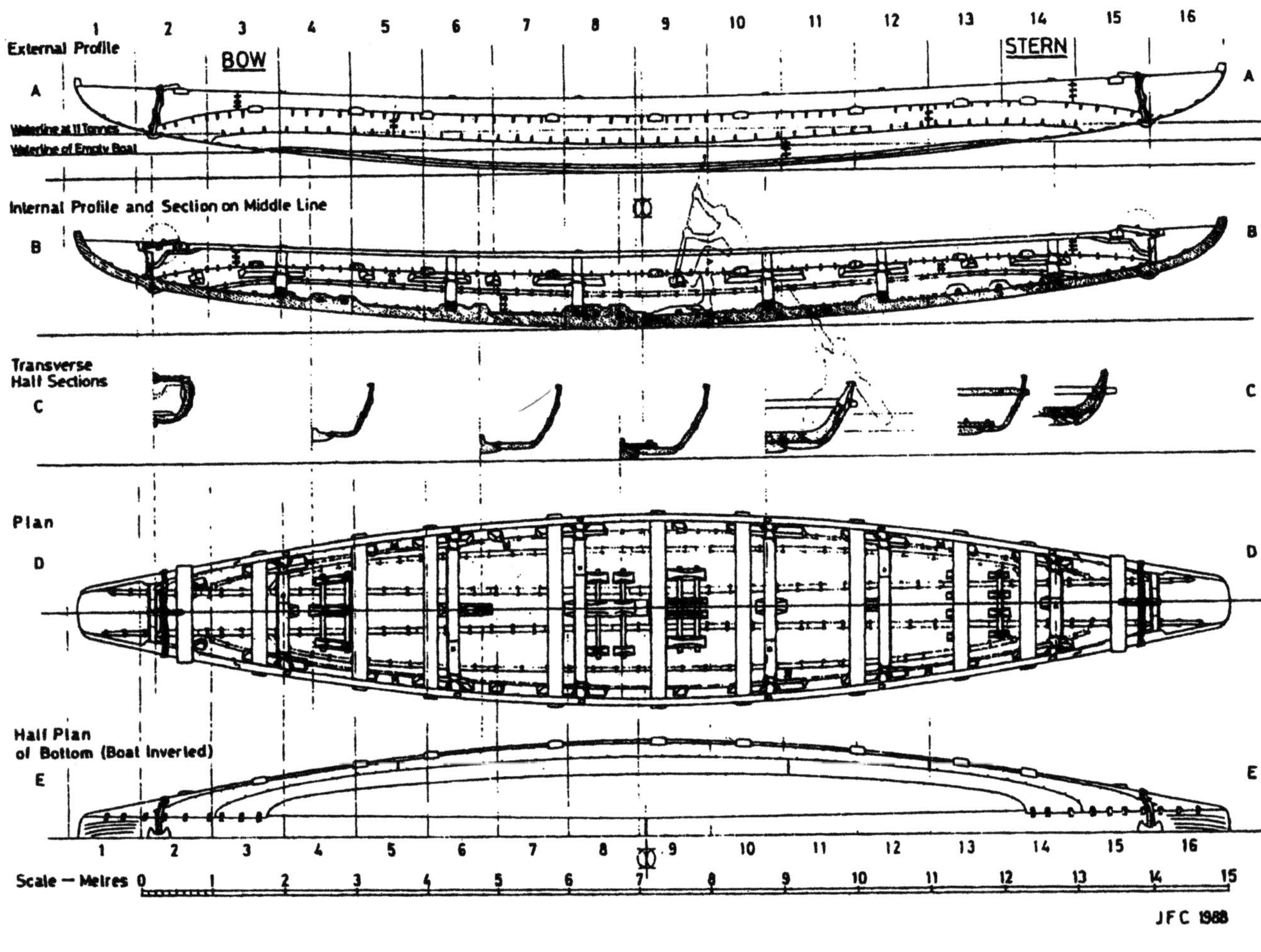

Fig. 8.9 Laminated pine keel plank.

Fig. 8.10 Nearly complete pine part model.

Fig. 8.11 Forward half of keel plank before steaming.

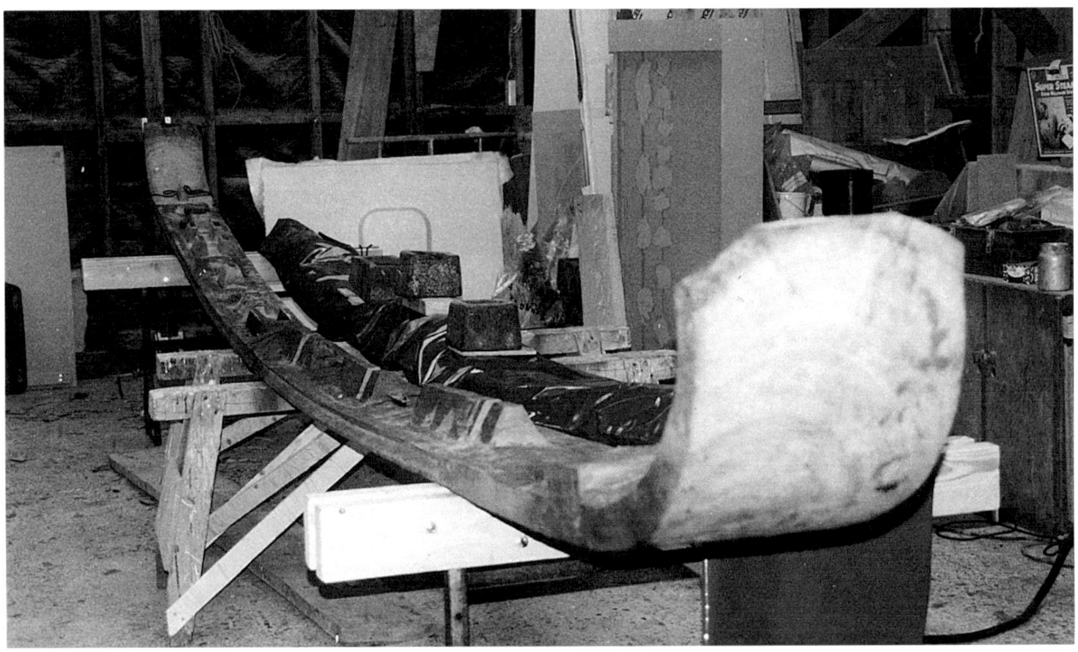

Fig. 8.12 Both parts of keel after steaming, PVC sleeve alongside.

an inverted arch. This has two beneficial effects. Firstly, the top strake being in tension would force inwards and there would be no need for the thwarts to lock into this strake to resist an outward force. This would greatly simplify building. Secondly, since the force on stitches is always in one direction there would be less wear on them.

This realisation impressed us with the Bronze Age builders' profound understanding of the forces in a structure. Equally impressive was the way in which the central part of the lowest side strake, despite being almost straight, fitted exactly the rockered elliptical bottom side plank with little steaming. Some difficulty was encountered in the three-dimensional carving of the plank hood ends both in Shropshire and in the final fitting to the keel plank in Hampshire, but speed increased with experience. This was the big step forward by Early

Bronze Age shipwrights when they learned to create the shape of the hull by building up with planks instead of hollowing out from logs (Fig 8.14).

As assembly progressed, we introduced two of the frames, which had been made from templates from the drawings, as a temporary measure to ensure a correct shape in the hull (Fig 8.15). Fitting the second side strakes caused no problems; being virtually straight they followed the shape dory fashion. The top strake was a different matter (Fig 8.16). The inverted L-shape section was based on Ferriby 4 and was intended to hold down the frames and to locate the thwarts where they passed through the planking (Fig 8.17). The frequency of notches required for frames and thwarts meant that the heavy plank had to be offered up many times (it was a three-man lift) and it also needed several three hour steamings. The realisation later that there was no structural need to notch the thwarts through the planking was welcomed by our shipwrights.

Stitching over the laths covering the seams went stage by stage, temporary stitches being used to hold the parts together while finalising the fit. A tool different from that found and experimented with by Ted Wright was developed by Jeff Bird, the leading shipwright, to enable the stitches to be tightened and wedged by one man (Fig 8.18). Whether this could be used on full-size yew withies is yet to be tested. The stiffness of the completed structure was impressive.

Although no frames were found at Ferriby, gaps between the blocks on the keel plank made their position clear. Each frame was built from two oak crooks provided by Damian Goodburn from Kentish woods. These were scarfed and lashed together, with a single peg to prevent sliding (Fig 8.19)

During construction, the parts were sprayed with water daily and with linseed oil thinned with white spirit each night. Two years have elapsed since the oak trees were felled, and it is hoped that further shrinkage will be limited. Nevertheless, space has been left at the top of the frames to allow for some movement. This gap will eventually be filled by wedges.

Launching

Prior to launching, the hull was one third filled with water and found to be tight except for a few places, mainly where there were small knots in the timber. These were easily stopped and during trials the leakage was negligible. This might well be different with moss caulking and it is intended to replace some of the mastic joint filler with moss before next season's trials.

The weighbridge weight of the empty hull was 570kg compared with the calculated weight of 480kg based on moderately dry oak. The hull floated to a water level only 5mm above that calculated (Fig 8.20).

Fig. 8.13 Cleats and transverse timbers, hood ends with birdsmouth and rebated joints.

Trials

The first trial was made by one man with two oars to test the ability of the vessel to run straight and to turn. This it could do well, but required strong correction after making a sharp turn, as would be expected in a rockered hull. With a crew of paddlers steering was more difficult (Fig 8.21), possibly because of the variety of experience of crew members. A longer steering paddle improved matters. Carrying capacity was tested satisfactorily with nine people on board, equivalent to seventy-two in the full-size ship. A double sculler rig with two experienced rowers gave good speed and manoeuvrability and little need for steering with the paddle. During the next trials two strong rowers on

Fig. 8.14 Fitting of hood ends.

Fig. 8.15 Frames temporarily fitted with two side strakes.

Fig. 8.16 (left) Top strake.

Fig. 8.17 (below) Top strake fitted over thwarts and frames.

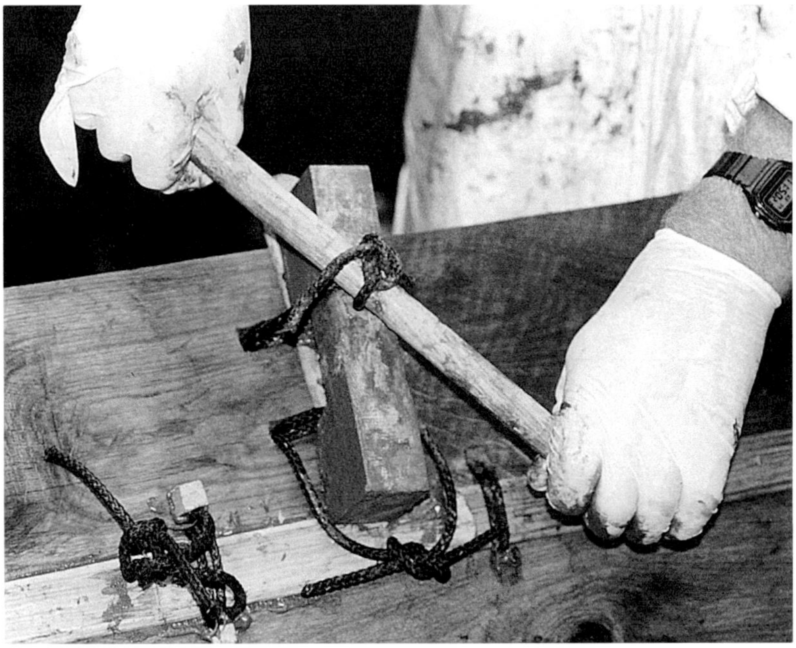

Fig. 8.18 Tightening and wedging stitches.

Fig. 8.19 Model nearing completion, showing frame detail.

Fig. 8.20 Launching.

Fig. 8.21 Building team paddling.

Fig. 8.22 Two shipwrights rowing.

Fig. 8.23 'Saddle feature' at right, butt-joint amidships.

a smooth sea reached a speed of 4.4 knots equivalent to a speed of just over 6 knots in the full-size ship with sixteen rowers (Fig 8.22). With such a crew, or twenty-two paddlers, working alternate four-hour watches, an average speed of about 4 knots should be possible.

The presence of two 'saddle features' on the keel plank, one amidships (Fig 8.23) and one near the next frame forward, suggests the possibility of a mast for sailing, for which the hull shape is suitable. A very small sail was set amidships (Fig 8.24) and in a light breeze, the model reached a GPS measured speed of 2.2 knots when running and reaching. This agrees with John Coates' prediction of 6–7 knots for the full-size ship running in a fresh breeze (Coates 1990, 115). The forward position for the mast might be preferred for certain conditions of wind or loading. During the sailing trials waves were small but the model was tested by sailing through the short, steep wash from another vessel which it

Fig. 8.24 (left) Model under sail

Fig. 8.25 (below) Comparison of mid-ship cross-sections of Ferriby I and Sae Wylfing.

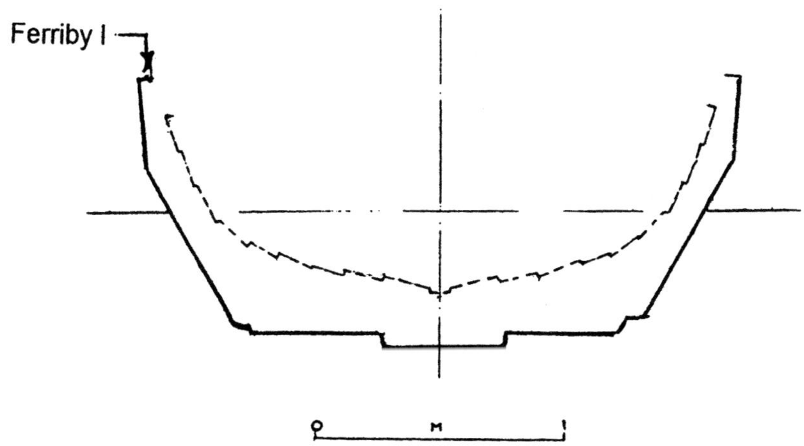

rode well, taking practically no water on board. Throughout these trials the stability of the model was impressive and the freeboard adequate.

The seaworthiness of the full-size Ferriby ship can be deduced by comparing its mid-ship section with that of the half-scale Sutton Hoo ship, Sae Wylfing, which has proved to be a fast, seaworthy vessel in a variety of conditions of wind and sea. It can be seen from Fig 8.25 that the Ferriby ship, which has greater beam, depth and freeboard and is nearly two metres longer, would also have been a seaworthy vessel. We conclude that sailors in the Early Bronze Age had ships capable of taking them across the North Sea.

Acknowledgement

Figures 8.5 and 8.6 are by Peter Rooley and Margaret Kay respectively.

List of references

Barnaby, K 1967 *Basic Naval Architecture*, London: Hutchinson

Coates, J F 1990 'Performance', in E V Wright, *The Ferriby boats: Seacraft of the Bronze Age*, London, 113–116

Fenwick, V 1978 The Graveney Boat, British Archaeological Reports (British Series), **53**

Gifford, E and Gifford, J 1996 'The Sailing Performance of Anglo-Saxon Ships as derived from the Building and Trials of Half-Scale Models of the Sutton Hoo and Graveney Ships Finds', *Mariner's Mirror*, **82.2**, 131–153

Goodburn, D 1994 'Anglo Saxon Boat Finds from London: are they English?', in C Westerdahl (ed), *Crossroads in Ancient Shipbuilding*, Oxford: Oxbow Monograph, **40**, 97–104

Goodburn, D M 1993 'A Side Rudder from the London Waterfront' , in J Coles, V Fenwick and G Hutchinson (eds), *Spirit of Enquiry – Essays for Ted Wright*, 56–60

Wright, E 1990 *The Ferriby boats: Seacraft of the Bronze Age*, London

9. Dover to Bevaix, from the Middle Bronze Age to Gallo-Roman times, from lashing to nailing: a page of naval archaeology illustrated by the evolution of techniques, tools and the discovery of new materials

Béat Arnold

The construction of Altaripa (Fig 9.1), a replica of the Gallo-Roman lighter of Bevaix (Fig 9.2), led to the conclusion that the vessel belonged to an older generation of boats as suggested by the special dimensions of the sawn planks (Arnold 1999a). In this instance, it was noted that in spite of the use of pit-saws, mastery of the art was not yet reached. This boat belongs to what has been termed the 'Celtic tradition' as opposed to the techniques used in the Mediterranean and Scandinavia. The use of this term was followed by much criticism owing chiefly to the absence of discoveries dating from the second half of the first millennium BC (Marsden 1974). Under such circumstances, the primitive aspect of the Bevaix lighter prompted a further study into Bronze Age craft with emphasis on the specificities of the Celtic tradition followed by an explanation on why the changes that occurred were

Fig. 9.1 Altaripa: replica of the Bevaix *Gallo-Roman lighter: (right) bending by direct and localized heating of the large bottom planking; (far right) carving of the spoonplanks by working away the wood.*

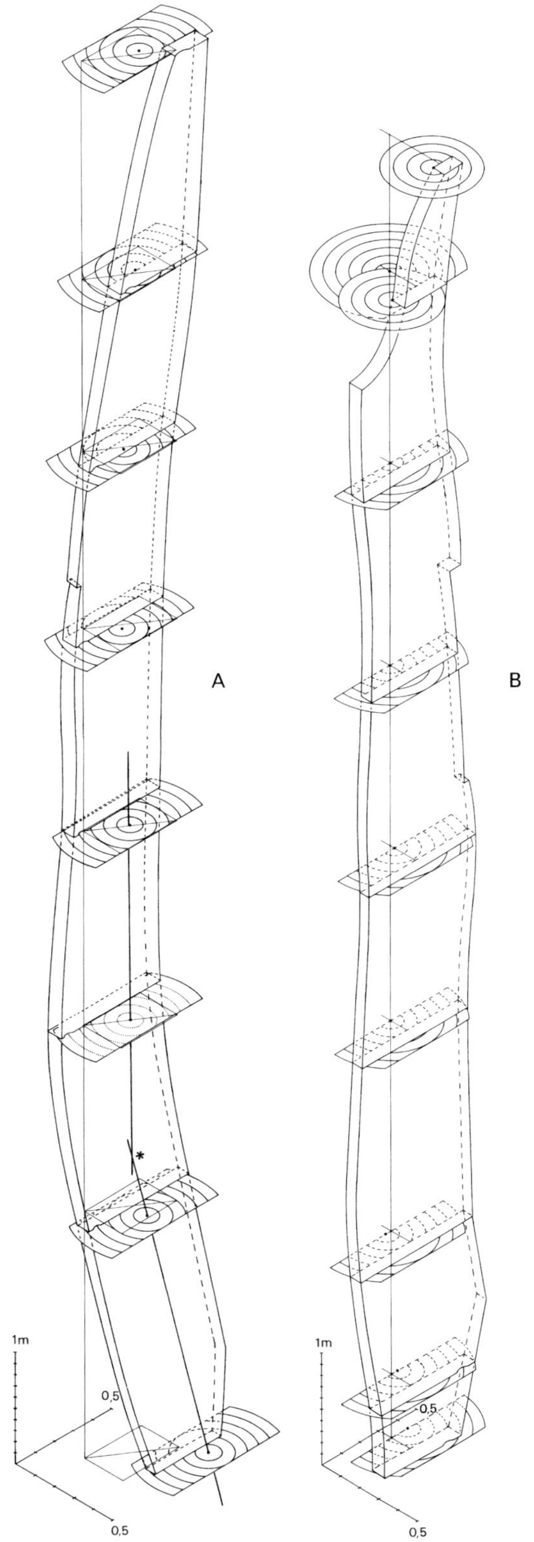

Fig. 9.2 (far left) Photomontage constructed by 194 slides of the Bevaix *Gallo-Roman lighter, close to its state of discovery (Arnold 1999a, 16-17).*

Fig 9.3 (left) Carving of the Bevaix *Gallo-Roman lighter planks, A and B; the first one presents an abrupt change of direction along its longitudinal axis due to localized heating of the plank when bending (Arnold 1992, 58-59).*

so definite and complete on the Continent as well as on the Atlantic coast of Europe (Arnold 1999b).

This paper proceeds in a chronological order starting with Bronze Age craft, the majority of the observations being based on the Dover boat. The planks of this Middle Bronze Age vessel were hewn out entirely by means of bronze axes and/or adzes and wooden wedges. This involved carving massive pieces out of single oak logs (or radially split half-logs; Darrah 2004). The above technique was then well mastered as can be seen on many planks and beams found on lakeshore sites dating from the Bronze Age.

The Helvetian carpenters followed the same procedure with the chine-girders of the Bevaix boat and, in some way, they did not alter the large plank structures even though these had been shaped by means of a pit-saw (Fig 9.3). This tool, a novelty to the carpenter's set, started to develop only when a previously unknown metal was found and mastered: the iron ore and the forge. In the case of the Bevaix, although the boat builders carried on manufacturing the longest and broadest possible planks, it was at the cost of excessive effort resulting in this technique being discarded, seen in the conservation of sap wood on the plank sides and the introduction of small supplementary pieces to rectify the natural irregularities encountered when shaping large size planks. In the present case, the discovery of a new material, iron, and the invention of a new tool, the pit-saw, did not bring about significant changes. Small bronze saws were already used during the Bronze Age although not exceeding 200 mm in length. The basic concept with reference to the sawing technique, which consists of wearing off part of the matter, had already been widely used, for instance to shape polished stone axes during the Middle Neolithic.

With regard to the construction of the Dover boat, two complementary processes had to be mastered: maintaining the planks together and giving a specific line to the assemblage. Technical solutions to these problems were scarce during the Bronze Age but the one that was chosen consisted of lashing planks one to the other. Others could have been used as, for instance, the dovetail tenons or the H-tenons placed on seams (as on the Appleby 1934/GB-5 logboat; Dudley 1943), or small tenons fixed to each plank by a small treenail. The latter technique, which developed particularly well in the Mediterranean, was already used during the Bronze Age, for example on the 14th century BC wreck at Ulu Burun (Steffy 1994, figs 3–15). To improve the process and minimize movement of the planking, lashing and sewing were reinforced by means of treenails pegged into the edge of the plank. This can be observed on Greek shipwrecks of the 6th century BC found in 1992–1993 at Marseille/Place Jules Verne (Fig 9.4; Pomey 1997, 90–93). North of the Alps, the concept of the last two processes were

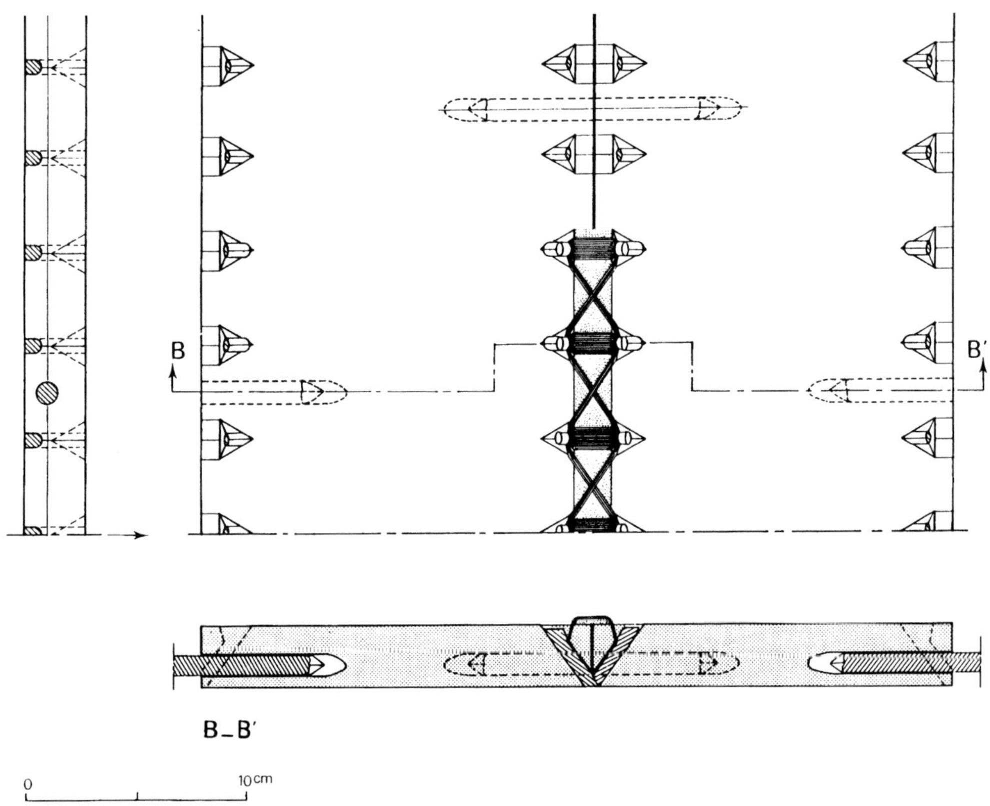

Fig. 9.1 Plan and cross-section of two planks from the Greek Marseille/Place Jules-Verne 11 *shipwreck (Pomey 1997, 92).*

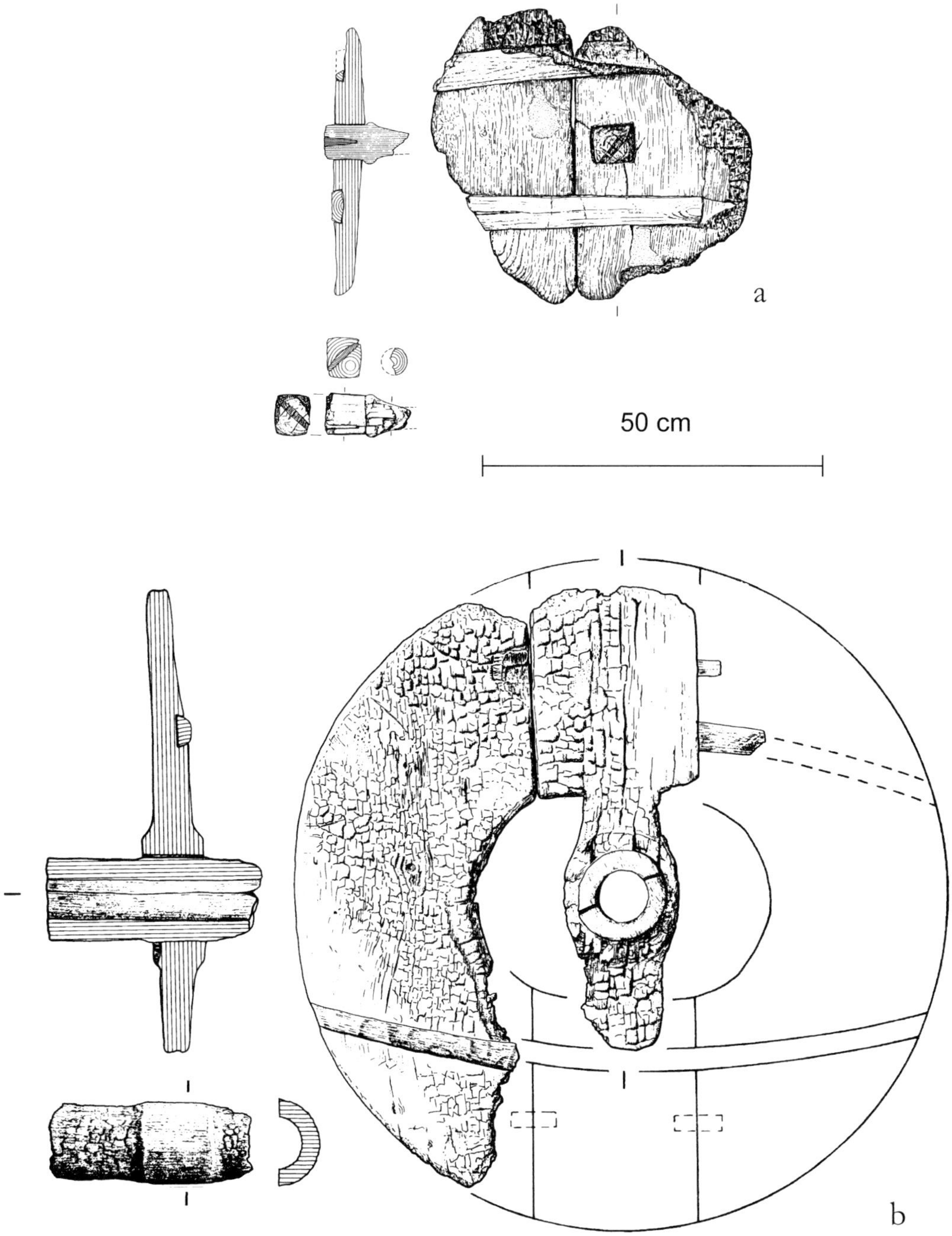

Fig. 9.5a The Neolithic wheel of Fenil/Vinelz (the trapezoidal timbers fasten the planks together and a wedge blocks the axis; (b) the Corcelettes Final Bronze Age wheel (showing a combination of trapezoidal timbers and tenons; b) give an illustration of the high level of workmanship displayed by the carpenters of each period when building exceptional objects (Winiger 1987, figs 3 and 6; Pugin et al *1988, figs 2 and 3). Scale 1/10.*

acknowledged, but were rarely used and in a specific way only. Examples are found on the Middle Bronze Age logboat of Douanne-Gare 1975/CH-53 (Arnold 1995, 97) where a long trapezoidal timber was driven into a dovetail fashioned groove on the stern, or on the wheel from Corcelettes dating from the Final Bronze Age where tenons and trapezoidal timbers were used (Fig 9.5; Pugin *et al* 1988). The scarcity and complexity of this type of construction are due to the lack of a tool best suited for this type of assembly: the spoon-drill. A number of them were discovered in a cache in Bologna (Zannoni 1888, pl.28a/14–33). Nothing similar has been found north of the Alps and if by chance such a tool were to be found, it would not only confirm its rarity but also its resulting uncommon utilisation.

The second problem to solve was that of the support to be given to the general shape of the boat. Once again, the number of solutions was limited because of the unavailability of a tool that would have allowed an intensive use of treenail fastenings (the spoon-drill). The other possible technique, the lashing of transversal pieces to the planking, was not chosen in this case although it was used, as proved by other examples such as the Scandinavian Iron Age boat, the Hjortspring (*c.* 350 BC; Rosenberg 1937), and subsequently the Nydam boat (4th century AD; Engelhardt 1865). It is also applied in archaic and traditional constructions around the world and can still be seen in use along the southern coast of India. The tenon-mortise assemblies, a widespread technique during the Bronze Age was made use of. It was adapted in the case of the Dover as well as on the North Ferriby (Wright 1990) and the Brigg boats (McGrail 1981), where a number of cleats were left upstanding on the surface of the planks into which massive mortises were carved, the size of the sharp edge of an axe blade. The tenons were replaced by large rods or transverse timbers that passed through a number of aligned mortised cleats giving the same constant inclination to the planking (Fig 9.6). In this context, the small elements that held together both planks, one on each side of the middle seam of the Dover, played the same role and can be considered as so many more transverse rods. It can be noted that the direct tenon-mortise fastening does not function as efficiently as the lashing of the framework to the planking. The weak points are not located in the lashings (easy to repair), but situated either on the mortises carved directly into the wood mass during construction, therefore impossible to mend, or on the transverse timbers, which meant having to dismantle the boat for repairs. It is possible that this difficulty encouraged the search for new solutions such as those found later in the Celto-Roman constructions.

The third element that remained to be solved was a way of keeping the hull watertight. The widespread technique used on lashed or sewn plank boats consisted of stitching small bundles of vegetable fibres onto the seams.

The study of the masula, a small fishing boat found along the south-eastern coast of India (Fig 9.7a), close to Madras, which is built of narrow sewn planks, underlines the double function of these small bundles:

To keep the hull watertight at the different joints;
To guarantee the tightness of the lashing/sewing and to even out stress at the joints of each plank. Just the rounded shape given to the joints by the watertight bundles relieves stress; this lashed material remains elastic when compressed and is important in reducing excess stress applied on the joints during navigation (Fig 9.7b).

In this context, it can be noted that the stitch-holes drilled right through the planks of the masula are not plugged by treenails on the upper part of the hull and are therefore not watertight: only reduction of stress is required.

The observations described above may explain the similarities found on 'primitive' craft throughout the world: the technical solutions for assembling the different parts of a hull are initially very limited; the same applies to those involved in keeping the line of the boat during construction. This accounts for the uniformity in shape of boats from all continents. In this context, the inefficiency of the Bronze Age direct tenon-mortise fastening, as for instance on the Dover, will lead to particularly dynamic changes.

The discovery of new materials (bronze and iron), new tools (a variety of saws of greater dimensions, drills, much heavier axes and adzes both fitted with sharper blades) and new methods of fitting (treenails, rivets, iron nails) generated an endless evolution through time and space. Nevertheless, it should be borne in mind that this evolution does not follow directly the discovery of a new technique but depends on the one that offers the best solutions to a variety of problems. These solutions remain associated to serial production and efficiency, both based on the criteria of the least possible effort.

With regard to the studies of Celto-Roman vessels, it should be stressed that the main elements of naval architecture of that time, which initiated a specific tradition, were not identified before the

Fig. 9.6 The Brigg *Iron Age boat (drawn on the basis of the 1888 and 1975 plans).*

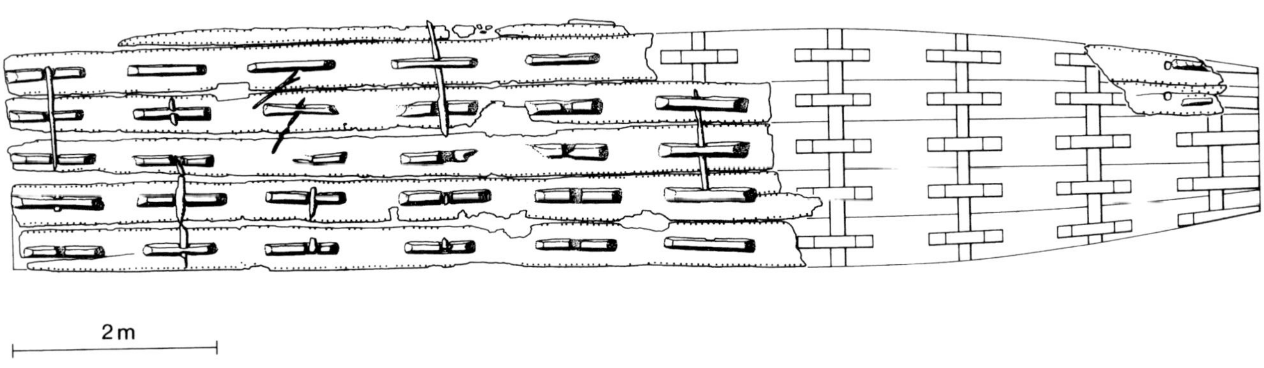

a b

Fig. 9.7
a. Masula: a small frameless fishing boat used along the southeastern coast of India.
b. On the upper part of the sides the stitch-holes meant to lash the planking together are not plugged. The lashed material is used only to reduce excess stress applied on the joints during navigation and is not waterproof.

building of Altaripa. These had to have a fundamental principle to allow their diffusion over the seas and inland waters of the vast territories occupied by the Celts, as well as to resist influences due to Roman occupation. The main element or the primary feature of Celtic naval architecture as opposed to that of the Bronze Age or that from the Mediterranean and Scandinavia, is the discarding of the lashing/sewing of the different parts of the boat without replacing it with another equivalent technique: rivets to fasten clinker planking in Scandinavia, or the mortise-tenon-peg system in the Mediterranean region. Other techniques could have been used such as the nailing of clinker-built planking or the treenailing or the edge-fastening of flush-laid planks. In order to compensate for the loss of that device it became necessary to build a heavy framework firmly attached to the planking.

In order to maintain these two structures together, the Celtic builders chose iron nails in preference to treenails (Fig 9.8). Nailing was a popular technique then as it brought many solutions to the problems encountered; it was widely spread over the Celtic territory such as in the construction of the wooden frameworks of the *murus gallicus,* the fortified walls of many hillforts. The nailing technique was not a novelty at the time but belonged to various fitting methods and it gained momentum from the beginning of the Iron Age when intensive mining of iron ore was started. One such example is the use of turned iron nails on wagon wheels found in a number of Hallstatt mound burials.

The roots of the Celtic tradition are undoubtedly to be found in the Bronze Age period (and the boats of that time found in England with heavy carved planking are good examples of this). Its distinctive feature, the discarding of the direct fastenings of the planks, was replaced by another technique to solve the problem of stress on the hull caused by navigation, namely the nailing of a massive framework. The evolution of this system was encouraged by a) the use of a carved and heavy planks, b) the introduction of a new and plentiful material, iron, with which thousands of nails of all dimensions were forged, and c) the subsequent development of the spoon-drill that could have helped Bronze Age naval architecture find an early way towards an intensive use of treenailing. Until the replacement of iron nailing by treenailing from the Middle Ages onwards in continental and northern Europe a 'heavy' method was used. In Scandinavia, on the other hand, a 'lighter' way was followed with the use of slender planks, small mortised cleats just big enough to allow the passage of a tying material to hold a lightly constructed frame and finally the lashing of clinker-built planking; this last way of binding was subsequently replaced by the use of rivets.

Axial or bottomed-based constructions

Axial-based boats are built with a central element that finally extends to include a keel, stempost and sternpost. The centre part of this structure is formed either by a plank of equal height and width (a true keel), or by one wider than high (in this case, thicker than the neighbouring planks), or else by two (Fig 9.9) or three juxtaposed planks (Blackfriars, St-Peter-Port). The other concept of boats is based on the following principle: one roughly flat bottom with well-marked chine-girders. It is characteristic of flat-bottom constructions to which the Gallo-Roman river craft (including the Bevaix) belong.

Recent studies on naval architecture have shown that some of the techniques used in shell-first construction stem from the skeleton sequence of construction (and vice-versa). The same procedure can be applied to the bottom-oriented vessels, which carry a heavier central element combined to an approximately flat bottom. In this regard, the Bronze Age craft displays a particularly interesting ambivalence arising from the use of large rods passed through a number of lined up mortised cleats left proud on the bottom planks. The Brigg boat belongs unquestionably to the bottom-based type. The question remains unresolved in both the North-Ferriby 1, which has a central plank against which the garboards rest and where the chine-girders are shaped into an L and the Dover with its two planks fitted on a central axis. The centre-line concept is clearly underlined by the V-shape intended to accommodate one of the ends of the boat. But the use of rods in mortises left proud on the bottom indicates that the bottom was considered as one undivided unit that could not be built piece by piece.

The application of these two principles on both boats is interesting; it might indicate that the

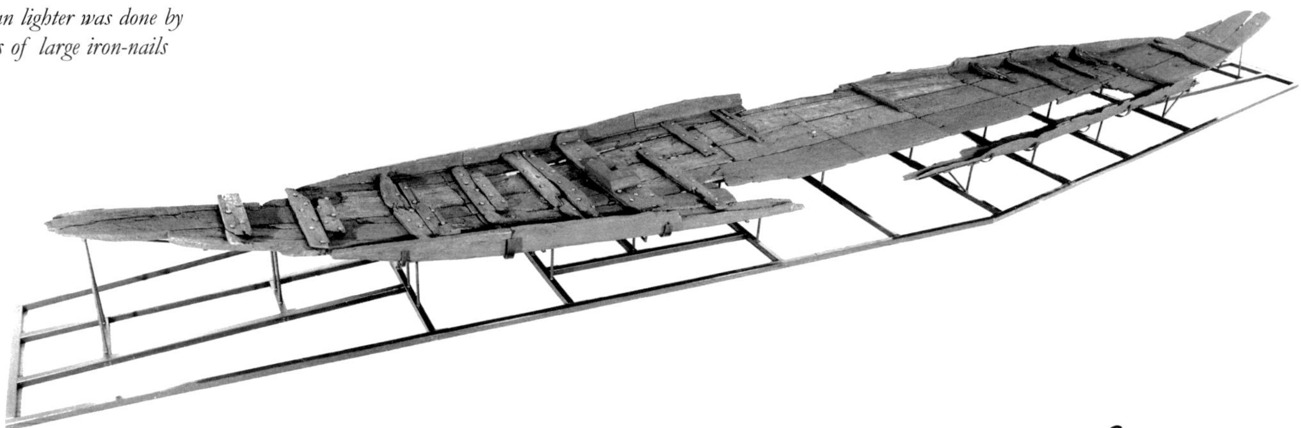

Fig. 9.8 The assembling of the Bevaix *Gallo-Roman lighter was done by means of large iron-nails only.*

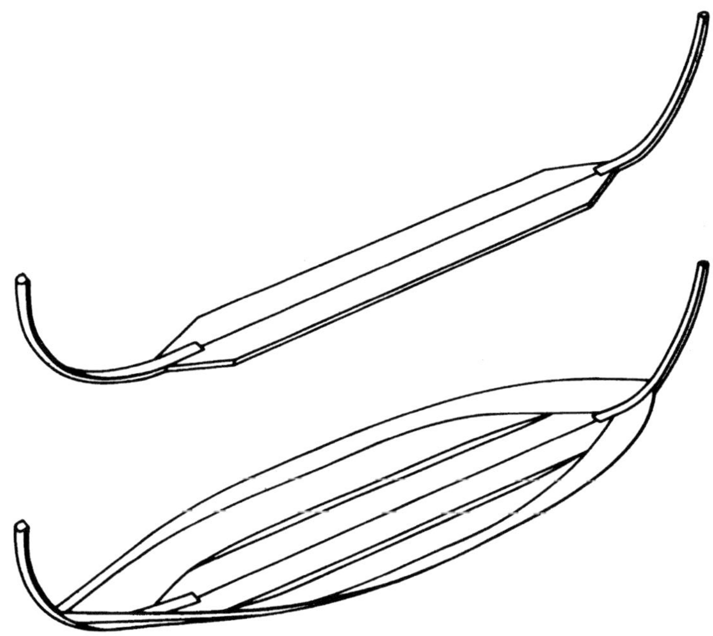

Fig. 9.9 Reconstruction of the first steps in the building of the Blackfriars 1.

replacement of rods and sewn techniques by iron nails to steady the massive framework led carpenters along two paths: one in which the central element becomes predominant, and the other in which the flat bottom constitutes a single unit.

The Dover boat will no doubt be the matter of further discussions on techniques and building principles including the origin and the evolution in shape of plank boats.

Acknowledgement

Translated by Dominique Robert Bliss.

List of references

Arnold, B 1992 *Batellerie gallo-romaine sur le lac de Neuchâtel, tomes 1 et 2*, Saint-Blaise: Editions du Ruau, Archéologie neuchâteloise, **12 et 13**

Arnold, B 1995 *Pirogues monoxyles d'Europe centrale: construction, typologie, évolution, tome 1*, Neuchâtel, Musée cantonal d'archéologie, Archéologie neuchâteloise, **20**

Arnold, B 1996 *Pirogues monoxyles d'Europe centrale: construction, typologie, évolution, tome 2*, Neuchâtel, Musée cantonal d'archéologie, Archéologie neuchâteloise, **21**

Arnold, B 1998 'Embarcations romano-celtiques et construction sur sole', in E Rieth (éd), *Concevoir et construire des navires: De la trière au picoteux*, Ramonville Saint-Agne: Editions Erès.

Arnold, B 1999a *Altaripa: archéologie expérimentale et architecture navale gallo-romaine*, Neuchâtel, Musée cantonal d'archéologie, Archéologie neuchâteloise, **25**

Arnold, B 1999b 'Some remarks on Romano-Celtic boat construction and Bronze Age wood technology', *International Journal of Nautical Archaeology*, **28/1**, 34–44

Darrah, R 2004 'Woodland Management and Timber Conversion', in P Clark (ed), *The Dover Bronze Age boat,* English Heritage, 106–123

Dudley, H 1943 'The one-tree boat at Appleby, Lincolnshire', Antiquity, 17, 156–161

Engelhardt, Conrad 1865 *Nydam Mosefund 1859–1863*, Copenhague

McGrail, S (ed.) 1981 *The Brigg 'raft' and her prehistoric environment*, British Archaeological Reports (British Series), **89**

Marsden, P 1974 'The County Hall ship, London', *International Journal of Nautical Archaeology and Underwater Exploration*, **3/1**, 55–65

Pomey, P (ed.) 1997 *La navigation dans l'Antiquité*, Aix-en-Provence: Édisud

Pugin, C, Corboud, P et Castella, A-C 1988 'Une roue du Bronze final sur la station littorale de Corcelettes (Grandson VD)', *Archéologie Suisse*, **11/4**, 146–154

Rosenberg, G 1937 *Hjortspringfundet*, Copenhague, Nordisk Forlag, Nordiske Fortidsminder, **3/1**

Steffy, R 1994 *Wooden ship building and the interpretation of shipwrecks*, College Station: Texas A and M University Press

Winiger, J 1987 'Das Spätneolithikum der Westschweiz auf Rädern', *Helvetia Archaeologica*, **71–72**, 78–109

Wright, E V 1990 *The Ferriby boats: Seacraft of the Bronze Age*, Londres et New York: Routledge

Zannoni, A 1888 *La fonderia di Bologna, scoperta e descritta*, Bologna: Società tipografica Azzoguidi

10. The Humber, its sewn-plank boats, their contexts and the significance of it all

Robert Van de Noort

Introduction

The world of prehistoric maritime archaeology remains somewhat remote from those practitioners who are safely based with two feet on the land. In recent major contributions to the study of boats (e.g. McGrail 2001), we learn much about the technology of shipbuilding and the practical aspects of using boats in prehistory, but we find very little here on what the significance of boats, transport and seafaring was to past societies in terms of socio-political and economic aspects of life. Conversely, our terrestrial-based colleagues happily discuss the long-distance exchange of prestige goods and the spread of intellectual concepts during prehistory without the slightest consideration for the craft and the mariners that enabled such processes in the first place (e.g. Barrett 1994; Bradley 1984).

This paper attempts to take in both fields of study, i.e. maritime and landscape archaeology. It revisits the sewn-plank boats of the Humber estuary, in particular those at Ferriby and Kilnsea, and their landscape contexts. In doing so, it aims at gaining understanding the significance of the boats, their use and their relationship to socio-economic change in the Early Bronze Age. This paper addresses the Humber estuary, the sewn-plank boats from the region and their landscape contexts, before considering what new information has been obtained from this approach.

The Humber…

We are most fortunate with the rich maritime heritage from the Humber estuary and its tributaries. Apart from the Early Bronze Age sewn-plank boats from North Ferriby and Kilnsea, which will be discussed in some detail below, it includes an additional Later Bronze Age sewn-plank boat from

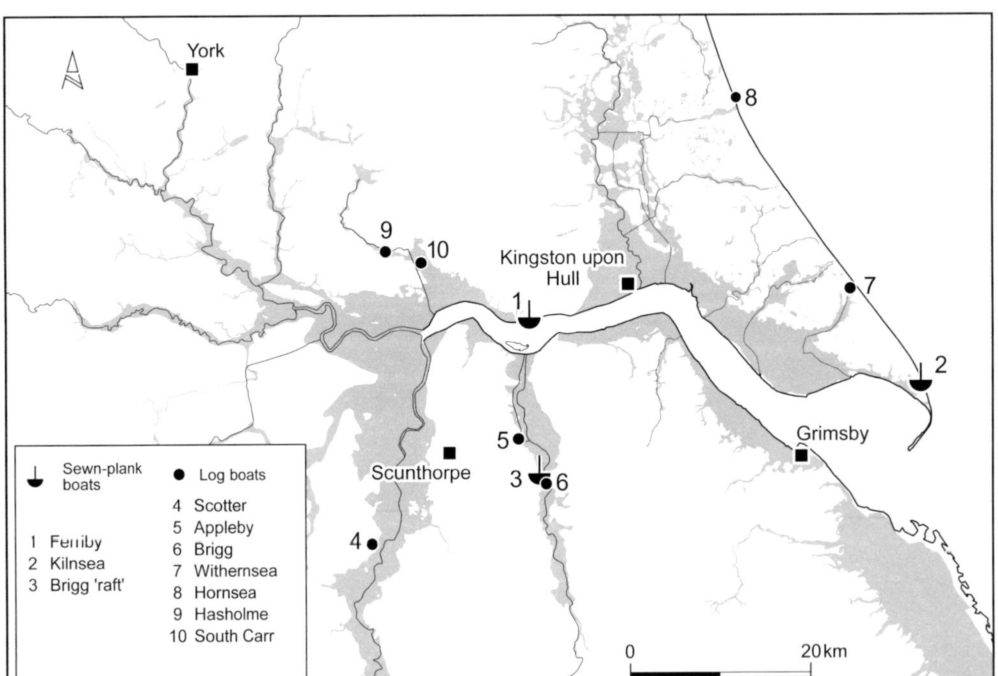

Fig. 10.1 Location of all prehistoric boats in the Humber Wetlands.

Brigg and prehistoric logboats from Brigg, Appleby, Scotter, Hasholme and elsewhere, studied and published to varying standards (Fig 10.1; McGrail 1990; Millett and McGrail 1990). In part, the richness of this resource is the result of the enthusiasm and persistence of local archaeologists, most notably Ted Wright, but natural forces are important here too.

Several research projects under the Land Ocean Interaction Study (LOIS) umbrella have recently addressed the environmental history of the southern North Sea basin during the Holocene period. In terms of the evolution of the Humber estuary and its surrounding wetlands, this research has shown that the Humber became a tidal inlet around 6000 cal BC (calibrated radiocarbon years) and that a range of 'eutrophic' wetlands, including saltmarsh, reedswamp and alder carr, developed on the Humber shores (Metcalfe *et al* 2000). By the Early Bronze Age, the highest regularly occurring sea-level (or mean high water of spring tides = MHWST) was at or around modern Ordnance Datum (OD) (e.g. Long *et al* 1998). Subsequent sea-level rise resulted in further marine transgression during the first millennium BC, thus burying the older 'eutrophic' wetlands. The sewn-plank boats from North Ferriby and Kilnsea were found just below modern OD. With reference to the Bronze Age period sea-level, these boats were submerged by tidal water and the sediments it contained during high- or spring tides. In other words, these boats did not sink, but were overwhelmed by the water whilst resting at their natural landing places. Archaeological evidence, as presented below, corroborates such an interpretation.

Apart from the discoveries of the boats over a period of 60 years, and the research by the LOIS group, another research project has been active in the Humber estuary; the Humber Wetlands Project. As part of this English Heritage funded research, sites such as the North Ferriby foreshore were further investigated, the boat plank from Kilnsea was studied and additional research was undertaken on the beach where the plank was found. It also provided a framework for the re-dating of the Ferriby boats (Wright *et al* 2002), and of more extensive research in the region including extensive field survey and the collation and re-analysis of previous archaeological work and discoveries (e.g. Van de Noort and Ellis 1995; 1999).

…its sewn-plank boats…

The discovery of the Ferriby boats between 1937 and 1963 and, in particular, the remains of what have become known as Ferriby 1, 2 and 3 (or F1, F2 and F3) have been well-documented by the discoverers themselves and many others (McGrail 2001; Wright and Wright 1939; Wright 1990). The boats are all of the same principle design. They are made of oak planks with bevelled edges, sewn together using individual stitches of yew withies and with an internal system of integrated cleats and transverse timbers that provide rigidity to the hull. The remains of F1 are the most complete and, fittingly, this boat has received most attention from maritime archaeologists (Fig 10.2). Debates on the exact technical details of the boat, its reconstruction and its performance are ongoing and will probably never be resolved to the full satisfaction of the participants to this debate. Nevertheless, it may be worth repeating here some figures from John Coates (1990), who on the basis of one of his theoretical reconstructions calculates that the boat could reach a maximum speed of 6 knots, and could have carried a maximum load of 11 tons. F2 comprises a near-complete keelplank, and F3 consist of the remains of an outer bottom plank stitched to the remains of a lowest side strake.

Recently, we successfully re-dated the Ferriby boats (Wright *et al* 2001). The quest to obtain accurate dates for F1, F2 and F3 became an important issue with the growing realisation that cocktail of chemicals, used during the last six decades to conserve the Ferriby boats, made previous radiocarbon dates unsafe and unreliable. The re-dating places F1, F2 and F3 in the early second millennium BC, the Early Bronze Age, rather than the Middle Bronze Age. F3 is now the oldest known plank-built boat in Western Europe, with a date range of 2030–1780 cal BC.

The Kilnsea boat plank was discovered in 1996 during a fieldtrip of the Hull Natural History Society on the beach of Kilnsea, *c.* 4 km north of Spurn Point in Holderness. The plank is probably part of a keel plank or lower bottom strake and the remains of the integral cleats are well preserved. The edges of the plank, on the other hand, were badly eroded, and we could not determine whether this plank had been stitched to another. The plank closely resembles, in terms of its size and the dimensions of the cleats, the lower bottom strakes of F1. The Kilnsea boat plank was dated by radiocarbon assay to 1750–1620 cal BC (Van de Noort *et al* 1999). McGrail (2001, 190–1) argues that we must question the identification of fragmentary remains such as that from Kilnsea as the remains of a sewn-plank boat. However, as cleats have as yet never been found on other Bronze Age wetland sites in Britain or abroad, and considering that such a construction would not be particularly useful in standing structures, this concern may be misplaced.

Discussions whether the boats from Ferriby and Kilnsea, and others in this group including Caldicot 1 and the Dover boat (Fig 10.3), could have been used for seafaring, or were merely used for cross-estuary and riverine transport, are ongoing. If the seafaring capacity of the sewn-plank boats is tested

Fig. 10.2 F1 stored at the National Maritime Museum, Greenwich.

against modern concepts of health and safety, than these boats will plainly fail. But if we ask whether these boats could have occasionally crossed the North Sea, under the right weather conditions, than the answer is most probably affirmative. Given the reconstructed performance of F1, with a speed of 6 knots, it could reach the Dutch coast in just over 24 hours from Spurn Point. The shorter crossing from the East Anglian coast would last merely 15 hours. If the crew waited for favourable wind, the latter journey could be readily achieved during the hours of light on a suitable summer's day.

What kind of cargo could these boats have carried? We know that people crossed the North Sea to trade or exchange goods, ideas and possibly people with Continental Europe ever since Britain became the British Isles, after *c.* 6000 cal BC. The introduction of early farming must have involved the transport of seedcorn for crops and domes-ticated animals, alongside the ideas for the production of new tools and the construction of buildings and long barrows. The dearth of Neolithic craft that could have been used for this transport must be attributed to a bias in the archaeological record.

By the late Neolithic and the Bronze Age, people continued to exchange goods, ideas and probably people across the North Sea, but the character of the long-distance exchanged commodities had changed. In this period, it included a range of prestige items, such as Beakers, elaborate flint daggers and early bronzes, and jewellery of gold, amber, jet and faience, recovered from burials from both sides of the North Sea (Cunliffe 2001, 213–60). The emergence of the 'rich burials', a term coined by Flemming (1973), in late Neolithic and the Early Bronze Age Britain has been equated with the rise of new elite groups in prehistoric communities, or their manifestation in the material culture (Bradley 1984). The matching development of the Beaker on either side of the North Sea has been frequently invoked as a demonstration of the exchange of ideas and of elite networks that developed over much of western Europe. At the start the second millennium BC, we note an important 'step-change' in the deposition of these exotic artefacts, with the wealthiest graves becoming richer still; the richest graves from southern England dated to 2000–1400 BC, and these provided the basis for Stuart Piggot's concept of the 'Wessex Culture'. Within these graves, amber from the Baltic Sea has been found repeatedly, and also early bronzes of apparent Continental origin (Beck and Shennan 1991; Rohl and Needham 1998). Rich burials have also been found in most regions of England and Scotland.

The re-dating of the Ferriby boats provides now a convincing group, together with the boats from Kilnsea, Dover and Caldicot 1 (Clark 2004; McGrail 1997), suggesting that the appearance of plank built boats in the early second millennium BC is more than a coincidence. If this group represents an important stage in maritime development technology, adopting the sewing of parts from hide boats, but with more robust hulls and possibly of greater capacity (McGrail 1993), then what was the reason for this? It is plausible that the new type of boat was developed to enable the expansion or maintenance of the elite networks across the North Sea and the English Channel. Hide boats, despite their absence from the archaeological record, were likely to have been used for travel during exceptionally favourable weather. The more robust plank boats, however, would have extended the windows of opportunity to gain access to the goods and ideas that facilitated the expression of rank and status around 2000 BC.

Fig. 10.3 Location of sewn plank boats in England and Wales.

...their context...

North Ferriby is situated at the southernmost point of the Yorkshire Wolds (Fig 10.4). As its name indicates, it functioned in the Middle Ages as one of the main cross-estuarine natural harbours, and it seems probable that it was used as such for much of the prehistoric period. It was well situated for contact with people living on the Lincolnshire Wolds on the opposite side of the Humber estuary. F1, F2 and F3 were found in intertidal creeks in what was a saltmarsh environment. Despite the standing of F1, the contexts of F2 and F3 are more relevant to the discussion presented here. The remains of these appear to have been carefully put aside; F2 was found on a single alder roundwood and F3 on top of a bundle of alder logs, as if they were stored there awaiting reassembly with the rest of the boat. What exactly happened with these remains, we will never know; maybe the part of the boats known to us as F2 and F3 were simply not good enough for reuse; or maybe they were lost in a storm or during an unanticipated spring high tide. But what makes these contexts significant is that this indicates that boats were built, repaired or refashioned at North Ferriby. This, and also the frequent finds of oak wood chips with evidence of bronze axe facets from the area, makes the North Ferriby foreshore the oldest known shipyard in the world.

The location of the North Ferriby foreshore reinforces the sense that this is an important place. The Yorkshire Wolds is a region where elite formation in the Early Bronze Ages is exemplified by the set of 'Great Barrows' and some early

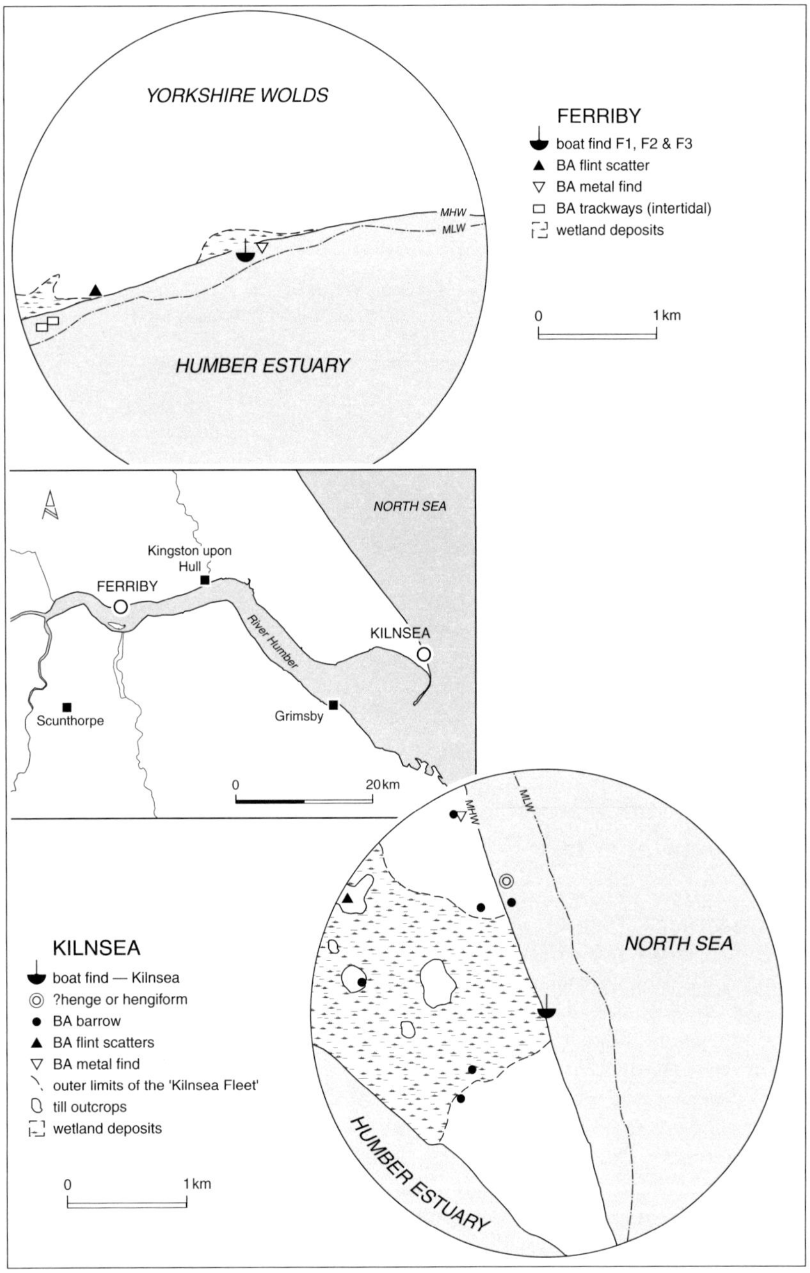

Fig. 10.4 The North Ferriby and Kilnsea sites in their landscape context.

ringforts, and where during the Early Bronze Age rich burials were created (Manby 1980; 1988a). Some rich beaker burial graves, containing amber, are also known from the Yorkshire Wolds, for example at Acklam Wold and Kellythorpe (Beck and Shennan 1991, 145, 160). This evidence points once more at the emerging elite in Yorkshire, and their contacts with Continental Europe.

However, in terms of archaeological remains, the landscape context of the North Ferriby foreshore is surprisingly bare. In contrast to the central and northern parts of the Yorkshire Wolds, its southernmost parts which form the hinterland of North Ferriby contain little in terms of significant monuments, including barrows. Nor do we have any evidence of the practice of votive deposition of metal artefacts which at this point in time emerges elsewhere in Britain, albeit not yet at a significant scale in the Humber Wetlands (*cf* Needham 1988). Could it be that this area had been set aside, or was treated differently, because of its important functions in trade and exchange? Suggestions that farming was not undertaken here, for example to retain woodland resources, appear unfounded. Pollen analysis from North Ferriby indicates that by *c.* 1700 cal BC, tree pollen were relatively rare and woodland was not extensive in this area, reflecting the general picture of the Humber Wetlands (Wright and Churchill 1965).

Remains of hurdle trackways had been noted by Ted Wright (1990) and dated to the 17th century BC. A reconstruction drawing of the North Ferriby foreshore in the Bronze Age shows the arrival of Ferriby 1 (Fig 10.5). The drawing shows trackways, made of woven hurdles of hazel, which provide a semi-permanent landing place, reinforcing the suggestion that the North Ferriby foreshore was one side of the cross-estuary traffic. I would like to question this representation.

During the Humber Wetlands Project, similar trackways were excavated on the nearby Melton Foreshore, and likewise dated to the Middle Bronze Age, in this case the 15th and 14th century BC. These latter trackways were found to have been staked into the ground at angles across former intertidal creeks. Our interpretation of this landscape is that the trackways provided an effective way to evacuate livestock to higher and dryer ground during spring high tides, when the saltmarshes, excellent feeding grounds, were flooded (e.g. Van de Noort and Fletcher 2001). In the past, this interpretation has been attacked on the basis that cattle would never walk over hurdle trackways. It is true that the trackways were practically undamaged, but this is due to their very short functional lifespan; one period of high tide could be enough to bury the trackway beneath sediments and render it invisible and useless to the Bronze Age farmers. However, following recent experimental archaeology trials undertaken by Exeter student Sarah Bidgood, it is clear that modern Dexter cattle, without ever having seen hurdle trackways or without any encouragement from the farmer, can use and probably used such structures without hesitation to travel over boggy and muddy areas.

Our understanding of the North Ferriby foreshore, and *ergo* the landscape context of the Ferriby boats, should be reinterpreted in the light of new research. The trackways from North Ferriby did not form part of some kind of waterfront facilities; the re-dating of the Ferriby boats and the very short life-span of such structures below

Fig. 10.5 The arrival of F1 at North Ferriby; reconstruction drawing by John Craig (in Wright 1990).

MHWST proves that the trackways were never contemporary with the boats. Nor do we have any other evidence of maritime structures on the foreshore. However, if the trackways from North Ferriby were used in a way similar to those at Melton, it means that by the 17th century BC the North Ferriby saltmarshes were probably used for grazing.

To all sense and purpose, we must conclude that the landscape context of the North Ferriby boats does not contain any significant indication that the activity of boat building or the daily operation of the boats in cross-estuarine traffic was considered special; in this landscape, we cannot identify any activities as such. We have no monuments, no deposition of valuable goods, and no exclusion of daily farming practices that could indicate this. All this, despite the undoubted importance of trade and exchange to the elite groups of Yorkshire and thus, one might expect, the importance that was attributed to the boats, the boat builders and the mariners. In other words, we must conclude here that the boats were perceived as tools in the everyday existence of the Bronze Age community, and that the use of the boats was part of everyday life.

The Kilnsea plank was found on the beach, seaward from a developing dune system, but this coastal location is due to more recent marine erosion of Holderness (Fig 10.4). On the beach are both clay and peat deposits visible during low tide; these deposits are of estuarine rather than marine origin, with the clays containing numerous fossils of the *Scrobicularia* mollusc, and the Kilnsea plank must have been preserved in these deposits. They belong to the Kilnsea Fleet, a natural elongated depression in the till clays of southern Holderness. Sometime before *c.* 4000 cal BC, this and similar large elongated glacial and glaciofluvial depressions in Holderness became estuarine wetlands, following sea-level rise, linking them with the Humber estuary (Dinnin and Lillie 1995). In terms of navigation, after *c.* 4000 cal BC, the Kilnsea Fleet was the outermost navigable inlet of the Humber estuary, the ideal location for boats departing to cross the North Sea. Alternatively, it was the first inlet safe for landing boats on the north bank of the Humber estuary when arriving from the east.

Whereas little more can be said about the boat remains from Kilnsea, its landscape context, and particularly the north bank of the Kilnsea Fleet, is rich and diverse. This is somewhat surprising, as the Holderness region it forms part of is particularly poor in terms of prehistoric monuments (*cf* Manby 1988). The prehistoric landscape at Kilnsea embodies up to 1500 years of human activity. This activity is represented in the archaeological record by a Neolithic house and several hearths (Mackey 1998), a late Neolithic or Early Bronze Age small henge, hengi-form monument or other circular structure, and two Early Bronze Age barrows, one on exactly the same location as the Neolithic house, the other overlying one of the Neolithic hearths. This group of sites does not equate to a form of continuous settlement or occupation; rather the landscape on Easington Beach appears to have been used, modified and reused according to prehistoric people's perception of their past. Radiocarbon dating has put the Neolithic phase around *c.* 3800 cal BC, whilst the circular henge or hengi-form monument was dated by a cremation burial in the outer ditch to *c.* 2600–2000 cal BC.

The two burial mounds on the beach were built around *c.* 2000 cal BC, again dated by radiocarbon assay. The structures themselves contained individual graves with grave goods, including Beakers and in one instance a jet button. Several more circular burial mounds can be found in the landscape context of the Kilnsea boat, but none has been excavated. The area was extensively inundated by the estuarine Kilnsea Fleet. With only the tentative evidence of a single sherd of unstratified pottery dated to the first millennium BC, this event appears to have taken place sometime in later prehistory. The inundation resulted in the deposition of grey clay within the ditches of the small henge or hengi-form monument and its partial destruction, and the discontinuation of monument building in the area.

In terms of context of the Kilnsea boat, to all sense and purpose this landscape appears to be dominated by ritual activities. By the Early Bronze Age, these are directly expressions of a manifestation of inequality in the form of individual burials beneath earthen barrows, using monuments for social reproduction. In terms of everyday activities, pollen analysis from the area suggests that by the Early Bronze Age, much of the forest remained intact, although clearances in the woodland were increasingly extensive (Lillie and Gearey 2000).

...and the significance of it all

The landscape contexts of the Ferriby boats and the Kilnsea boat provide us with stark contrasts. The landscape of the Ferriby boats is that of the activities of everyday life, without any indication in terms of monuments, finds or agricultural activities (as far as we can tell) of anything extraordinary happening here. On the other hand, the landscape context of Kilnsea boat is that of monuments and ritual activities, and within the wider context of the Holderness region where such monuments and activities appear absent, one is surely justified to call this area a small 'ritualised landscape'.

Of course, this understanding of the landscape context of the two boat sites could be to a degree coincidental. It may be, for example, that future archaeological discoveries will bring to light new evidence from North Ferriby which requires a comprehensive re-evaluation of the evidence, and maybe the location where the Kilnsea boat finally came to rest was the consequence of an ancient accident. However, if our current knowledge of the contexts of these two archaeological sites is correct, then we should consider the significance of it all.

The landscape context of the Ferriby boats indicates that what happened here in the Early Bronze Age was were not embedded with any 'special' meaning, but the activities formed part of the rhythm of daily life; the cross-estuarine exchange that was enabled by the boats formed part of this. Crafts of varying types had been used from the Mesolithic through to the later Iron Age for daily transport, and in the Bronze Age this must also have been the case. However, traffic across the North Sea was loaded with meaning and significance. This form of transport enabled elite groups in Yorkshire and further afield to express and manifest their status in death, as shown in the archaeological record by the amber, bronzes and beakers, and most likely also in life. The importance of this aspect of early Bronze Age communities is reflected in the landscape context of the Kilnsea boat; the landing place chosen for the seafarers was imbedded with references to the ancestors and their monuments, with the burial mounds of the emerging elite superimposed on this landscape, sometimes directly on top of the Neolithic remains.

Conclusion

The argument put forward here may be summarised as follows. Around 2000 BC, a new innovative technique of boat building was pioneered in the British Isles. Planks, rather than hides, were fastened together using yew withies through individual stitches. A system of integral cleats and transverse timbers provided rigidity to the hull; this method too may have been adopted from existing traditions of boat building. The period in which this innovation is introduced around the coast of England and Wales coincides with the increased inclusion of exotic and prestigious items in 'rich burials'; items included bronze tools and jewellery made from gold, amber, jet and faience that were important from Continental

Europe, and frequently Beakers. It is suggested here that the introduction of sewn-plank boats played a role in the development or maintenance of the expanding elite networks across Europe, which is reflected in the imported goods that found their way into the 'rich burials'.

Analysis of the landscape context of the boats has shown that the Ferriby foreshore was not, in any way, referring to monuments of the ancestors or charged with any special or religious meaning. The landscape contains neither monuments, nor any votive depositions, but the archaeology suggests that everyday farming activities took place here. Considering that this is the only known Bronze Age boat builder's yard, we may assume that the sewn-plank boats, their makers or their crew did not receive exceptional treatment. The landscape context of the Kilnsea boat, on the other hand, includes ample reference to ancestral monuments and contains several Bronze Age barrows including at least one with a Beaker burial. If Kilnsea was indeed the sheltered harbour chosen by the seafarers, as argued here, than it appears that these journeys across the sea, undertaken to acquire exotic goods and maintain networks across Europe, were loaded with distinctive meaning expressed in the reference to the ancestors and their monuments (*cf* Bradley 1998).

If this interpretation is not too wide off the mark, this could indicate that by the Early Bronze Age, seafaring was not, or no longer, perceived as an everyday activity. Possibly, the reinforcement of the elite networks and the acquisition of the foreign prestige goods that signalled the wearer's status formed parts of a rite of passage for young men. The dangerous, or at least perilous, nature of the journey would be compatible with such rites, and the sea was a liminal place, only to be entered on distinctive occasions and with clear reference to the ancestors.

I admit that this interpretative archaeology presented here includes several issues that are not without a degree of supposition and conjecture. Nevertheless, I hope that this innovative approach of 'seamlessly' integrating practical and theoretical aspects of maritime and landscape archaeology opens up fresh avenues for research that addresses the role of boats in the wider socio-political, economic and religious aspect of prehistory.

List of references

Barrett, J 1994 *Fragments from antiquity; an archaeology of social life in Britain, 2900–1200 BC*, Oxford: Blackwell

Beck, C and Shennan, S 1991 *Amber in prehistoric Britain*, Oxford: Oxbow

Bradley, R 1984 *The social foundations of prehistoric Britain*, London: Routledge

Bradley, R 1998 *The significance of monuments: on the shaping of human experience in Neolithic and Bronze Age Europe*, London: Routledge

Clark, P (ed) 2004 *The Dover Bronze Age boat*, London: English Heritage

Coates, J F 1990 'Performance', in E V Wright, *The Ferriby boats: Seacraft of the Bronze Age*, London, 113–116

Cunliffe, B 2001 *Facing the ocean. The Atlantic and its people 8000 BC–AD 1500*, Oxford: Oxford University Press

Dinnin, M and Lillie, M 1995 'The palaeoenvironmental survey of southern Holderness and evidence for sea-level change', in R Van de Noort and S Ellis (eds), *Wetland Heritage of Holderness, an archaeological survey*, Hull: Humber Wetlands Project, University of Hull, 87–120

Flemming, A 1973 'Models for the development of the Wessex culture', *The explanation of culture change: models in prehistory : proceedings of a meeting of the Research Seminar in Archaeology and Related Subjects held at the University of Sheffield, 1971*, London: Duckworth, 571–585

Lillie, M and Gearey, B 2000 'The palaeoenvironmental survey of the Hull valley, and research at Routh Quarry', in R Van de Noort and S Ellis (eds), *Wetland heritage of the Hull Valley: an archaeological survey*, Hull: Humber Wetlands Project, University of Hull, 31–82

Long, A J, Innes, J B, Kirby, J R, Lloyd, J M, Rutherford, M M, Shennan, I and Tooley, M J 1998 'Holocene sea-level change and coastal evolution in the Humber estuary, eastern England: an assessment of rapid coastal change', *The Holocene*, **8**, 229–247

Mackey, R 1998 'A Round Barrow at Easington, East Yorkshire: The 1996 Excavation', *Bulletin Prehistoric Research Section*, **35**, 1–4

Manby, T G 1980 'Bronze Age settlement in eastern Yorkshire', in J Barrett and R Bradley (eds), *Settlement and society in the British Later Bronze Age*, Oxford: British Archaeological Reports (British Series), **186**, 307–370

Manby, T G 1988 'The Neolithic in eastern Yorkshire', in T G Manby (ed), *Archaeology in eastern Yorkshire: Essays in honour of T C M Brewster*, Sheffield: Department of Archaeology and Prehistory, University of Sheffield, 35–88

McGrail, S 1990 'Early boats in the Humber basin', in S Ellis and D Crowther (eds), *Humber Perspectives*, Hull: Hull University Press, 109–130

McGrail, S 1993 'Prehistoric seafaring in the channel', in C Scarre and F Healy (eds), *Trade and exchange in prehistoric Europe*, Oxford: Oxbow, 199–210

McGrail, S 1997 'The boat fragments', in N Nayling and A Caseldine, *Excavations at Caldicot, Gwent: Bronze Age palaeochannels in the Lower Nedern Valley*, York: Council for British Archaeology Research Report, **108**, 210–7

McGrail, S 2001 *Boats of the World*, Oxford: Oxford University Press

Metcalfe, S E, Ellis, S, Horton, B P, Innes, J B, MacArthur, J, Mitlehner, A, Parkes, A, Pethcik, J S, Rees, J, Ridgeway, L, Rutherford, M M, Shennan, I and Tooley, M J 2000 'The Holocene evolution of the Humber estuary: reconstructing change in a dynamic environment', in I Shennan and J E Andrews (eds), *Holocene land-ocean interaction and environmental change around the western North Sea*, Geological Society Special Publication, 97–118

Millett, M and McGrail, S 1990 'The archaeology of the Hasholme boat', *Archaeological Journal*, **144**, 1–68

Needham, S 1988, 'Selective deposition in the British Early Bronze Age', *World Archaeology*, **20**, 229–48

Rohl, B and Needham, S 1998 *The circulation of metal in the British Bronze Age: the application of lead isotope analysis*, London: British Museum

Van de Noort, R and Ellis, S (eds) 1995 *Wetland Heritage of Holderness, an archaeological survey*, Hull: Humber Wetlands Project, University of Hull

Van de Noort, R and Ellis, S (eds) 1999 *Wetland Heritage of the Vale of York, an archaeological survey*, Hull: Humber Wetlands Project, University of Hull

Van de Noort, R and Fletcher, W 2001 'Bronze Age human ecodynamics in the Humber estuary', in G Bailly, R Charles and N Winder (eds), *Human ecodynamics*, Oxbow: Oxbow Monographs, 47–54

Van de Noort, R, Middleton, R, Foxon, A and Bayliss, A 1999 'The 'Kilnsea-boat', and some implications from the discovery of England's oldest plank boat', *Antiquity*, **73**, 131–135

Wright, C W and Wright, E V 1939 'Submerged boat at North Ferriby', *Antiquity*, **13**, 349–354

Wright, E V and Churchill, D M 1965 'The boats from North Ferriby, Yorkshire', *Proceedings of the Prehistoric Society*, **31**, 1–24

Wright, E V, Hedges, R, Bayliss, A and Van de Noort, R 2001 'New AMS dates for the Ferriby boats; a contribution to the origin of seafaring', *Antiquity*, **75**, 726–734

Wright, E V1990 *The Ferriby boats: Seacraft of the Bronze Age*, London: Routledge

11. A search for the prehistoric harbours of Kent

Keith Parfitt

Introduction

After the end of the last Ice Age, sometime during the Mesolithic period, Britain was finally separated from the Continent by rising sea levels. From that time onwards, until the advent of air transport and the opening of the Channel Tunnel in the late twentieth century, any Continental settler, trader, visitor or raider, bringing commodity, custom or cult, has had to arrive in Britain via some type of sea-going vessel. Sean McGrail has previously provided us with some general considerations on prehistoric seafaring in the English Channel and the nature of such vessels (McGrail 1993, 202).

East Kent has always been the closest part of our island to mainland Europe. The shortest distance across the Strait of Dover – between the South Foreland, immediately north of Dover, and Cap Griz Nez on the French coast, is just 34 km (21 miles). From such basic geographical facts it will be readily apparent that people crossing the English Channel have very often passed through Kent, although other established but longer crossing zones also existed further to the west (McGrail 1993, 200).

Kent's geographical position makes the county a very special place in archaeological terms. 'Continental influences' are increasingly being recognised throughout the archaeology of pre-historic Kent. In practical terms such 'influences', be they ideas or actual artefacts, must ultimately have arrived here with people landing from a ship or boat. From this it must follow that a series of landing sites once existed at various locations along the Kent coast during the prehistoric period, just as they have throughout the historic past. The location and form of any such prehistoric harbour sites, however, remain largely unknown.

Kent and its changing coast-line

Kent is essentially a sea-girt peninsula, bounded by the Thames Estuary and North Sea along its northern margin and the Dover Strait of the English Channel on the east and southern sides. Over the centuries, these waters have served as both a protective barrier and communications artery. There has always been great potential for water transport. The extensive and intractable lands of the Wealden Forest have tended to form something of a natural landward boundary along the western edge of the county, and served to isolate it from the rest of the south coast region. The inhabitants of our county have thus often looked to the sea to provide links, not only with other parts of Britain but also the Continent.

The county's coast-line is a long one, totalling some 160 km (100 miles). Profound local changes have occurred since the prehistoric period, however. Sea-levels have changed considerably; the available evidence suggests that Bronze Age sea-level was perhaps around 5 metres lower than it is today (Long 1992). Great tracts of marshland now exist in areas where there was once open water. Of the two largest north Kent islands, Thanet and Sheppey, only the latter is still detached from the mainland. Elsewhere, there has been severe erosion, particularly along parts of the north coast, where the soft Tertiary sands and clays are easily removed by the sea (Champion 1980, 224–5). Even the high chalk cliffs of the east and south-eastern shore – the world famous White Cliffs of Dover – have receded. Every section of coast has seen change – a very rough estimate suggests that about half has been subject to regular phases of erosion and half to long periods of deposition.

Without doubt, Kent's prehistoric coastline must have looked very different to that of today. Yet it is within the much changed, modern coastal landscape – heavily eroded in some areas, greatly silted in others, that we must attempt any search for the harbours and landing places of prehistoric Kent. The task is a difficult, if not impossible, one. On the exposed and eroded sections of coast, large amounts of important information must have been swept away without trace, although occasional fortuitous exceptions occur, such as the remains from Langdon Bay, east of Dover Harbour. Here, bronze implements recovered from the sea-bed seem to relate to a Bronze Age wreck (Needham and Dean 1987). Elsewhere, in places where there has been deposition, prehistoric remains are likely to be buried at considerable depths; the Dover Bronze Age boat lay in riverine silts about 6 metres below modern street level.

All these factors combine to make archaeological research very difficult. Nevertheless, the discovery of the Dover boat has brought the whole question of prehistoric seafaring and in particular cross-Channel travel sharply to the fore. Apart from being a major discovery in its own right, surely this find must also potentially provide clear evidence for the existence of a Bronze Age 'harbour' in this part of Kent, situated at the shortest crossing of the English Channel.

What did a prehistoric 'harbour' look like?

It is at this stage that we need to further consider what exactly we might expect to find, in terms of structural evidence, at a site which served as a harbour or landing-place in prehistoric times. At its most basic, very little is actually required. A sheltered area of water in a bay, or a gently shelving beach, with some sort of access to settlements either close-by or some distance inland, has proved to be entirely adequate along many coast-lines, for many centuries (McGrail 1993, 206–7). Fairly certainly, there would never have been much more than this at the majority of prehistoric landing sites. Perhaps some sort of timber jetty might occasionally have been con-structed at regularly used sites but in the majority of cases there will be no remains for the archaeologists to discover, beyond (with great luck) a vessel that actually used the haven or perhaps concentrations of items that were being unloaded or traded there.

A few large chalk blocks were found around the outside of the Dover boat. These were the only traces of what might be regarded, in any way, as being 'harbour works'. They amounted to little more than a few 'stepping stones' and are unlikely to represent permanent arrangements for landing. Recent work in Poole Harbour, Dorset, however, has revealed that rather more formal arrangements were in existence there during the late Iron Age when two substantial jetties or moles, provisionally dated to *c.* 250–200 BC, were constructed (Markey *et al* 2002). Previous work at Hengistbury Head, also in Dorset, has revealed what appears to be a deliberately created gravel hard, of *c.* 100–50 BC, laid along the shore line of an inlet (Cunliffe 1987, 120–122). Such discoveries provide hope and inspiration for Kentish field-workers.

A prehistoric haven at Dover?

To fully comprehend the importance of Dover as a landing place it is best to view the site from the sea, as if making the short crossing from the Continent. As Caesar's scout Volusenus must have reported in the first century BC, towering chalk cliffs stretch away to the west and to the east but the narrow, steep-sided valley carved out by the River Dour (a Celtic river-name) offers a safe haven and a ready point of access into the fertile hinterland of east Kent. In fact, the River Dour has been central to Dover's very existence, originally providing both a sheltered haven for shipping at its mouth and a constant supply of fresh water for its inhabitants.

Whilst the river was without doubt a valuable source of fresh water for prehistoric people, its course, narrow width and short length strongly suggest that it was never much used for water transport. Whatever its exact purpose, it seems unlikely that a substantial vessel such as the Dover Bronze Age boat could have ever successfully plied such a small river beyond the lower reaches adjacent to the sea.

Other Possible Prehistoric Harbour Sites

A brief survey of the Kent coast-line will now be undertaken in the hope of pinpointing some other likely areas where prehistoric harbours may once have existed. From the outset it has to be acknowledged that evidence is in short supply and somewhat diverse in nature. Nevertheless, it is hoped that the following notes will be of some interest.

Romney Marsh

In the south of the county lies a vast tract of marshland known collectively today as the Romney Marsh. This is protected on its seaward side by the great shingle barrier of Dungeness. Across this region there was once open water; now there is land, but its evolution has been long and complex. A network of creeks and streams probably crossed much of the area in prehistoric times and water transport must have been essential to the inhabitants of this region.

Here, we may usefully note the discovery of a small hoard of Early Bronze Age low-flanged axes in a gravel pit north of Lydd (Needham 1988). This find seems to imply that the formation of the Dungeness shingle had begun by the Early Bronze Age and that this area was habitable and in use by this time. The Romney Marsh Research Trust has done much in recent years to chart the complex development of the area (Eddison 2000) and it is to be hoped that future work by the Trust will turn up a major new site. The low-lying, water-logged nature of much of the ground here will allow for good preservation of organic remains in many areas and the possibility of another Flag Fen-type settlement or a boat find seems high.

Folkestone and East Wear Bay

Continuing eastwards around the coast, we pass the old medieval ports of Hythe and Folkestone, situated at the end of the Greensand Ridge. In the context of the Dover boat it is of particular interest to note that a thin layer of glauconitic sand (glauconite is the mineral which colours greensand) was found on the inboard surface of the vessel (Green, this volume). Sand with this composition does not occur at Dover but it is to be found on the foreshore in the area of Hythe and Folkestone, only 10–15 km from Dover. Although similar greensand deposits also occur along the French coast opposite, it is perhaps most logical to assume that the sand in the Dover boat originated in the Folkestone area.

Just beyond Folkestone lies East Wear Bay. Here, the sea has eroded the soft Gault clay to form a bay between the Greensand headland of Copt Point and the chalk escarpment of the North Downs. Today, there is a gentle, sandy foreshore here (glauconitic sand), strewn with rocks and boulders derived from the adjacent greensand cliff face. Aside from the major Roman villa situated at the top of the cliff, the region is of some archaeological interest for a number of reasons and it would seem that this has been an important place for many centuries.

We should note that a Bronze Age pot-rim discovered adjacent to the Dover boat seems to have been manufactured from Gault clay, strongly implying a source somewhere in the Folkestone area.

Overlooking East Wear Bay, below the villa complex, evidence of pre-Roman occupation includes late Iron Age pottery, cremation burials and coins (Winbolt 1925), whilst a scatter of earlier prehistoric struck flints occurs on the top of Copt Point. Clearly, there was pre-Roman activity in this area. Possibly of relevance to those in search of evidence of a prehistoric haven here, is a late Bronze Age sword dredged from the sea bed about 40 metres off the shore in 1951 (Cowen 1952). How did this object arrive in the sea – fallen from some long eroded cliff, or cast/lost overboard from a Bronze Age boat using the bay?

On the foreshore numerous examples of quernstones, many unfinished, may be found (Keller 1988, 59–68; 1989, 193–200). Stylistically, these are of late Iron Age and Roman types. Stratified soils that have slumped down the cliff-face have included layers of greensand dust and chippings, produced during the manufacture of such querns. It thus seems fairly clear that natural boulders found on the beach were being worked throughout the late Iron Age and earlier Roman period to produce quern-stones. These stones are very heavy and sea-borne transport would have provided by far the most efficient way of moving them off site.

Taken in conjunction with a quite significant number of late Iron Age coins, fragments of imported Dressel 1 Italian wine amphora and fine-ware pottery, there is now a very convincing case to be made for East Wear Bay being the site of a late Iron Age trading port and landing place (Frere 1991). The exact nature of the coastal topography here during the prehistoric period must remain uncertain. However, if we are correct in surmising that it was of broadly similar form to today, even if further out, we seem to have all that is needed for a regular landing place – a location virtually on the shortest sea crossing; a sheltered bay with a gently shelving beach; and a ready link with the adjacent prehistoric North Downs trackway which runs inland along the chalk scarp above the site.

The discovery of pieces of Folkestone greensand on prehistoric sites across east Kent and beyond indicates that this rock source was being exploited much earlier than the late Iron Age. Neolithic pits on Mill Hill at Deal have produced a few small fragments of greensand, whilst another at Wingham, some 19.5 km north of Folkestone has yielded a saddle quern and a stone rubber, both seemingly derived from the Folkestone Beds (Greenfield 1960, 66–7). A complete saddle quern of this rock-type also comes from a late Bronze Age pit on Mill Hill, Deal (Keller 1988, 65–66; Parfitt 1985, 213–214). Further afield, two Folkestone Beds quernstones were discovered at the Iron Age hillfort of Hunsbury, Northants (Keller 1989, 200) and most recently another quern has been found in a Bronze Age context at Flag Fen, (Buckley and Ingle 2001; Middleton and Bowman 2001). Were consignments of rock, either worked or unworked, regularly shipped out from a prehistoric haven at East Wear Bay?

Folkestone to Dover

Between Folkestone and Dover the English Channel cuts through the North Downs, giving rise to sheer, vertical chalk cliffs between 100 and 170 metres high. Even allowing for erosion of these cliffs, it seems unlikely that there could ever have been any practical landing places in this area. A narrow strip of beach might have been usable by the occasional small boat but there was probably no way to scale the adjacent cliffs.

Two archaeological features are of interest in this area, however. The first is the North Downs trackway, widely held to be a long distance routeway of prehistoric origin. Today, this terminates at the edge of the high cliff just behind the Valiant Sailor public house, over-looking East Wear Bay. However, Ronald Jessup (1970, 19) has speculated that this downland track is of such great antiquity that it once continued on along the crest of the downs to France – in short, it pre-dates the formation of the English Channel. Could it represent a Mesolithic (and earlier) route, perhaps originally created by herds of migrating animals?

The second site of note is a Bronze Age round barrow at Capel, situated some 2.4 km along the cliffs from the end of the track-way. This is a large mound, partially excavated in the 1950s (Grinsell 1992, Capel-le-Ferne 1). It produced an early-middle Bronze Age biconical urn, with applied horseshoe handles (Parfitt and Grinsell 1991), which is now on display in Dover Museum. Today, the barrow lies virtually on the cliff edge. In Stukeley's day it seems to have been one of a pair, the other mound having presumably since collapsed down the eroding cliff. Could these mounds have once served as Bronze Age sea-marks for vessels in the Straits making for East Wear Bay? Clearly, this question is closely bound up with erosion rates for the chalk cliffs here and how far back from the cliff-edge the mounds were originally placed.

Another Bronze Age cremation urn has been recovered from Round Down Cliff, to the north-east of Capel (Jessup 1930, 124). It is not impossible that this burial was also originally contained within a cliff-top round barrow, although there is no record of this.

Dover to Kingsdown

The lack of suitable landing places along the 8 km of coast-line between East Wear Bay and Dover is readily apparent and serves to emphasise the importance of the gap created by the River Dour at Dover. This provides the only significant break in the cliffs anywhere between Folkestone and Kingsdown (20 km) and there is ready access to the Kentish hinterland from here. There seems little doubt that the site served as a regular landing place throughout prehistory. The Dover boat surely provides tangible evidence for such a landing place and the finds from Langdon Bay seem to provide further, if less direct, evidence.

The high cliffs continue north-eastwards from Dover, past the South Foreland. As the sea cuts across the downs in this area, it truncates a series of dry chalkland valleys. Greater erosion into these has resulted in the creation of a series of small, shallow bays – Langdon Bay, Fan Bay, St Margaret's Bay and Oldstairs Bay. Today, these are generally of little use to those wishing to land from a boat, because of the limited access up the cliffs. Presumably, the same was true in the past.

Points of archaeological detail occur at two of these bays, however. The first is in Langdon Bay, situated immediately outside Dover Harbour. Here, in 1974, divers of the Dover Sub-Aqua Club recovered a large quantity of bronze implements from the sea-bed (Muckelroy 1981; Needham and Dean 1987; Stevens 1976). Regular dives since have produced more pieces and these now total over 450 individual items. The majority of the implements are Continental types datable to about 1100–1000 BC and many show signs of damage or deliberate breakage, indicating that this was scrap material.

There seem few reasonable alternatives to the theory that these bronzes represent the cargo from a vessel that foundered whilst trying to make the safety of the Dour estuary when sailing from the Continent fully laden with scrap intended for re-casting. As one likely scenario, Muckelroy (1981, 288) has postulated that a craft sailing from the French coast was driven past the haven mouth by a strong south-westerly gale and foundered on the rocky shore below the South Foreland.

The find-spot lies some 500 metres out from the present shore-line and it is worth giving some consideration to the question of cliff erosion rates in this area. Clearly, all the exposed cliff faces along the Kent coast have receded to some extent since prehistoric times. Estimates of erosion for this section of coast-line suggest that around 600 metres of land may have removed here. Yet if our interpretation of the Langdon Bay discovery is correct, the bronzes were lost in open water, presumably at too great a depth to have been retrieved by any survivors or local shore-based witnesses. The notion that this was a Continental hoard originally contained within a pit on the cliff-top has been previously considered but has not found much favour with researchers. It may be noted in passing, however, that there are extensive scatters of Neolithic-Bronze Age struck flints to be found on the cliff-top in this area (Parfitt 1976), so prehistoric people certainly do seem to have been active here. But it appears more likely that the Langdon Bay bronzes were lost at sea, at some distance out from the shore. If so, this implies that there has been rather less cliff erosion here than estimated.

At St Margaret's Bay, just north of the South Foreland, there is today access from the beach to the top of the cliff and this may have also been the case in the past. In historic times this little bay has occasionally served as a haven for a few small vessels; perhaps this was also the case in prehistoric times. At the top of present-day Bay Hill, on a ridge-top over-looking the sea, a Bronze Age round barrow survived until quite recently (Grinsell 1992, St Margaret's at Cliffe 4). It seems possible that, like Capel, this might have been visible from out to sea.

In dry valley deposits just above the beach, investigations by Dover Archaeological Group have revealed a deposit containing significant amounts of Neolithic-Bronze Age flint-work, some pottery and quantities of locally collected marine mollusc shells. Fairly certainly, this material is derived from some sort of coastal occupation site and we are again returned to the issue of cliff erosion rates and coastal formation. The South Foreland valley which gives rise to St Margaret's Bay runs in from the south-west and strikes the shore-line at an angle. Allowing for the retreat of the cliff line it seems likely that any prehistoric fore-runner of the present-day bay would actually have lain further to the north-east. The occupation site, with its discarded marine shells, however, implies that the prehistoric seashore lay at no great distance.

During 1938 a fine Bronze Age Picardy Pin was discovered in the garden of a house in the South Foreland valley (Rowlands 1976). This import could have arrived at its find-spot as a direct import from the Continent, perhaps acquired from some trading vessels that put into the bay. It is presently on display at Dover Museum.

Continuing north from St Margaret's Bay, the cliffs gradually decrease in height but remain a definite obstacle to landing. Another cliff-top find of passing interest is a Middle Bronze Age barrel urn containing a cremation, found south of Kingsdown, in 1936. This was contained in a small pit located some 30 metres from the present cliff edge (Stebbing 1936, 235). There was no evidence that it was ever covered by a barrow but this remains a possibility.

Deal and the Wantsum Channel

The chalk cliffs finally end north of Kingsdown and are replaced by a level plain of brickearth, edged with a steeply shelving beach of shingle. It is here that the great Roman general Julius Caesar and his legions are believed to have landed, having decided that the cliffs to the south were impossible to scale. Despite quite a long period of archaeological research in the area, Caesar's extensive bridgehead camp has remained elusive. One thing does seem quite clear, however – there was no established port here that could have been used, even by a fraction of his great fleet.

To the north of Deal, throughout the prehistoric period lay a broad water-way, the Wantsum Channel, which separated mainland Kent from the Isle of Thanet. The channel seems to have finally silted up during the medieval period but before this time it formed an important water-way, providing a more sheltered alternative to rounding the North Foreland for vessels travelling between the English Channel and the Thames estuary/southern North Sea.

The Wantsum seems to have been formed at the start of the Neolithic period, if not before, and by the Bronze Age the silting-up process must have been well underway. On the evidence of the finds recovered from the surrounding area, however, it would seem that the shores of the Wantsum Channel were particularly well populated, at least during the middle and late Bronze Age. We may imagine that a series of landing places lay along both sides of the Wantsum – many associated with adjacent settlements. It seems likely that there were settlements of some size and importance here.

Ann Ellison (1980, 135) has recognised a group of large Middle Bronze Age defended enclosures, perhaps representing major redistribution centres, that are set at fairly regular intervals across central southern England. Characterised by concentrations of metal-work in the immediate hinterland, she predicts the existence of another similar centre somewhere in east Kent. As yet, no likely sites have been identified but it seems quite possible that any such site was situated adjacent to the shores of the Wantsum Channel. Provided with a safe harbour, such a site could have been an important trading centre with the Continent (Drewett *et al* 1988, 117). Although no such Bronze Age site has been identified, the recent discovery of a large Neolithic causewayed camp on the southern shore of the Isle of Thanet, overlooking the eastern entrance to the Wantsum channel (Shand 2001), provides hope that such a site might yet be located.

There has been some research on the marshlands of the Lydden Valley at the southern end of the Wantsum. Here, it would seem that a substantial tract of ground was dry land during the Bronze Age, only becoming inundated at a later date. An extensive submerged land-surface occurs between North Deal and Worth and finds of Beaker pottery in particular indicates early Bronze Age settlement here (Halliwell 1981; Halliwell and Parfitt 1985). No doubt the activities on such settlement sites were closely bound up with the exploitation of the adjacent wetlands. Small havens and landing places must have existed and Long has been able to trace the course of a silted-up prehistoric deep water channel running through this area (Long 1992).

Excavations for a new sewer in 1936 at Great Downs Bridge, south-east of Sandwich, revealed the remains of a dug-out canoe (Cook 1937). This was made of oak and still showed clear traces of tool marks. It is tempting to see this as a prehistoric craft which plied the local water-ways – but so often, similar vessels have turned out to be much later in date. Nothing of the present vessel now seems to survive, so no further research is possible.

Moving to the late Iron Age, five sites scattered along the shores of the former Wantsum Channel have been identified as producing considerable quantities of Celtic coins. The sites are Worth (Temple), Worth Hill, Archers Low, Richborough (island) and Ebbsfleet on Thanet. The exact status and function of most of these sites in the late Iron Age remains uncertain but it may be suggested that each one represents a port site, where regular trading occurred, hence the large quantities of coins (including imports). Imported pottery also occurs at several of the sites. It is of particular interest to find the internationally important Roman site of Richborough present on the list. Did the Roman legions decide to disembark at Richborough in AD 43 precisely because this was a well-established landing-site, already regularly used by merchants and traders?

The North Kent coast

The Isle of Thanet is rich in important prehistoric remains and in part this must be a reflection of its geographically advantageous position in relation to the Kentish mainland and the near-Continent. From the available evidence Perkins has previously envisaged Thanet's Bronze Age and early Iron Age shoreline as being 'ringed with villages, some of them perhaps functioning as havens and entrepôts' (1994, 309). On the exposed north coast evidence of submerged Bronze Age settlements have been located at both St Mildred's Bay and Minnis Bay. Both sites originally seem to have been coastal sites situated on higher ground above the shoreline, but now both lie below the high water mark, due to rising sea levels. At St Mildred's Bay fragments of a dugout canoe, perhaps 4 metres long, were discovered (Jay 1990, 276; Perkins 1988) and it seems likely that the inhabitants of both these settlements were closely involved in sea-faring activities. Such sites provide clear evidence for coastal erosion but also show that in some eroded areas traces of ancient coastal sites may yet survive.

Further west, the chalk cliffs of the Isle of Thanet are replaced with much softer Tertiary rocks on mainland Kent. These have been subject to extensive erosion in the region between Minnis Bay and Whitstable. As an illustration of this, we may take the example of the Roman Fort of the Saxon Shore at Reculver. Situated on the present-day shoreline at the northern end of the former Wantsum Channel, this site in the third century AD perhaps lay around 1.5 km from the north coast. The prehistoric coastline would have been even further out, implying a very considerable loss of land in this region over the centuries.

At Swalecliffe, west of Herne Bay, the remains of another quite extensive submerged Bronze Age site have been discovered. Traces of what appear to be wicker lined pits are visible on the beach at low tide and formal excavations just inland have revealed a series of Bronze Age wicker-lined water-holes (Masefield *et al.* 2003), quite possibly associated with a settlement site. As with the two Thanet sites, any such settlement must have originally been set a little back from the Bronze Age coastline.

As a conclusion to our survey of the Kent coast we must briefly consider the area around the mouth of the River Thames and Medway. Here, the Isles of Sheppey, Harty, Grain and the Hoo Peninsula are separated by a complex arrangement of channels, creeks and inlets. The present-day configuration of the coastline in this area clearly reflects rising sea levels and the drowning of the original estuary. Early land-surfaces have been submerged and prehistoric horizons must lie at a considerable depth (Evans 1953). The Bronze Age shoreline will have had a very different appearance to that of today. Nevertheless, the area was without doubt quite extensively occupied, since it provided local communities with opportunities to exploit the resources of the open sea, coastal wetlands and fertile high ground, all within quite close proximity. Later Bronze Age hoards from the higher ground on the Isle of Harty, Allhallows, Cliffe and Stoke provide clear evidence for activity in this area, just as around the shores of the Wantsum. Water-craft must have provided one of the easiest means of moving around the region.

Of particular significance in this region is an important late Iron Age site discovered on the Isle of Grain. This extensive settlement lies on a gravel bluff over-looking the Thames estuary, close to the point where it is joined by the River Medway, Kent's largest river (Philp 2002, 139–143). Covering around 20 acres, the settlement seems to have been occupied during the second and first centuries BC. Extensive evidence for salt production has been revealed, suggesting that this was a major salt producing site, whilst the location would have allowed water-borne trade links with the Kentish hinterland via the Medway; the Thames valley, the Essex coast and the Continent. Quite possibly, comparable sites of earlier date await discovery. A possible Beaker burial comes from Cliffe on the Hoo Peninsula (Kinnes *et al* 1998).

Conclusion

There can be little doubt that in the extensive Kentish coastal zone, with its evidence for widespread prehistoric settlement, water-craft were widely used throughout prehistory. No doubt, coastal inhabitants were regularly engaged in a variety of maritime activities; transportation and fishing were probably the most common forms, but communication, ceremonial journeys and warfare are also possible.

It seems clear that maritime activity was not entirely confined to short, locally based sea trips. Throughout the prehistoric period imported artefacts demonstrate that rather more extensive journeys were also being made and cross-Channel trade seems to have occurred regularly. That trading vessels arrived at, and operated from, various settlements located adjacent to havens placed all around the Kent coast seems very probable.

In our brief survey we have attempted to identify some possible landing places for such vessels, even if with only limited success. Nevertheless, it seems clear that there are very few regions of the Kent coast where there is absolutely no potential for some significant new discoveries to be made. Thus, diligent field-workers undertaking detailed survey and investigation work along virtually any part of the Kent coastline are unlikely to go completely unrewarded.

List of references

Buckley, D G and Ingle, C J 2001 'The saddle querns from Flag Fen', in F Pryor, *The Flag Fen basin: Archaeology and environment of a Fenland landscape*, English Heritage Archaeology Reports, 322–328

Champion, T 1980 'Settlement and Environment in Later Bronze Age Kent', in J Barrett and R Bradley (eds), *The British Later Bronze Age; Part i*, British Archaeological Reports (British Series), **83**, 223–246

Cook, N 1937 'Note', *Archaeologia Cantiana*, **49**, xivii

Cowen, J D 1952 'A Bronze Sword from Folkestone', *Archaeologia Cantiana*, **65**, 90–92

Cunliffe, B 1987 *Hengistbury Head, Dorset. Vol. 1: The Prehistoric and Roman Settlement, c. 3500 BC–AD 500*, Oxford

Drewett, P, Rudling, D and Gardiner, M 1988 *The South-East to AD 1000*

Eddison, J 2000 *Romney Marsh, Survival on a Frontier*, Tempus

Ellison, A 1980 'Settlements and Regional Exchange: A Case Study', in J Barrett and R Bradley (eds), *The British Later Bronze Age; Part i*, British Archaeological Reports (British Series), **83**, 115–126

Evans, J H 1953 'Archaeological Horizons in the North Kent Marshes', *Archaeologia Cantiana*, **66**, 103–146

Frere, S S 1991 'Roman Britain in 1990: Folkestone', *Britannia*, **22**, 291

Greenfield, E 1960 'A Neolithic Pit and Other Finds from Wingham, East Kent', *Archaeologia Cantiana*, **74**, 58–72

Grinsell, L V 1992 'The Bronze Age Round Barrows of Kent', *Proceedings of the Prehistoric Society*, **58**, 355–384

Halliwell, G, 1981'Flint Artefacts from the Deal-Sandwich Marshes', *Kent Archaeological Review*, **65**, 113–6.

Halliwell, G and Parfitt, K 1985 'The Prehistoric Land Surface in the Lydden Valley: an Initial Report', *Kent Archaeological Review*, **82**, 39–43

Jay, L 1990 'The Trust for Thanet Archaeology: Excavations and Evaluations, 1989–1990', *Archaeologia Cantiana*, **108**, 271–277

Jessup, R F 1930 *The Archaeology of Kent*, Methuen

Jessup, R F 1970 *South East England*, London

Keller, P T 1988 'The evidence for ancient quern production at Folkestone', *Kent Archaeological Review*, **93**, 59–68

Keller, P T 1989 'Quern production at Folkestone, South-east Kent: An Interim Note', *Britannia*, **20**, 193–200

Kinnes, I, Cameron, F, Trow, S and Thompson, D 1998 *Excavations at Cliffe, Kent*, British Museum Occasional Paper, **69**

Long, A J 1992 'Coastal responses to changes in sea-level in the East Kent Fens and south-east England, UK over the last 7500 years', *Proceedings of the Geological Association*, **103**, 187–199

Markey, M, Wilkes, E and Darvill, T 2002 'Poole Harbour: An Iron Age Port', *Current Archaeology*, **181**, 7–11

Masefield, R, Branch, N, Couldrey, P, Goodburn, D and Tyers, I 2003 'A Later Bronze Age Well Complex at Swalecliffe, Kent', *Antiquaries Journal* **83**, 47–121

McGrail, S 1993 'Prehistoric Seafaring in the Channel', in C Scarre and F Healy (eds), *Trade and Exchange in Prehistoric Europe*, Oxbow Monograph, **33**

Middleton, A P and Bowman, S G E 2001 'Report on the examination of four Bronze Age quernstones from Flag Fen', in F Pryor, *The Flag Fen basin: Archaeology and environment of a Fenland landscape*, English Heritage Archaeology Reports, 328–329

Muckleroy, K 1981 'Middle Bronze Age trade between Britain and Europe: A maritime perspective', *Proceedings of the Prehistoric Society*, **47**, 275–297

Needham, S 1988 'A group of early Bronze Age Axes from Lydd' in J Eddison and C Green (eds), *Romney Marsh: Evolution, Occupation, Reclamation*, Romney Marsh Research Trust, 77–82

Needham, S and Dean, M 1987 'La Cargaison de Langdon Bay a Douvres', Actes du Colloque de Bronze de Lille – R. A. P. / S. P. F., 1987.

Parfitt, K 1976 'A Neolithic-Bronze Age Site at St Margaret's at Cliffe', *Kent Archaeological Review*, **46**, 141–146

Parfitt, K 1985 'Some Iron Age Sites in the Deal Area', *Kent Archaeological Review*, **79**, 206–219

Parfitt, K and Grinsell, L V 1991 'A Bronze Age Urn from Capel-le-Ferne', *Archaeologia Cantiana*, **109**, 334–335

Perkins, D R J 1988 'A Middle Bronze Age Hoard from a Prehistoric Settlement Site at St Mildred's Bay, Westgate-on-Sea', *Archaeologia Cantiana*, **105**, 243–249

Perkins, D R J, Macpherson Grant, N and Healey, E 1994 'Monkton Court Farm Evaluation, 1992', *Archaeologia Cantiana* , **114**, 237–316

Philp, B 2002 *Archaeology in the Front Line, 50 years of Kent Rescue, 1952–2002*, Dover

Rowlands, M J 1976 *The Organisation of Middle Bronze Age Metalworking*, British Archaeological Reports (British Series), **31**

Shand, G 2001 'Ramsgate Harbour Approach Road', *Canterbury's Archaeology 1998–1999*, CAT 23rd Annual report, 18–22

Stebbing, W P D 1936 'Discoveries in the Neighbourhood of Deal during 1936', *Archaeologia Cantiana*, **48**, 235–237

Stevens, S 1976 'Major Discovery of Bronze Age Implements at Dover', *Kent Archaeological Review*, **43**, 67–73

Winbolt, S E 1925 *Roman Folkestone*, Methuen

12. An environmental context for the Dover boat?

M G L Baillie

(Note on convention: in this article absolute dates derived from dendrochronology are termed BC and those from calibrated radiocarbon cal BC; all dates are therefore comparable in real time, limited only by the precision on the calibrated radiocarbon estimates).

Dendrochronological dating, even when allowance has to be made for missing sapwood, still provides a tight range within which to work. In the case of the Dover boat, a combination of high-precision radiocarbon wiggle-matching and direct dendrochronological dating tells us that the boat was constructed using timbers felled between the calendar dates 1575 and 1525 BC (Bayliss *et al* 2004). It seems reasonable to suggest that the most likely date would be in the vicinity of 1550 BC. This is useful because it restricts the period for which an environmental story is required. We can compare this refined situation with the more normal one where some routine site or object is dated only by one, or a few, routine radiocarbon dates. Often in such cases the site or object is only fixed, after the radiocarbon dates have been calibrated, to a range of one or two calendar centuries at best. In such cases the search to begin to understand the contemporary environment is hindered by the fact that most environmental information is also gleaned from carbon-dated sources such as peat profiles or glacial advances. As the resolution of such evidence is normally no better than one or two centuries, the compound vagueness of any relationship soon becomes apparent.

So, the question about the contemporary environment of the Dover Boat is a relatively refined one, and reduces to that of the nature of the environment in Northern Europe in the sixteenth century BC. In attempting to provide even an initial insight into the answer to this question we can look at two broad sources. There is what might be called the conventional wisdom – what is generally understood to have taken place in the sixteenth century BC? Then there is the secondary question, what can a dendrochronologist, or, more generally, the dendrochronological world, add to refine the conventional wisdom. In this short paper I will attempt to provide a little colour to the period bracketing the sixteenth century.

Events of sorts: The backstop

Anyone discussing the sixteenth century BC probably has to set a backstop of some kind and we are provided with a useful marker in the form of the 1628/1627 BC tree-ring event as originally identified by LaMarche and Hirschboeck (1984) and Baillie and Munro (1988). Much discussion has taken place on whether or not this environmental downturn was due to the environmental impact of the eruption of Thera in the Aegean. Currently the discussion reduces to whether Thera erupted in 1628 BC (the Irish and American tree-ring suggestion) or close to 1645 BC (the Anatolian tree-ring and Dye3 ice-core suggestion; see Hammer 2000; Manning *et al* 2001). What is not in doubt is the fact that the Irish, English, German and American chronologies pretty well agree that the environmental downturn was in the years following 1628 BC (Baillie 2002). If Thera erupted at that time then it probably caused or contributed to the environmental event; if it erupted around 1645, then clearly it did not and the cause of the 1628 BC environmental event will have to be sought elsewhere (see for example Baillie 1999). So the backstop for any discussion of the Dover Boat is that there was an abrupt downturn in the 1620s BC.

In terms of well-dated information, we also know that in constructing a long oak chronology in East Anglia it was possible to build a continuous chronology from 3196 BC to 1681 BC. In addition, a single bog-oak site at Croston Moss, Lancashire yielded a chronology from 3198 BC to 1682 BC and another from 1584 to 970 BC. So, in two low-lying areas of England long-term occupation by oaks seemed to be interrupted around or shortly after 1680 BC (Baillie 1995; Brown and Baillie 1992), the interesting point being the resumption of oak growth in 1584 BC at Croston Moss. Gunnarsson *et al* (forthcoming) curiously have a gap in their Swedish pine chronology from 1650–1633 BC.

These pine chronologies span 2893–1650 BC and 1633 BC–AD 887, making the gap exceptional by any standards, the only gap in nearly four millennia of continuous chronology. It is probably worth recording that Lara and Villalba (1993) in Chile report a mega-long Fitzroya chronology that runs from the present day to 1636 BC. One could be forgiven for imagining that in Chile and Sweden seedlings rooted in the years just before the 1628 BC event were released to grow by the event (in a similar way another Irish tree-ring event at 1159–1141 BC sees the initiation of an 800 year chronology in Eastern England, namely the Swan Carr chronology, at 1155 BC). So several tree-ring chronologies hint strongly at environmental change in the 17th and 16th centuries BC. Overall, in the run-up to the sixteenth century BC there are plenty of parameters to investigate at high resolution.

Events of sorts: The fore-stop

In terms of a fore stop, one interesting observation is a relatively tight cluster of archaeological tree-ring dates from Ireland that seem to cluster between 1525–1475 BC (Baillie and Brown 2002). This cluster of activity is interesting because it suggests a change of some kind. In Ireland there are almost no archaeological tree-ring dates between 2250 BC and the period around 1000 BC, except for the *c.* 1500 BC cluster. Since most of the sites represented are wooden trackways or lake-side settlements it seems fair to suggest that what had changed around 1500 BC was the relative dryness of the environment. This can be claimed because some of the sites, e.g. Cullyhanna Hunting Lodge, Co. Armagh (Hillam 1976) are lake-side settlements and since the timbers have survived it has to be assumed that the lough levels were relatively *low* when the timbered sites were constructed; the timbers being preserved by subsequent higher water levels.

This suggestion was originally backed up by two other observations, namely a short colonization around 1500 cal BC of an English bog surface by pine trees (Grant 1995), and the occurrence of a substantial timber settlement in a bog at Siedlung Forschner in South Germany (Billamboz 1992). Both of these observations seemed to suggest a relatively dry pulse centred around 1500 BC (Baillie and Brown 1996). We now know that Siedlung Forschner is just part of a pattern of precisely-dated archaeological activity that is specified in two pulses between 1660–1590 BC and 1520–1490 BC (Fig 12.1; Billamboz 1996). The close juxtaposition between the European 1520–1490 BC and the Irish 1525–1475 BC site clusters suggests some macro-scale change to dryer conditions making lake-side settlements possible. This assertion could of course be entirely wrong and the building episode straddling 1500 BC could have something to do with changes of some other kind, though Occam's razor would seem to argue in favour of dry conditions.

The conventional wisdom

The question of conventional wisdom, regarding the environment of the sixteenth century BC, has recently been helped by the publication of a useful summary paper by Hughes *et al* (2000). They make it clear that a number of lines of enquiry point towards 'a wet event' (but see below) that, fairly consistently, provides calibrated ages around 3400 or 3500 cal BP. In fact, if one plots the centre points of their calibrated dates (Hughes *et al* 2000, table 4) there is the clear impression of two separated events centred on 1550 cal BC and 1450 cal BC respectively (given the vagaries of radio-carbon dating, and the shape of the calibration curve, it is quite possible that there is just one event, but for the purposes of this article we will accept the double structure as suggested). If one plots these wet events, deduced from bog evidence, against the distribution of Irish archaeological tree-ring dates, it is clear that the two 'wet events' from bog evidence bracket the apparently 'dry' phase around 1500 BC suggested above on the basis of archaeological sites in wet contexts (Fig 12.1).

We can start to pull in other strands of evidence to bulk out the picture. The *c.* 1550 BC construction date for the Dover Boat is of interest due to the recent recognition that a short pine tree-ring chronology from the base of a bog at Hanvedsmossen some 50 km SW of Stockholm, Sweden, dates across this period. Although not

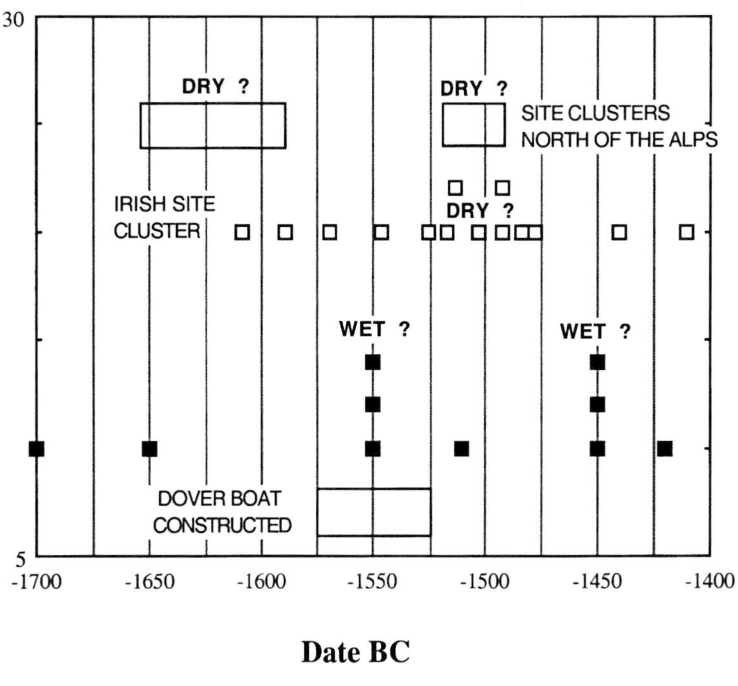

Fig. 12.1 The likely construction range of the Dover boat with evidence for wet mire conditions (Hughes et al *2000), for Irish archaeological sites (Baillie and Brown 2002) and for phases of site construction north of the Alps (Billamboz 1996).*

precisely dated by dendrochronology, the 204-year floating chronology is well dated by a radiocarbon wiggle match to the range 1686–1483 ± 23 cal BC (Gunnarsson 1999). Of the 48 trees that started to grow on the pre-bog surface, more than 50% started to grow within 30 years. The 'germination rate decreases slowly with the last pine germination taking place 100 years after the first'. Tree death shows two periods of differing rates. The first 'commences at 1581 ± 23 cal BC and ends at 1510 ± 23 cal BC', the second, with twice the rate of deaths, lasts from 1510–1483 ± 23 cal BC, with the growth decreasing rapidly in the last 20 years.

Gunnarsson hazards that around 1550 cal BC 'the climate at Hanvedsmossen shifted to wetter conditions'. What makes this episode interesting is that Boswijk (in preparation) reports an almost identical pine episode at Goole Moor, part of the Thorne Moors complex in Yorkshire, UK. This dense woodland phase is dendrochronologically dated and spans 1690–1489 BC with all the trees starting growth between 1690 and 1643 BC. Apart from the short pine colonization recognised by Grant, noted above, there are radiocarbon dated pines from the west of Ireland consistent with a short, isolated, mid-second millennia BC growth episode (Caulfield *et al* 1998). It seems unlikely that this synchronous evidence for pine in widely dispersed areas is purely coincidental, and much more likely that it is a common response to changed conditions across northern Europe (drying out of bog surfaces during the seventeenth century BC with the trees being affected by changing conditions in the 16th century and ultimately killed by wetter (?) conditions in the early 15th century BC. However, how this sits with the suggestion, above, that the Irish archaeological sites might be a response to dryer conditions is unclear. This raises the question, what other evidence do we have? In England the 1681–1594 BC tree-ring gap in the Croston Moss oaks was bridged by a separate bog-oak chronology from Hasholme that spanned 1687–1362 BC. Does this help? Not obviously. One reason why the bog oak evidence may be at variance with the other apparently wet/dry evidence is that oaks are able to grow for long periods and presumably set seed in suitable well-spaced episodes. In addition in the English sites in both Lancashire and East Anglia the areas are extremely low lying and may have been influenced by water table changes influenced by the sea.

So in order to get a different oak perspective, a plot was made of the widest and narrowest growth rings in any year in the Irish oak chronology (ie from all the dated trees the record was searched by date. The three widest rings and the three narrowest rings in any calendar date were accumulated and plotted as a smoothed curve. The result, Figure 12.2, shows that there is a notable depression in the growth of Irish oaks close to 1540 BC and others around 1470 and 1430 BC. One is tempted to see these growth depressions as direct reflections of the wet events suggested by the mire evidence. Interestingly, a recent publication by Leuschner *et al* (2002) shows a very notable growth depression in combined German and Dutch oak chronologies across 1550 BC, with others at 1470 and 1410 BC, the first two in remarkable agreement with Figure 12.2. The figures do suggest a general downturn close to 1550 BC neatly separating the archaeological evidence for possibly dry events around 1600 and 1500 BC respectively.

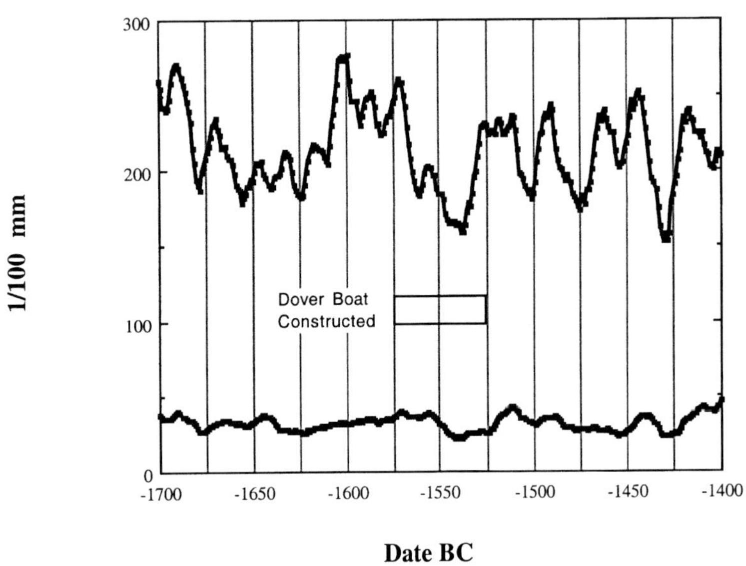

Fig. 12.2 By selecting the widest, and narrowest, growth rings in each year it is possible to plot an envelope of Irish oak growth. It can be seen that the Dover boat was constructed in the vicinity of a notable growth downturn. This is also seen in German and Dutch oaks (Leuschner et al *2002).*

Other factors

It would be possible to look at other well-dated environmental factors from a variety of sources. For example, the radiocarbon calibration curve has a relatively flat portion from around 1680 to around 1520 BC, where all the calibration ages are constrained to values around 3300 radiocarbon years BP (Baillie 1995, fig 7.2). Overall, there do not appear to be any large scale changes in radiocarbon content of the atmosphere across the 16th century BC (see for example Pearson *et al* 1986; Stuiver and Becker 1993), something that implies relatively little change in solar output. However, one more parameter will suffice here simply as an example of what may be possible in the future. From experience in Ireland, most bog oaks, as recovered from peat bogs, occur as trunks rather than stumps. Logically these trees were preserved because they blew down. By plotting the death dates of bog oaks across a period it should be possible to obtain a crude index of 'storminess'. Figure 12.3 shows a first attempt at such an approach (this can only be modelled crudely as not all tree-ring patterns run to the underbark surface). In the figure, the plot of the number of death dates per decade has been smoothed. Surprisingly, the likely construction date of the Dover Boat sits in a blow-down 'trough' ie a period when relatively few oaks blew down. This at least allows for the possibility that the Dover Boat was constructed during a relatively calm period when storms were relatively infrequent (not enough bog oaks are available from England during this period to allow an equivalent diagram; though this very absence may itself argue in favour of the hypothesis).

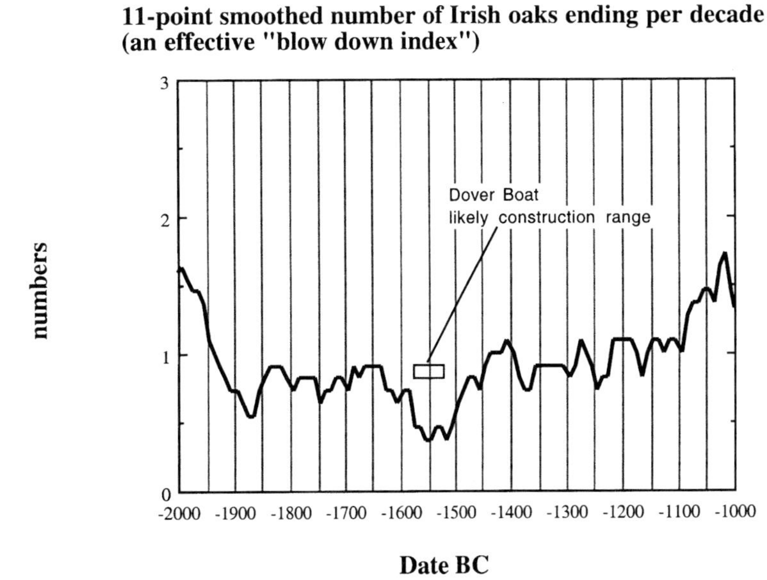

Fig. 12.3 As Irish sub-fossil bog oaks mostly blew down and were preserved as trunks, by accumulating the numbers of death-dates per decade we get an impression of changing 'storminess' through time. While this is a provisional diagram, it is interesting that the likely period of construction of the Dover boat does sit in the period of lowest bog oak occurrence in the second millennium BC, i.e. possibly the period with the least storms.

Conclusion

The stimulus for this article was a request for information on the environment as it might have been around the time the Dover Boat was constructed. As can be seen, dendrochronology allows a number of well dated strands of evidence to be drawn together. These, when combined with the independent suggestions of wet mire conditions, allow the development of a 'picture' of what might have happened in the middle of the 16th century BC.

However, this author would suggest the following scenario. Because of the lack of sapwood on the Dover Boat timbers, we cannot be certain that the boat was constructed close to 1550 BC, let us consider that it may actually have been constructed closer to 1525 BC (note that this is still within the probability range; Bayliss *et al*, 2004). If this were the case then we could argue that the boat was constructed as conditions were moving from a wet/cold phase into a dry phase ie conditions were improving. It would also put the construction further into the suggested 'calm' phase. If this were the case then one could see why the construction of the boat would be an attractive proposition – calm, warm, generally better conditions; better growth, increased confidence. This sounds like a scenario that might be consistent with cross-Channel trading. The alternative is to accept the idea of a *c.* 1550 BC construction in what may have been a wet episode when oak growth from Ireland to Germany was depressed. If one preferred this scenario, then it would be possible to imagine construction when water levels were relatively high and river or lagoon navigation might have been a factor in the use of the boat. The problem is that the lack of an exact date for the boat leaves us, as usual, with an inadequate target date for comparison with the other, better dated, records. The final word, as given in the original lecture, is 'would you prefer the Dover Boat to have been constructed in a wet or in a dry period?'. Currently the reader is at perfect liberty to choose.

List of References

Baillie, M G L 1995 *A Slice through Time: dendrochronology and precision dating*, London: Routledge

Baillie, M G L 1999 *Exodus to Arthur: Catastrophic encounters with comets*, London: Batsford

Baillie, M G L 2002 'Future of Dendrochronology with Respect to Archaeology', *Dendrochronologia*, **20(1)**, 67–83

Baillie, M G L and Brown, D M 2002 'Oak dendrochronology: some recent archaeological developments from an Irish perspective', *Antiquity*, **76**, 497–505

Baillie, M G L and Brown, D M 1996 'Dendrochronology of Irish Bog Trackways', in B Raftery, B, *Trackway Excavations in the Mountdillon Bogs, Co. Longford*, Transactions of the Irish Archaeological Wetland Unit, **3**, Department of Archaeology, University College, Dublin, 395–402

Baillie, M G L and Munro, M A R 1988 'Irish tree-rings, Santorini and volcanic dust veils', *Nature*, **332**, 344–346

Bayliss, A, Groves, C, McCormac, F G, Bronk Ramsey, C, Baillie, M G L, Brown, D M, Cook, G T and Switsur, R V 2004 'Dating', in P Clark (ed), *The Dover Bronze Age Boat*, English Heritage, 250–255

Billamboz, A 1992 'Tree-Ring Analysis from an Archaeodendrochronological Perspective. The Structural Timber from the South West German Lake Dwellings', *Lundqua*, **34**, 34–40

Billamboz, A 1996 'Structures D'Habitat et Économie Forestière à L'Âge du Bronze. L'Apport de la Dendrochronologie', *Acta Archaeologica*, **67**, 299–306

Boswijk, G 2003 *Tree-Ring Analysis of Oak and Scots Pine to Study the Early Development of Lowland Raised Mire at Thorne Moors, Yorkshire, UK*, (in preparation)

Brown, D M and Baillie, M G L 1992, 'Construction and Dating of a 5000 Year English Bog Oak Tree-Ring Chronology', *Lundqua*, **34**, 72–75

Caulfield, S, O'Donnell, R G and Mitchell, P I 1998 '14C Dating of a Neolithic Field System at Céide Fields, County Mayo, Ireland', *Radiocarbon*, **40**, 629–640

Grant, M E 1995 *The dating and significance of Pinus sylvestris L. macrofossil remains from Whixall Moss, Shropshire: palaeoecological and modern comparative analyses*, Unpublished PhD thesis, University of Keele

Gunnarsson, B E 1999 'A 200-year tree-ring chronology of pine from a raised bog in Sweden: implications for climate change?', *Geografiska Annaler*, **81A**, 3, 421–430

Gunnarsson, B E, Borgmark, A and Wastegård, S forthcoming 'Holocene humidity fluctuations in Sweden – inferred from dendrochronology and peat stratigraphy',

Hammer, C U 2000. 'What can Greenland Ice-Core data say about the Thera Eruption in the 2nd Millennium BC?', in M Bietak (ed), *The Synchronisation of Civilizations in the eastern Mediterranean in the Second Millennium BC*, Austrian Academy of Sciences, **19**, Vienna, 35–37

Hillam, J 1976, 'The Dating of Cullyhanna Hunting Lodge', *Irish Archaeological Research Forum*, **3**, 1, 17–20

Hughes, P D M, Mauquoy, D, Barber, K E and Langdon, P G 2000 'Mire development pathways and palaeoclimatic records from a full Holocene peat archive at Walton Moss, Cumbria, England', *The Holocene*, **10**, 4, 465–479

LaMarche, V C Jr and Hirschboeck, K K 1984 'Frost Rings in Trees as Records of Major Volcanic Eruptions', *Nature*, **307**, 121–6

Lara, A and Villalba, R 1993 'A 3620-Year Temperature Record from Fitzroya cupressoides Tree-Rings in Southern South America', *Science*, **260**, 1104–1106

Leuschner, H H, Sass-Klaassen, U, Jansma, E, Baillie, M G L and Spurk, M 2002 'Subfossil European bog oaks: population dynamics and long-term growth depressions as indicators of changes in the Holocene hydro-regime and climate', *The Holocene*, **12**, 6, 695–706

Manning S W, Kromer B, Kuniholm I P, and Newton M W, 2001. 'Anatolian Tree Rings and a New Chronology for the East Mediterranean Bronze-Iron Ages', *Science*, **294**, 2532–2535

Pearson, G W, Pilcher, J R, Baillie, M G L, Corbett, D M and Qua, F 1986, 'High-Precision 14-C Measurement of Irish Oaks to Show the Natural 14-C Variations from AD 1840 to 5210 BC', *Radiocarbon*, **28**, 911–34

Stuiver, M and Becker, B 1993 'High-precision decadal calibration of the radiocarbon time scale, AD 1950–6000 BC', *Radiocarbon*, **35**, 35–65

13. Sea faring voyages and rock art ships

Kristian Kristiansen

'But when it comes to men, I feel that few or none can rival me in wealth, for it took me seven years and great hardship to amass this fortune and bring it home in my ships. My travels took me to Cyprus, to Phoenicia, and to Egypt. Ethiopians, Sidonians, Erembians, I visited them all; and I saw Libya too…' (Homer, 'The Odyssey', Book 4, 75–85)

The signature of the rock carver

Voyaging was the dominant way of life in the Bronze Age; it was the way to status and renown, and a prerequisite for the movement of metal. The ship is the transport of the sea, and has therefore been surrounded by rituals that ensure the success of the journey[1] As such, the ship has a prominent symbolic role in the Bronze Age conceptual world, as shown recently by Tore Artelius (1996; 1998) and Flemming Kaul (1998). This is why the chiefly symbol, the razor, was in the shape of a ship during the entire Bronze Age period, why the women of the Late Bronze Age wore necklaces with the ship as a symbolic amulet, why the sun sailed on a ship and why important rituals took place on the ship. The ship was connected to a multitude of values; it crossed borders, meeting with the other and the unknown on all levels, from the journey in search of renown to the last journey of life to the realm of the dead.

But to own and equip a ship was only possible for a chieftain who could provide warriors and a work force, who could equip the ship with food, goods and oarsmen. And where did they travel to? Answers to that question have traditionally been based on the study of metalwork – its origins and distribution – and in this way map connections between Bronze Age societies. In the same way, artefacts made in the same workshop show that there is quite long distance communication, not least by the artefacts themselves (Kaul 1998, fig 85; Kristiansen 1998 a, 88), and some prestige goods could even travel from Central Europe to the Nordic countries. The problem with bronze is – who or what travelled? – the people or the artefacts? Burial studies where men and women are buried with their personal belongings (jewellery or weapons) have, however, shown that direct relationships were maintained – political alliances – between chiefs that were up to 100 to 200 kilometres apart (Jockenhövel 1991). In some instances the weapons and personal belongings indicate even longer distances were involved (Kristiansen and Larsson manuscript).

The rock carvings, however, contain concealed information about the voyages and the distances covered. The carvings, like the bronzes, are created by craftspeople and artists that naturally adhered to the artistic practices of that time, but often asserted their own personal expression. Sometimes even a single hand can be identified (Bengstsson 2002). In addition, variations in the rock carvings of ships and their prototypes, like the bronzes, display regional and local variation. As rock carvings are immovable, there is a correspondence between the place and the carving. The artist was there, on the site. If there is a carving in foreign style amongst the local carvings then we can be relatively certain that the artist was a visitor to the place, or that a local artist had spent time elsewhere learning another style.

It is of course difficult for us today to know to what extent the standardised tradition of ship carvings followed specific artistic traditions or to what extent these traditions reflected (for example) the art of ship construction. However, when we find the same chronological development of the stem and the prow on both the bronzes of Southern Scandinavia and on the rock carvings, this surely ought to reflect actual developments in stem shape and decoration (Kaul 1998, figs 53–54). This basic construction, however, changed relatively little throughout the entire Bronze Age period. The plank-built Hjortspring boat construction technique (Kaul 1998, figure 73) has continuity a long way back in time, as can be seen, for example, in the Sagaholm burial ship carvings from the early Bronze Age (Goldhahn 1999). But it is also evident in the rock carvings rendered with plank construction from the early Bronze Age (Fig 13.3; Högberg 1988, Tanum 22.2, fig 76).

The regional and local variations thus ought to reflect actual variations in ship construction traditions, and as such the rock carvings depictions of these chronological and geographical variations ought to vary from place to place. I therefore propose that a closer study should make it possible to identify visiting chieftains from distant chiefdoms that carved their signature in the guest book of the rock in their own local style, or chieftains that copied depictions seen on their travels when they returned home. If it is possible to identify the origins of a style, it is possible to map the length of the voyage. The most well known and most complicated example is of course the famous Kivik burial with eight pictorial slabs. But let me begin with a couple of easier examples, and return to the matter of Kivik later on.

The destination of the voyage

Amongst the many carvings in Bohuslän there is a group from the Early Bronze Age Periods 1–2 (*c.* 1700–1300 BC), carved on a large area of rock in Torsbo (Fredsjö *et al* 1981, 172–189; Fig 13.1). Here we find a small group of ships with their own distinctive character – the ships are short and compact and the rails are high. This is in part a local variant of the Rørby sword's general ship type from Period 1 (*c.* 1700–1500 BC). But these ships are found alongside a lower, slightly longer alternative. The distinctions are so consistent that we must consider them as representing two distinct ship types with different uses. Both have solidly carved hulls. One of the ships has an unusual detail – an oar which slants down against the keel extension (Kaul 1998, fig 46). The closest parallel to this ship can be found in North Jutland, more precisely on the Truehøjgård grave stone in Himmerland (Glob 1969, fig 18a–f). But there was no local rock carving tradition in this area so it may be that the chief of Torsbo, in Boshuslän carved his signature to mark his visit. An alternative is that the stone was carved during a visit to Torsbo and taken back to Himmerland, to be buried later on with the well travelled chief (it is quite small; 270mm x 170mm). He carved both the high, compact version and the longer, slender one, like the ones at home in Torsbo. Both ships participated in the voyage (Fig 13.1). We know that direct connections were maintained over the Kattegat between Bohuslän and Himmerland/ Thy during the Late Bronze Age. In Period 5 (*c.* 800 BC) one woman carried her own jewellery with her to Bohuslän from Himmerland, and a male chieftain from Thy was buried in Bohuslän – his razor is one in a series of locally manufactured razors from the Periods 4–5 (*c.* 1100–800 BC; Kristiansen 1998b, 87). Truehøjgård is also an interesting example in that it is one of the few closed contexts where several carving motifs appear in connection with burial. Over and above the paired ships we find the phallic chief (or god) with a pronounced head like the one in Kivik, and on the back there are carved footprints with the toes clearly defined. Are these possibly Bohusländic trademarks? In several studies

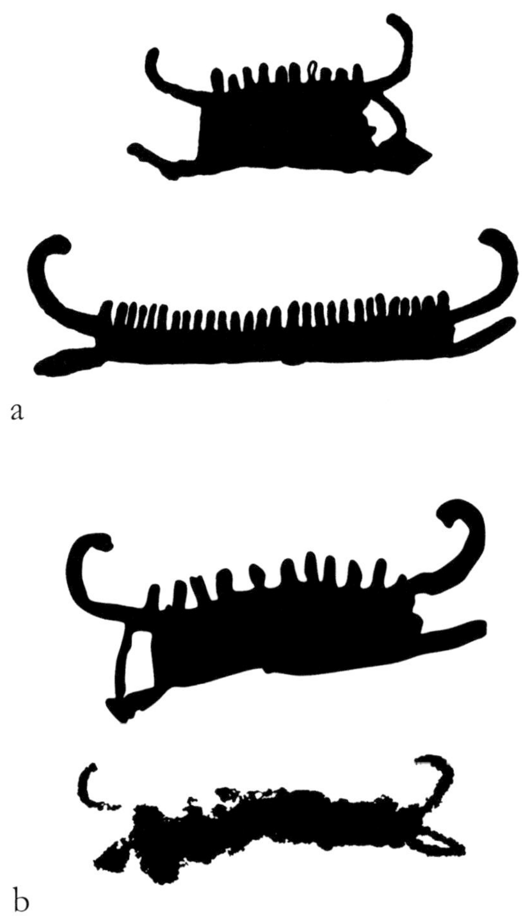

Fig. 13.1 (right) The voyage of the Torsbo chiefly carver. Identical carvings from (a) Torsbo in Bohuslän and (b) Truehøjgård in North Jutland (reproduced in Glob 1969 and Fredsjö et al *1981). Various scales.*

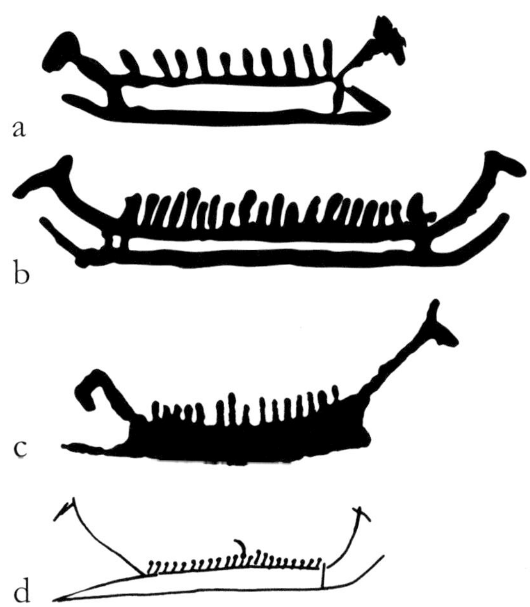

Fig. 13.2 (far right) East Swedish/ Baltic style ship carvings from Early Bronze Age (periods 1/2) from a) Boglösa, Uppland, b) Simris, Scania c) Himmelstalund, Östergötland and d) the Wismar lur, Mecklenburg (after Althin 1945; Coles 2000). Various scales.

of Indo-European mythology and carvings the Spanish researcher Marco Garcia Quintela has shown that the footprints were part of initiation ceremonies for a new king (or chief) who was to walk in the carved footprints as part of the crowning ritual (Garcia 1999). Truehøjgård, then, shows us three central symbols needed to attain chieftain status and possibly even divine status – the symbols of the voyage, fertility/manhood and the divine symbol to attain chiefdom– the footprints. That is why the stone is buried along with the chief, as testimony to his status and achievements.

The long maritime voyages between Limfjorden and Bohuslän were part of the normal activities of a chief and we consequently get some idea of the significance of the ship carvings – the ship was carved at the onset of a long voyage, or on reaching a destination. On returning home with new, foreign goods they were probably carved too. The rocks displayed the chief's achievements, but these were also the place where rituals were carried out to ensure safe and successful voyages. And in death, the ship was probably both the symbol for the journey to the realm of the dead and the symbol for the expeditions' chief (Artelius 1996).

But who visited Bohuslän? On one carving from Kville we find a ship where the hull is covered in circular- or spiral decoration (Fredsjö *et al* 1981, nr. 60 and 56). This is quite unique in Bohuslän, but is characteristic for a group of ships in Östergötland on the east coast of Sweden, the most famous of which is the Ekenberg ship (Selinge 1989, 160). On the same carving in Kville we also find one depiction which includes full hilted swords and axes, again motifs from Östergötland. The parallel between this carving and the corresponding ones from Östergötland is quite remarkable, and may be explained by the presence of a visiting chief, or a chief having returned home, with new ships and prestige goods, from a lengthy stay in Östergötland, who perhaps saw the carving of Ekenberg. But the chieftains from Bohuslän also journeyed south and east, via Simris and Kivik to Östergötland, and we also find a couple of Bohuslandic ship types further north in Uppland (Coles 2000, Plates 76 and 79). Here we find ship carvings of the distinct Östergötlandic type with the typical straight stems and animal headed prows dominate, for example in Boglöse (Coles 2000, plates 84, 101 and 142). This ship type is closely related to the ship figures known from the bronze horn from Wismar and belongs as such to Periods 1–2 (*c.* 1700–1300 BC; Fig 13.2; Kristiansen and Larsson manuscript). On the Boglöse carving, other motifs that point to a connection with Kivik can be found, namely the three dimensional carved battle wagon scene (Coles 2000, plates 78–79), along with the typical southern Scandinavian Rørby ship and the ship with Östergötlandic stem, all from Periods 1–2 (*c.* 1700–1300 BC). The triangular

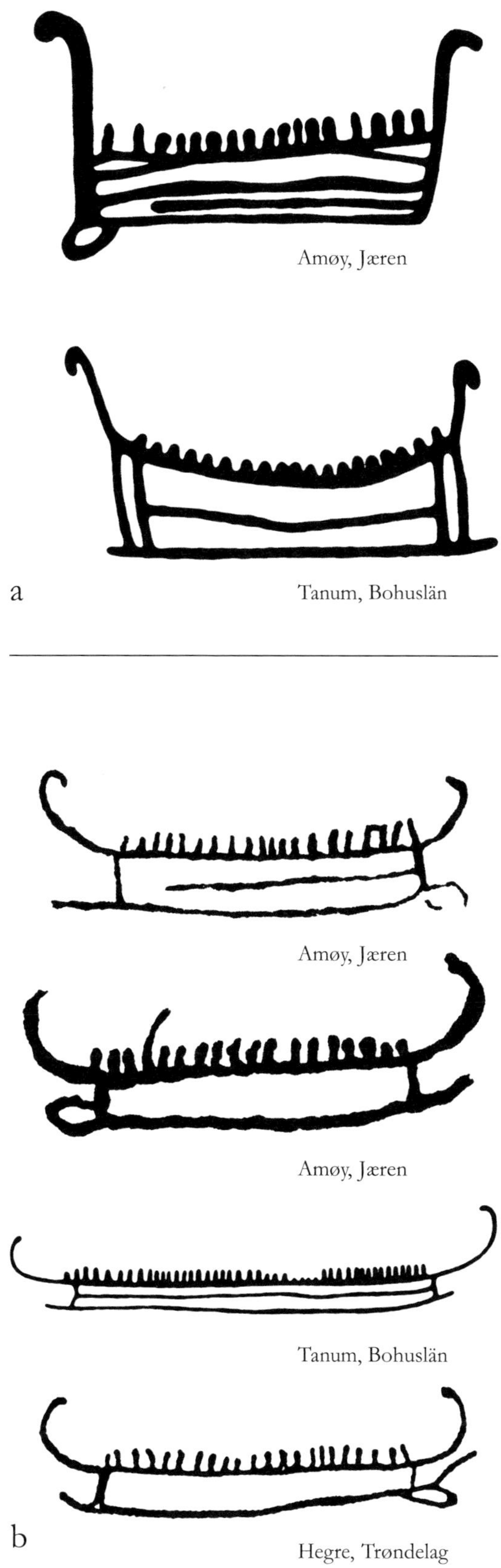

Fig. 13.3 South-west Norwegian ship types with planks from Jæren carved in Bohuslän, and Bohuslandic ship types without planks carved in Jæren and Trøndelag (after Fett and Fett 1941; Högberg 1988; Sogness 1998). Various scales.

Fig. 13.4 A pair of axe-bearers on the Simris carvings and their imported prototypes from Austria–Central Europe, period 1 (after Althin 1945).

shaped ends (presumably the helm) are also an Östergötlandic trademark, which also can be found on a couple of ships in Torsbo and on one ship at Åmøy on Jæren (Fett and Fett 1944, plate 16). The Bronze Age maritime chiefs travelled far and wide and learned from each other.

The chiefs of Bohuslän sailed even further north to southern Norway and to Jæren during the Early Bronze Age. Here we find a distinctive ship type (Åmøy and Nag type) with a vertically raised stem and with the board planks engraved horizontally (a plank built ship), a ship type that can be found along the entire length of the Norwegian coast with origins in the Neolithic. But north of Jæren this type most often has vertical frames (Mandt 1991, bind 2, fig 12.42 and volume 1, fig 8.18; Sognes 1998, plates VI–VII, Røkke and plates XIV–XV, Auran). But in this same area, on Nag and Åmøy, the new long and slender southern Scandinavian ships of the Rørby type also appear, and these are exactly like the ones found in Bohuslän (Fett and Fett 1941, planche 3 and 17–19). The characteristic finishing keel rudder was copied on to some of the short local ship carvings, so there is little doubt that these were contemporary. One Rørby type ship was carved with vertical planks as preferred by local tradition. The ship types of south-west Norwegian tradition also appear sporadically in Bohuslän, for example as mentioned above, in Torsbo (Fredsjö *et al* 1981, planche 184) and in Tanum, where even the Rørby ship with vertical planks is found (Högberg 1988, figs 71, 76 and 78–79) – these carved signatures in the guest book of rock testifying to visits by south Norwegian chiefs (Fig 13.3). They arrived at Östergötland too, far from home; at Ekenberg we find a couple of unfamiliar carving of the Jæren type, with horizontal planks (Norden 1923, tafel 38).

When the maritime chiefs on Jæren became skilled at building and carving ships in south Scandinavian style, they continued to sail further north spreading their new-found knowledge on the art of ship building and metallurgy. Not long after they carved their signatures over the earlier, hunter carvings in Bardal in Central Norway – three large ships of the Rørby type with many crew strokes (Sognnes 1999, 118); but these might even be Bohusländic. They also continued to build the traditional fishing boat here, but added prows with animal heads, as in the Røkke example (Sognnes 1999, 37).

But the voyages also went south over the Baltic Sea to the Oder Estuary, and from there they continued to sail even further south establishing alliances and trading contracts with the chiefs of Central Europe. During the Early Bronze Age these long voyages departed from Simris and Kivik (Kristiansen and Larsson manuscript).

Kivik, Simris and the voyaging chiefs

During Period 1 (from 1700–1500 BC), particularly during the latter part, Scanian chiefs from Simris and Kivik on the south-east coast established relations with chiefs in Central Europe. This was to be the beginning of a widespread exchange of goods and knowledge that would create the conditions necessary for a Nordic Bronze Age. Simris, which is situated *c.* 20 km south of Kivik, was at that time a departure point for such voyages. We see the results in the carvings – the axes, which the twin chiefs carried in their procession, were imported from Austria-Hungary (Fig 13.4).The ships are all of Period 1 type (Rørby), and on one of them the imported paired axes are carved above the ship, which is again equipped with the twin crew strokes. This suggests that the ship type belonged to the twin chiefs, successfully returned home from their voyage (Althin 1945, tafel 11). This particular trade mark, the twin crew strokes, which can also be found on the Rørby ship itself, is also found in solitary ships in Bohuslän, Östfold, and Sagaholm (Fig 13.5) corroborating once again that these regions had connections. It is a southern Scandinavian ship type,

Fig. 13.5 Ship carvings with twin crew strokes from Simris, Bohuslän, Östfold and Sagaholm (after Althin 1945; Goldhahn 1999; Bengtsson et al *2000; Østmo 1990; Vogt 2000). Various scales.*

Onsøy, Østfold

Tanum, Bohuslän

Tanum, Bohuslän

Berget

Sagaholm, Småland

The sword from Rørby, Sjælland

Simris, Scania

but in south-eastern Scandinavia the stem pointed forward, as on the Wismar ship and the type from Östergötland.

This means that the twin-axe gods, the 'Divine Twins' (Ward 1968), had already been introduced during Period 1 (*c.* 1700–1500 BC), and are connected with regular voyages to Central Europe, from whence one returned home with both prestige goods (ie full hilted swords and axes) and new myths and stories (Kristiansen 1999). So it is possible to reconstruct one or more of the trading routes during this period, from Oder and even further down to Hungary. Personal jewellery (that was not part of the trading business), shows that Hungarian chiefs travelled north to establish relations (Rittershofer 1983), whilst Nordic chiefs sailed over the Baltic Sea to the Oder Estuary and then south, as we have seen. Once this has happened over two or three generations a lot more knowledge had been gained in many spheres, from metal casting to new gods and new ways in which to organise society, knowledge that could be incorporated into a distinct Nordic format, and this is what happened after 1500 BC. Central to this new development were the voyaging chiefs from Simris or Kivik.

But why did they travel and what did they travel for? To bring back metal and knowledge about its use was but one reason; but what in any case did they have that was more valuable to exchange for the vast quantities of metal that now came to the North and enabled Nordic bronze founders to develop into the most advanced in Europe in the course of only a few generations?

The Bronze Age was the age of the voyage and the 'Odyssey' is the archetype story of the significance and perils of voyage. This was the prerequisite for fame and fortune; voyages lasting many years were normal, as we have heard Menelaus tell Telemachus; 'But when it comes to men, I feel that few or none can rival me in wealth, for it took me seven years and great hardship to amass this fortune and bring it home in my ships. My travels took me to Cyprus, to Phoenicia, and to Egypt. Ethiopians, Sidonians, Erembians, I visited them all; and I saw Libya too…' (Homer, 'The Odyssey', Book 4, 75–85).

It was, however, not only during the Bronze Age that voyaging occurred; the voyage has in all pre-state societies been the path to honour and renown for a chief. That which came from geographically distant places – prestige goods, metal works, warriors, etc – always had extraordinary magical powers and ensured more status and prestige to the chief that could bring it to his house. The American anthropologist Mary Helms has, in several books, researched and described the importance of the voyage and the acquisition of esoteric knowledge and goods in the establishment and maintaining of local power (Helms 1988; 1993; 1998). The voyage and war were two elements around which the lives of the male members of a chief's family revolved. The warriors travelled with their chief and whilst some stayed and served on foreign soil, others returned home and established themselves with the honour and prestige achieved after participating in adventurous and successful expeditions. The chief that had voyaged was closer to the ancestors that brought the new gods and rituals home only a few generations earlier and as such had also become more sacred. A geographical voyage was also a voyage through time, back to society's origins, that either originated in Central Europe, in Kivik or Zealand. This explains why travels and trade with the outside world was essential in establishing and maintaining sacred and political power. But the voyages followed known routes, at least to begin with. Alliances through marriage were established with chiefs on the other side of the Baltic Sea down along the shores of the Oder. Typical distances between such allied chiefdoms were 100–200 km (Kristiansen 1998a, fig 206 and 207). Via networks of alliance the chiefs and their warriors could travel many hundreds of kilometres in relative safety, voyages that took them either from Trondheim to Jæren, from Bohuslän to Östergötland or from Simris to the Oder and, as we shall see, at times even further south.

These voyages also had material content. This was necessary for the exchange of goods needed to maintain the new chiefdoms – bronze travelled north whilst amber travelled south. Amber was known as the 'gold of the North', and there is no doubt as to its value. We can follow the amber route during Period 1 (*c.* 1700–1500 BC), from Oder and down through Hungary, Rumania to Mycenae and Crete. In Hungary there were other goods that the Minoans and Mycenaeans desired – well trained horses for the many chariots, and gold (Penner 1998). A network of well organised transactions connected the North to the Med-iterranean (Engedal 2002; Larsson 1997; 1999). Just like Ulysses, the Nordic chief that voyaged all the way to the Mediterranean, who saw and understood the new and the strange, was already a legend by the time he returned home. This status was enhanced if he had with him never before seen curiosities such as chariots, knowledge of new casting techniques, of wagon and ship building, perhaps even the foreign craftspeople themselves, as well as the stories about far-off settlements and gods, in addition to which he could even draw or carve. One such man was the chief of Kivik.

Pictorial stones and rock carvings – the historical importance of Kivik

The monument they raised in his honour when he died was exceptional. His grave was a stone cist made of eight uniquely decorated pictorial stones. But we have to imagine that the chief had already drawn and carved these motifs that were to appear on the cist slabs long before. For years these motifs had been admired by chiefs that came from far and wide to stay with the chief of Kivik. They visited him to hear his stories and learn his technical skills. Kivik became a chiefly centre of learning, and as was the case in the majority of chiefdom societies around the world during the Bronze Age, technical accomplishment and chiefly status went hand in hand. This is why we see attempts to repeat the motifs from Kivik throughout southern Scandinavia. The pictures created a new kind of art engraved in the rock. But these rock art depictions were first and foremost passive symbols – the wheel, the ship, etc – which could easily be copied. The more complex narrative scenes exceeded what one could transfer on to the hard surface of the rock – with a few exceptions – and the result was almost always simplification.

I will not go into a closer interpretation of the cosmology of the Kivik images (Goldhahn 1999; Randsborg 1993), but state only what can be known with some degree of certainty – namely, that the images show us two side of burial – an active and a passive side. They show us rituals with processions, a chariot race, bull fighting, music (horn blowers), dance and possibly offerings (in the altar scene). The other drawings show us the chiefs' most important possessions in symbolic, fragmented or arranged formation. The paired cult axes arranged in Minoan fashion (as for example the burial scene on the Hagia Triada frieze; Winther 2002, fig 9.7), the pair of ships, the pairs of wheels of two chariots and the accompanying pairs of horses. Is this a symbolic offering through pictorial reproduction?

The paired arrangement has its counterpart in the world of the gods (twin gods, or 'Divine Twins' with the same attributes; Ward 1968) and in the political organisation of society in the form of the twin chiefs that represented the gods (Kristiansen 1999; 2001). The language of the images shows us that they have now accepted and created a new religious and political order, a political/ religious institution centred on a new warrior aristocracy based on the twin chiefs and gods, with origins on Crete and in the Aegean. Only in Kivik do we find the Minoan/Mycenaean iconography directly represented, as an expression of personal connections and voyages. But the foreign influences in material culture were numerous, from drinking vessels, chariots and weapons to the very particular style of simplified ship image carved on the Rørby scimitar with oblique crew strokes and a small dot on top to symbolise the head. It is modelled after ships depicted on Late Middle Helladic ceramics from Aegina, produced and exported throughout the entire Aegean region during the period that corresponds to the Nordic Period 1 (*c.* 1700–1500 BC), where its style was adopted in rock art (Fig 13.6).

From Östergötland to Bohuslän and Jæren we find carved testimony to the fact that the chiefs of these regions visited the renowned chief in Kivik and tried to imitate his magical pictorial world. As I have demonstrated, the local characteristics of the ship carvings show that the chiefs of these regions – the maritime chiefdoms in southern Scandinavia – were in regular contact with each other. The examples could also include other motifs with origins in Kivik. On a carving in Boglöse, Uppland,

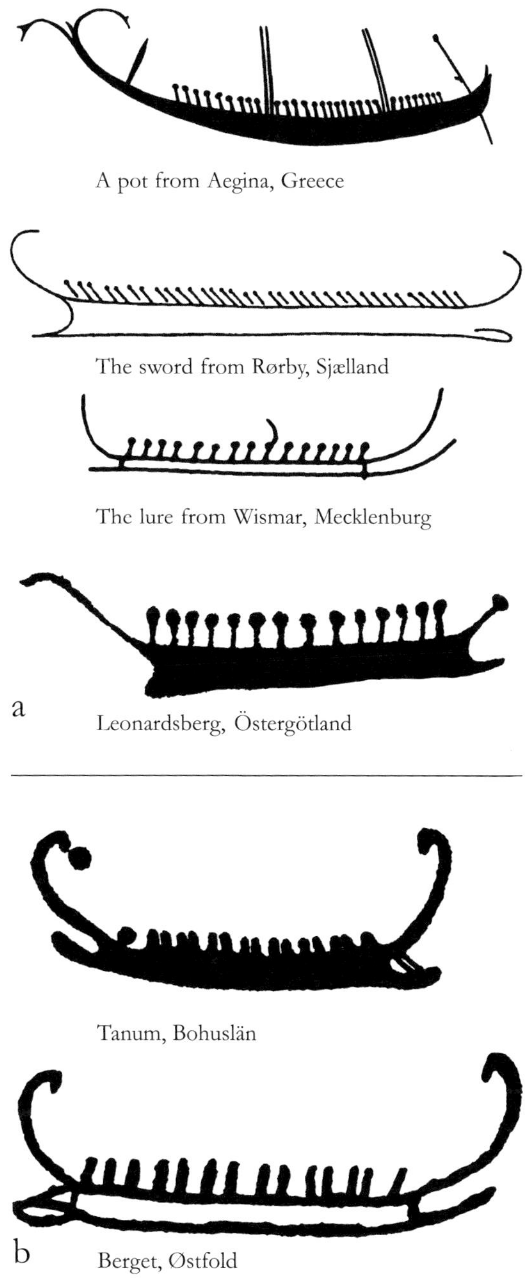

Fig. 13.6 Periods 1/2 ship drawings from the Mediterranean to the North. Stylised ship images on ceramic vessels from the small island of Aegina which, during the Bronze Age period 1, produced ceramics for the entire Aegean region. The ship type is Minoan and can be found reproduced in naturalistic form in the frescoes on Thera (Marinatos 1988:Fig.35). Please note the inrolled stem with animal head, which can also be found on several of the Nordic ship carvings from the same period, and of course the oblique crew strokes with a dot on top, which can also can be found on contemporary Nordic depictions on bronzes and rock carvings. Here is a selection (after Lindblom 2000; Østmo 1990; Bengtsson et al *2000; Malmer 1981 and Kaul 1998). Various scales.*

there is a chariot scene and a ship in typical, southern Swedish Period 1 style and a similar, fully carved, Period 1 ship of south-west Swedish tradition is found nearby the much later Brandskog ship (Hyenstrand 1989, 182–183). Guests from Simris and possibly Bohuslän have carved their signature in the rock here. There were also visits between Kville (in Bohuslän), Kivik and Simris, because in Kville there are chariot scenes, but first and foremost there are the typical paired reproduction of the four-spoked wheels of the chariot from Kivik, for example on Solbräcke (Fredsjö *et al* 1981, numbers 43–44). These can be found in several other places, including Ven; even the unusual Hungarian wheel type, with an extra ring from the Wismar lur, is carved on the Krapperup stone (Althin 1945, abb 61 and 63). When this wheel cross was used as the body of a spear-bearing warrior chief or god, we may date these figures to Period 1 (*c.* 1700–1500 BC; Högberg 1988, figs 58, 54–55). The Klinta stone on Öland likewise resembles some of the Kivik motifs (Randsborg 1993, fig 39), and the particular shape of the crew, with clearly drawn bodies and round heads are also to be found on the solitary ship carvings in Kville, Bohuslän (Fredsjö *et al* 1981, number 63, S74) and these once again testify to the chiefs' long and regular voyages. But the most characteristic is the procession of armless cloak-clad men from the Kivik pictorial scenes, which we find in all the principal rock carving regions in Scandinavia, for example on Aspeberget in Tanum (Milstreu and Prøhl 1996, 70), Leirfall, Stjørdal I Trondheim (Sogness 1999, 50) and Ekeberget, Östergötland (Norden 1923, fig 14). This surely indicates, more than anything else, that the rituals were understood and received locally, but apparently only in the chiefly centres. The same procession of young men can also be found in the large fresco on Thera from the Minoan period, in the early 17th century BC (Marinatos 1988, 60). Over and above the chariot and procession motifs I would like to emphasise the paired ships from period 1 (*c.* 1700–1500 BC) which are an imitation of the motifs found on the Kivik grave. In most cases the motif is found on grave stones (on Jæren and in Järrestad), but in other instances on ordinary carved rocks, where the connection is more difficult to document (Fig 13.7). It is once again the symbolism of the twin gods and twin chiefs and their connections to sea faring voyages that is manifested.

The centres for the carvings and the voyages were specially chosen regions in Scandinavia that had specialised in the building of ships and long sea faring voyages. This was a demanding speciality that

Fig. 13.7 The twin ships from periods 1/2 on the gravestones from Haga, Jæren and Järrestad in Simris, and on the rock carving from Simris (after Fett and Fett 1945; Althin 1945). Yet another example of the iconographic influences of Kivik during this formative period. Various scales.

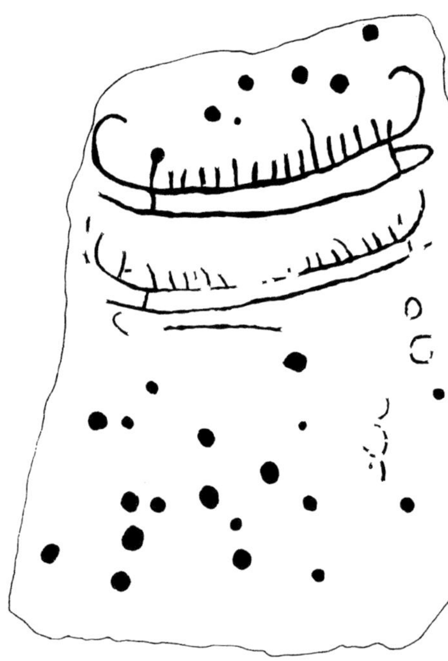

Haga, Jæren

Jârrestad, Scania

Simris, Scania

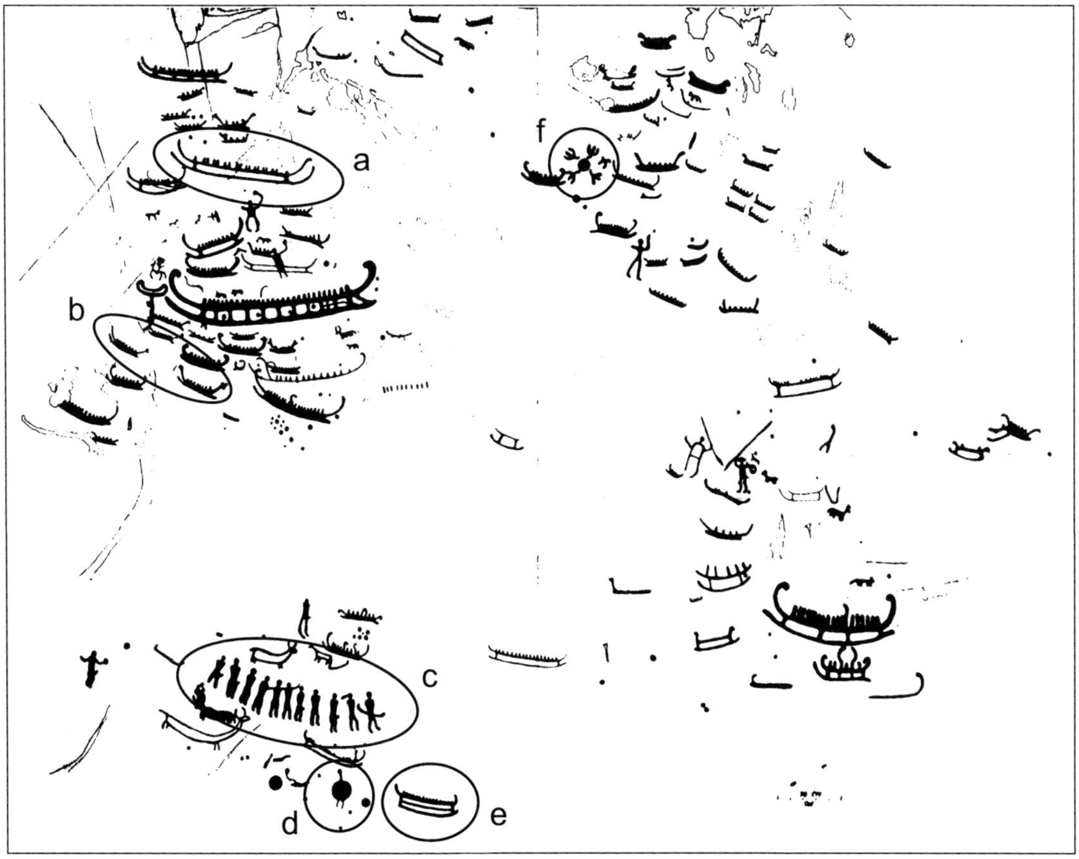

Fig. 13.8 A typical rock art panel from Tanum in Bohuslän with suggested foreign influences and carvings: (a) Twin crewstrokes from Simris; (b) Stems of Baltic type (Ostergotland); (c) procession inspired by Kivik; (d) Sunman with protruding neck from Uppland, Eastern Sweden; (e) Plank carved ship from southwestern Norway; (f) Three fingered horned god from Wismar.

not everyone could undertake (Kvalø 2000). They would then in turn provide the chiefly hinterland and neighbouring chiefdoms with news and goods from the journeys. The maritime chiefdoms of the past were situated where we find the most abundant and most complex carvings, first and foremost the ship carvings. They are situated with regular intervals from Uppland, via Östergötland, to Kivik and Simris, and from there Bohuslän/Östfold, Southern Norway, Jären, Bergen and Trondheim (Fig 13.8). In Denmark participation in the ship voyages occurred, but there were no rocks to carve on, but loose stone blocks were sometimes employed (they probably painted on the house walls instead). It is therefore difficult to localise the maritime chiefdoms here. The Danish ship carvings on loose blocks are most likely to be testimony of visits by chiefs from southern Scandinavia[2].

It is thus possible to demonstrate how the pictorial art of Kivik spread over southern Scandinavia. By studying the regional and local characteristics of the rock art ships of the early Nordic Bronze Age (Kaul 1998; Kristiansen in press), it has been possible to chart the voyages along the Swedish and Norwegian coasts, over the Kattegat and the Baltic Sea. An inconceivable activity, all of which occurred during Period 1 (*c.* 1700–1500 BC) and presumably the early part of Period 2 (*c.* 1500–1400 BC). This was the most expansive and communicative epoch of the Bronze Age. It also explains how and why the Nordic Bronze Age culture could be created and maintained, through regular voyages and the exchange of humans, goods and stories throughout a period of 1000 years.

Notes

[1] Bronze Age rock carvings are works of art and dominated by depictions of the ship (Malmer 1981).This observation is well known but has only recently acquired the attention it deserves (Kaul 1998; Hauptman Wahlgren 2000; Thedéen 2002).

[2] During the Late Bronze Age the voyages continued south, now using other routes and here we find direct testimony of personal contacts, including those to Val Camonica in the Alps where a motif, completely unknown in the North, was carved. This has, however, been carved on a lose stone block in a barrow from Storhøj in Central Jutland (Glob 1969, figs 115 and 169), even though nothing like it has been found in between these two regions. Here we surely find testimony to the fact that long, personal voyages were the order of the day even during the

Late Bronze Age. The voyages continued to Bohuslän because here we find direct motif parallels to Val Camonica (Glob 1969, fig 174, Askum RAÄ nr. 22:1, Archaeological Report 3). Single finds of Nordic women's jewellery from the same part of Europe support these connections (Sprockhoff and Höchmann 1979, taf. 323), which were part of the extensive distribution of new impulses from Italy to the North during Period 5 (*c.* 800 BC; Kristiansen 1998b, 161–188; Bartoloni 1998, fig 40). Also on Vestlandet in Norway, in Kyrkje-Eide, there is one unique rock art panel (Mandt 1991, fig 12.41), which has its closest parallel to the stelae from the Iberian peninsula from the Late Bronze Age (Gamito 1988, 246, No 29), where other similarities to the southern Scandinavian rock art have also been found (Celestino 2001). One grave stone from Rishaug in Trøndelag with a large collar (Sognnes 1999, 113) has its counterpart in Val Camonica as well (Briard 1987, 20), and this is also applicable to certain characteristic human figures (Sognnes 1999, 91; Briard 1987, 154). The examples of such direct personal ties could be made longer but we must also reckon with the fact that some motifs could easily have been copied from imported bronzes, Greek vases (Winther 2002), or wood carvings (Nordbladh 2001). The male figures which are lifting a huge spears with both arms, at times two people (Larsson 1997, fig 18 and figs 36–38), show a ritualised and formalised procession, which was also practiced in Greece during archaic times (Gods and Heroes, 182). In a similar way the Late Bronze Age stern with a round head with two ears or mouths resembles the corresponding heads that finish the handle on Italian knives from the Villanova culture. The number of motifs being transferred is so immense that it is not possible to explain merely in the context of random borrowing. It is the result of systematic voyaging at an elite level and as such is connected to the transmission of new rituals, depictions and myths that characterised the entire Bronze Age.

List of references

Althin, C-A 1945 *Studien zu den bronzezeitlichen Felszeichnungen von Skåne*, I–II, Glerup, Lund og Munksgård, København

Artelius, T 1996 *Långfärd och återkomst – Skeppet i bronsålderns gravar*, Riksanatikvarämbetet Arkeologiska Undersökningar, Skrifter 17, Kungsbacka

Artelius, T 1998 'Skeppsformade gravar I södra Sverige – Om projektion av religiösa och sociala meningsinnehåll I begravningstraditioner', in T Løken (ed), *Bronsalder I Norden – Regioner og interaksjon*, Foredrag ved det 7, Nordiske bronsealdersymposium I Rogaland 31 August 3–September 1995, Arkeologisk Museum Stavanger

Bartoloni, G 1998 'Ancora sulle urne a capanna rinvenute in Italia:nuovi dati e vecchi problemi', in P I Schauer (ed), *Archäologische Untersuchungen zu den Beziehungen zwischen Altitalien und der der Zone Nordwärts der Alpen während der frühen Eisenzeit Alteuropas*, Universität Regensburg, Rudolf Habelt, Bonn

Bengtsson, L Högberg, T and Olsson, C 2000 *Arkeologisk rapport 5, Vitlycke museum,* Världsarvsområdetscentrala del och Grebbestad, Vitlycke Museum

Briard, J 1987 *Mythes et symboles de l'europe preceltique. Les religions de l'age du bronze (2500–800 AV JC)*, Edition Errance

Celestino, S Perez 2001 *Estelas de guerrero y estelas didademadas, La precolonizacion y formacion del mundo Tartesico*, Bellatera arqueologia, Barcelona

Coles, J 2000 *Patterns in a Rocky Land. Rock Carvings in South-West Uppland, Sweden, Volumes 1–2*, AUN 27, Uppsala

Engedal, Ø 2002 *The Nordic Scimitar. External relations and the creation of elite ideology,* British Archaeological Reports (International Series), **1050**, Oxford

Fett, E and Fett, P 1941 *Sydvestnorske hellristninger. Rogaland og Lista,* Stavanger Museum, Dreyers Grafiske Anstalt

Fredsjö, Å with Nordbladh, J and Rosvall, J 1981 *Hällristningar Kville härad i Bohuslän, Kville socken,* Del 1 och 2, Studier i nordisk arkeologi, **14/15**, Fornminnesforeningen i Göteborg i samarbete med Göteborgs arkeologiska musem och Institutionen för Arkäologi, Göteborgs Universitet

Gamita, T J 1988 *Social Complexity in Southwest Iberia 800–300 BC: The Case of Tartessos*, British Archaeological Reports (International Series), **439**, Oxford

Garcia, M Quintela 1999 *Mitologia y Mitos de la Hispania Preromana III,* Madrid: Akal

Glob, P.V 1969 *Helleristninger i Danmark*, Jysk Arkæologisk Selskabs Skrifter, Bind VII, Århus

Gods and Heroes of the Bronze Age 1998 *Gods and Heroes of the Bronze Age: Europe at the Time of Ulysses*, 25th Council of Europe Art Exhibition

Goldhahn, J 1999 *Sagaholm-hällristningar och gravritua,* Studia Archaeologica Universitatis Umensis, **11**, Umeå

Hauptman Wahlgren, K 2000 'The Lonesome Sailing Ship: Reflections on the Rock-Carvings of Sweden and Their Interpreters', *Current Swedish Archaeology*, **8**, 67–96

Helms, M 1988 *Ulysses' Sail. An Ethnographic Odyssey of Power, Knowledge, and Geographical Distance*, Princeton University Press

Helms, M 1993 *Craft and the Kingly Ideal:Art, Trade, and Power*, Austin:University of Texas Press

Helms, M 1998 *Access to Origins. Affines, Ancestors and Aristocrats*, Austin: University of Texas Press

Högberg, T 1988 *Hällbilder på Aspberget*, Strömstads Tidning Tryckeri AB

Hyenstrand, Å 1989 'Uppland', in S Jansson, E B Lundberg, and U Bertilsson (eds), *Hällristningar och Hällmålingar i Sverige*, Forum, 182–183

Jockenhövel, A 1991 'Räumliche Mobilität von Personen in der mittleren Bronzezeit des westlichen

Mitteleuropa', *Germania*, **69**, 49–62

Kaul, F 1998 *Ships on Bronzes. A Study in Bronze Age Religion and Iconography*, PNM Studies in Archaeology and History, **3**, 1, Copenhagen

Kristiansen, K 1998a *Europe before History*, Cambridge University Press

Kristiansen, K 1998b 'Mellem centrum og periferi. Bohuslän I bronzealderen', I *Bronser. Bronsåldersfynd I Göteborg och Bohuslän*, Bohuslän Museum

Kristiansen, K 1999 'Symbolic structures and social institutions. The twin rulers in Bronze Age Europe', in A Gustavsson and H Karlsson (eds), *Glyfer och arkeologiska rum – en vänbok til Jarl Nordbladh,* Gotarc Series A, **3**, Göteborg, 537–552

Kristiansen, K 2001 'Rulers and Warriors: Symbolic Transmission and Social Transformation in Bronze Age Europe', in J Haas (ed), *From Leaders to Rulers. Fundamental Issues in Archaeology*, Kluwer Academic/ Plenum Publishers, 85–104

Kristiansen, K in press *Kivik og den nordiske bronzealders begyndelse*

Kristiansen, K and Larsson, T manuscript *The long journey. Symbolic transmission and social transformation in Bronze Age Europe*

Kvalø, F 2000 *Oversjøiske reiser fra Sørvest-Norge til Nordvest-Jylland i eldre bronsealder, En drøftning om maritim realisering og rituell mobilisering*, Hovesfagsopgave i arkeologi ved Universitetet i Oslo

Larsson, T B 1997 *Materiell kultur och religiösa symboler*, Arkeologiska studier vid Umeå Universitet, **4**

Larsson, T.B 1999 'TheTransmission of an elite ideology – Europe and the Near East in the second millennium BC', in J Goldhahn (ed), *Rock Art as Social Representation,* British Archaeological Reports (International Series), **797**, Oxford, 49–65

Lindblom, M 2000 'Krukor som märks', *Hellenika*, **91**, 16–19

Malmer, M 1981 *A Chorological Study in North European Rock Art*, Antikvariska Serien, **32**, Stockholm

Mandt, G 1991 *Vestnorske ristninger i tid og rom, Kronologiske, korologiske og kontekstuelle studier, Bind 1 og 2*, Bergen, Manuskript

Marinatos, N 1988 *Kunst und Religion im alten Thera, Zur Rekonstruktion einer bronzezeitlichen Gesellschaft*, Athens

Milstreu, G and Prøhl, H 1996 *Dokumentation och registrering av hällristningar i Tanum. No 1 Aspeberget,* Tanums Hällristningsmuseum Underslös, Scandinavian Society for Prehistoric Rock Art

Nordbladh, J 2001 Italienska träskulpturer som hällristningsfigurer, *Adoranten*, Årsskrift

Norden, A 1923 *Felsbilder der Provinz Ostgotland in Auswahl*, Werke der Urgermanen, Folkwang-Verlag Hagen und Darmstadt

Østmo, E 1990 *Hellristninger av sørskandinaviske former på det indre Østlandet*, Fylkene Buskerud, Akershus, Oslo, Oppland og Hedmark, Universitetets Oldsakssamling Skrifter, Ny Rekke Nr. 12, Oslo

Penner, S 1998 *Schliemanns Schachtgräberrund under der europäische Nordosten*, Studien zur Herkunft der Mykenischen Streitwagenausstattung, Saarbrücker Beitrage zur Altertumskunde, Band 60, Dr Rudolf Habelt Verlag, Bonn

Randsborg, K 1993 'Kivik. Archaeology and Iconography', *Acta Archaeologica*, **64**, 1, København, Munksgård

Rittershofer, K-F 1983 'Das Hortfund von Bühl und seine Beziehungen', *Ber. Der Römisch-Germanischen Kommission,* **64**, Mainz

Selinge, K G 1989 'Östergötland', in S Jansson, E B Lundberg, and U Bertilsson (eds), *Hällristningar och Hällmålingar i Sverige*, Forum, 147–165

Sprockhoff, E and Höchmann, O 1979 *Dei gegossene Bronzebecken der jüngeren nordischen Bronzezeit,* Römisch-Germanisches Zentralmuseum, Mainz

Sogness, K 1998 *Prehistoric Imagery and Landscapes. Rock Art in Stjørdal, Trøndelag, Norway*, Manuscript

Sogness, K 1999 *Det levende Berget*, Tapir forlag, Trondheim

Thedéen, S 2002 'På resa genom livet och landskapet – tankar kring bronsålderns skeppssymbolik', in J Goldhahn (ed), *Bilder av bronsålder – et seminarium om förhistorisk kommunikation*, Acta Archaeologica Lundensia, Series in 8; **37**, Almqvist and Wiksell International, Stockholm, 129–137

Vogt, D 2000 *Helleristninger i Onsøy*, Fredriksstad kommune, Østfold, Varia 50, Oldsakssamlingen, Oslo

Ward, D 1968 *The Divine Twins*, Folklore Studies, **19**, Berkley and Los Angeles

Winter, L 2002 'Relationen mellan Medelhavsområdets och Sydskandinaviens bildvärdar', in J Goldhahn (ed), *Bilder av bronsålder*, Acta Archaeologica Lundensia, Series in 8, **37**, Almqvist and Wicksell International, Stockholm, 201–222

14. Social and religious perceptions of the ship in Bronze Age Northern Europe

Flemming Kaul

Introduction

It is an astonishing fact that in Scandinavia and Denmark thousands of Bronze Age ship renderings are known, while no remains of Bronze Age ships or boats proper (apart from dugouts) have been found, whereas in Britain there is almost no Bronze Age ship iconography, but a number of interesting finds of Bronze Age boats proper. It is difficult to explain why the ship became so an important iconographical motif of the North, while it hardly occurs in Britain, where sea transport must certainly have been of great importance. At the beginning of the Early Pre-Roman Iron Age of Denmark, Sweden and Norway the ship iconography almost disappears, but still some examples are known, and from that period we have the well preserved Hjortspring boat from the island of Ȧls, Southern Jutland.

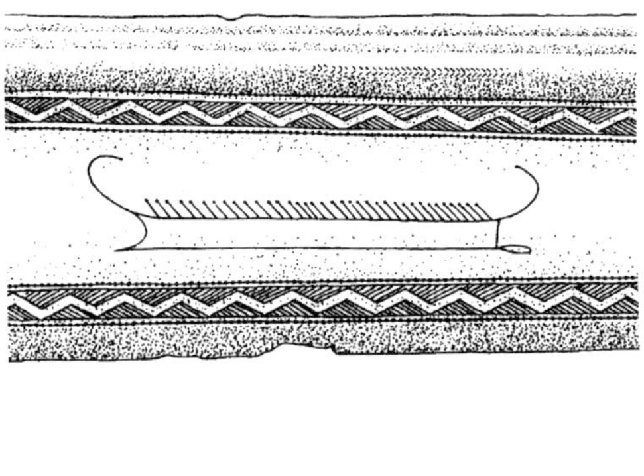

Fig. 14.1 The sword from Rørby, Western Zealand (Period IB of the Nordic Bronze Age, c *1600 BC), and its ship decoration, after Aner and Kersten 1976.*

Ship and iconography in a formative phase of the Nordic Bronze Age Culture

In an early part of the Nordic Bronze Age, at 1600–1400 BC, a formative phase of Bronze Age religion and society culminated. A distinguished aristocratic elite seems to have formed, and richly furnished barrow-graves turned up at the same time as a new iconography. For the first time for centuries figural art appears in Denmark and Southern Scandinavia, and motifs such as the ship, the horse, the fish and probably the snake were introduced. Some religious changes, with new and probably more complex ideas of the otherworld, must have taken place, and these ideas – to judge from the extent of this iconography – seem to have been accepted in a sort of standardized form in a relatively large area of Southern and Central Scandinavia, and later Northern Germany. Together with the new figural motifs also some new non-figural motifs occur, such as the fan shaped symbol and the wheel cross.

The most important and characteristic of these new figural motifs of the Nordic Bronze Age was the ship, which on rock carvings was introduced and spread over large areas of Denmark, Sweden and Norway within a relatively short span of time. A bronze sword found at Rørby on Zealand, Denmark from *c.* 1600–1500 BC (Period Ib; Vandkilde 1996, 231–232) carries the earliest datable Bronze Age ship rendering of the North (Fig 14.1). The shipshape is characterised by high stems turning inwards, and a horizontal or only slightly raised and pointed keel extension fore, and a horizontal stabiliser aft (Fig 14.2). The ship renderings on stone

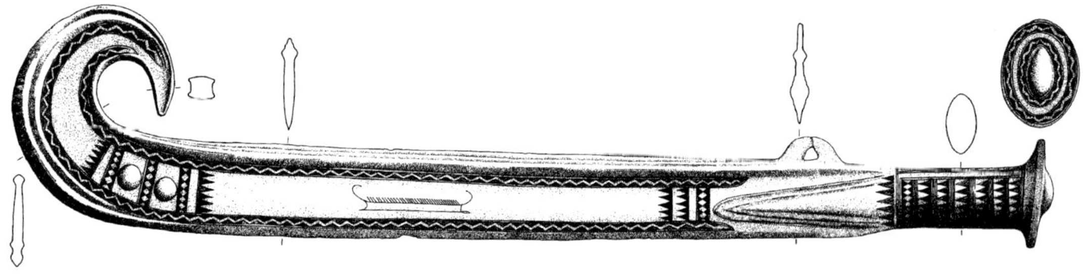

1

2

3

4

5

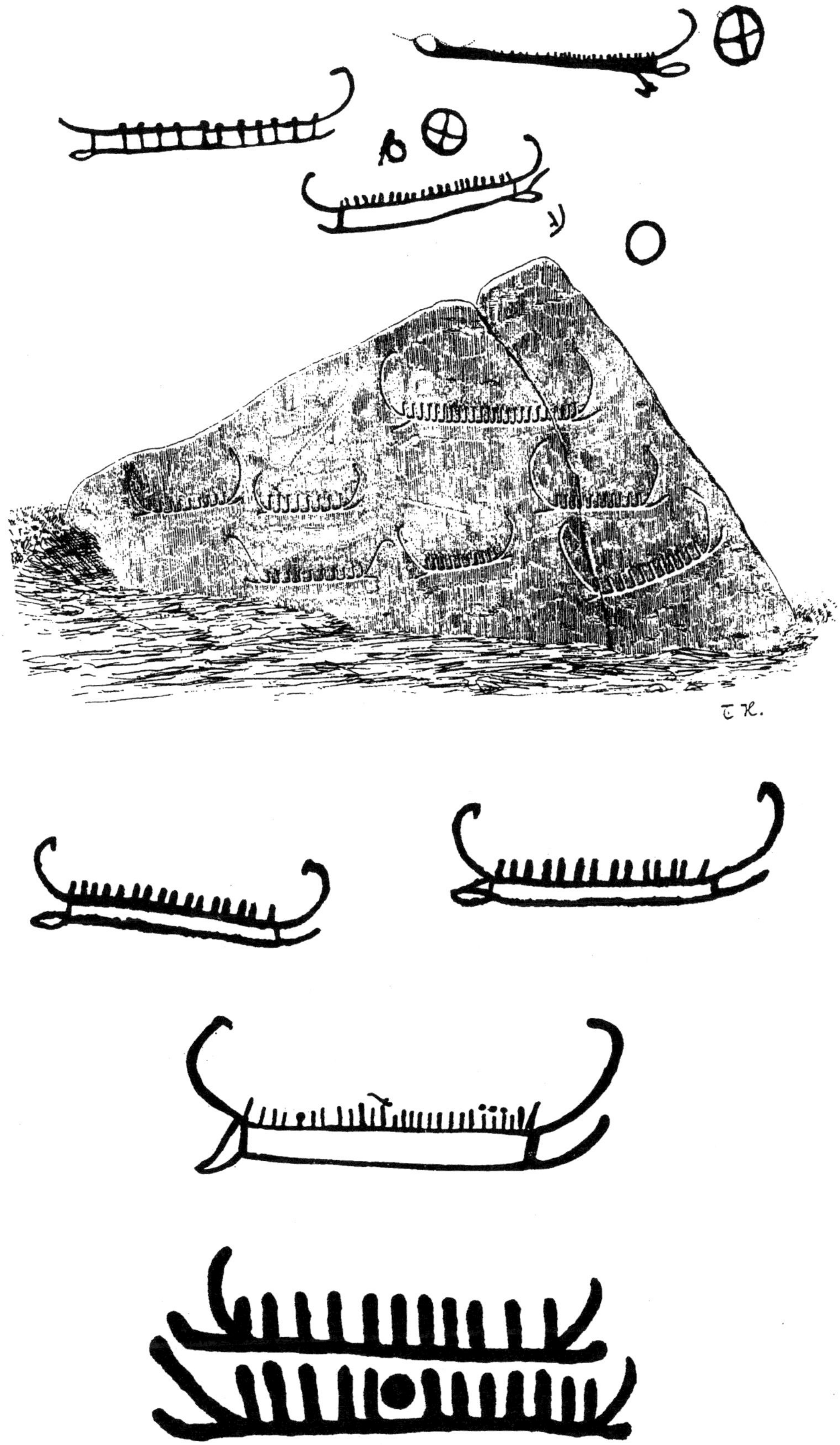

Fig. 14.2 Ship images of a shape like the rendering on the Rørby sword seems to have spread relatively swiftly over larger parts of Scandinavia. Such ships are characterized by inturned stems and a horizontal or only slightly raised keel extension fore, and a sort of stabilizer aft. 1: Ship images from Hegra VII, Stjørdal, Nordtrøndelag, Norway; 2: Ships from a larger now destroyed stone from Ølberg near Stavanger, Western Norway; 3: Ships from Berget, Buskerud, Southern Norway; 4: Ship rendering from Litslena 280 (Ulstämma A), Uppland, Central Sweden; 5: Two ship images on a smaller stone from Grevinge, Odsherred, and Northern Zealand, Denmark. All rock carvings; after Sognnes 1999, Myhre 1981, Østmo 1990, Coles 2000 Photo/photographic Kaul and Milstreu.

sharing this peculiarity should be placed – by analogy to the well-dated Rørby ship – in the same period, that is period I of the Nordic Bronze Age, and probably parts of period II (Kaul 1998, 73–79; Østmo 1990). During period II (1500–1300 BC) the horse's head seems to be introduced as stem adornments, and horse headed stems continue during the rest of the Bronze Age, until *c.* 500 BC. In the Late Bronze Age (1100–500 BC) the aquatic bird also turns up as stem adornments, as an influence from the Urnfield Culture. The ship renderings of the Late Bronze Age is furthermore characterised by a highly raised keel extension fore and a horizontal 'stabilizer' aft (Fig 14.3).

Bronze objects and rock carvings of the Nordic Bronze Age have yielded thousands of ship renderings. Ships on rocks are found in many parts of Denmark, Sweden and Norway, though in Denmark not as numerous as in the other Nordic countries, since larger suitable rock surfaces are only found on the Baltic island of Bornholm. Elsewhere in Denmark glacial erratics were used for rock carvings. The number of ship renderings on bronze objects is generally much lower than the number seen on the rocks, except in Denmark. The ships on bronzes – for instance on razors, knifes and neck-rings – have their main distribution in Denmark, where more than 800 ships are known from 422 bronze objects (Kaul 1998). Far fewer are known from Sweden and Northern Germany. Most of the ship renderings on bronze objects belong to the Late Bronze Age.

The central motifs of the Nordic Bronze Age iconography must somehow have been introduced from outside, although ships must for long have had a significant role as means of transport, contacts and communication in the sea-landscape of the North and the Baltic Sea area. The ship and the horse were chosen as important objects of symbolic value – the horse being the finest and most aristocratic animal known – with a certain ambivalence being somehow wild though controllable by man – the ship with its associations to transport, contacts and access to bronze. It is also important to weave these changes into a local background and ask how it was possible that (for instance) the ship was introduced into iconography during the formative phase of the Nordic Bronze Age culture. The ship must already have had a number of associations as to the social sphere. The ship meant wealth, power, control of resources, connections, news, and knowledge of the world. Already during the Late Neolithic, the distribution of flint objects in Western Norway coming from the flint mines of Northern Jutland demonstrates that one of the most treacherous waters of the north, between North Jutland and SW Norway was regularly trafficked (Solberg 1994). Particularly in the Early Bronze Age, the importance of ships and boats in the economical, social and political sphere must have increased dramatically – at a time when connections to the South and access to metal by sea and river transport became increasingly vital (Vandkilde 1996; 2000). Every drop of copper and tin had to be brought to Denmark, Sweden and Norway from areas far away. Between 1600 and 1500 BC the ship emerged as by far the most important figural motif of the iconography. In the formative process of Bronze Age religion and iconography the ship's social and political role became superseded by its role in the beliefs and myths related to the transempirical world. The ship, together with the other motifs or symbols, were together with large ceremonial bronze-axes and other cult objects kept in use during 1000 years, from *c.* 1500 BC to 500 BC.

But from where was the ship as symbol introduced? At the time of the introduction of the ship in the North, there are no signs of a rich ship iconography in Northern and Central Europe. However, on a number of bronze objects from the Apa-Hajdusamson horizon in the Hungarian-Rumanian area, as for instance the cult axes with '*Nackenscheibe*' (disc-butted axe) we sometimes find ship-like motifs (Fig 14.4; Kaul 1998, 277–284). Also the gold-discs from Graniceri, Rumania, probably contemporary with the Nordic Period I or Period II (1700–1300 BC), might evidence some iconography related to the ship (and the horse). On one of the gold discs we see horses moving around a central field, surrounded by hook-like shapes ending in spiralling forms (Randsborg 1993). On two other gold discs from Graniceri other ship-like shapes are seen (Fig 14.5). Such hook-like shapes are also found on the Early Period II cult axe from Bredebækgård, which could be interpreted as ship images sailing around a central sun image (Fig 14.6; Kaul 2001). It is particularly from these Middle-Danubian areas that the influences came at the beginning of the Nordic Bronze Age, and by means of these contacts the leaders of the North could have had a central role in discourses relating to the introduction of foreign elements and their meaning. In the North, the implementation of the ship in iconography and cosmology had an almost explosive impact and distribution, where it was kept as the leading motif for centuries to come. In Central Europe the ship as an iconographical motif almost vanished or held an inferior position. But a few centuries later, in the Urnfield culture of central Europe, the ship gained an important place in the iconography (see below).

In respect to the background for the emergence of the ship iconography of the North, the recent find of the bronze disc – *Die Himmelscheibe von Nebra* – in Sachsen-Anhalt is of great interest (Fig 1.9; Meller 2002). On the disc from Nebra we find gilded motifs interpreted as the sun, the moon, stars, a ship, and the heavenly vault. This Northern European manufactured cosmological/mythological narrative

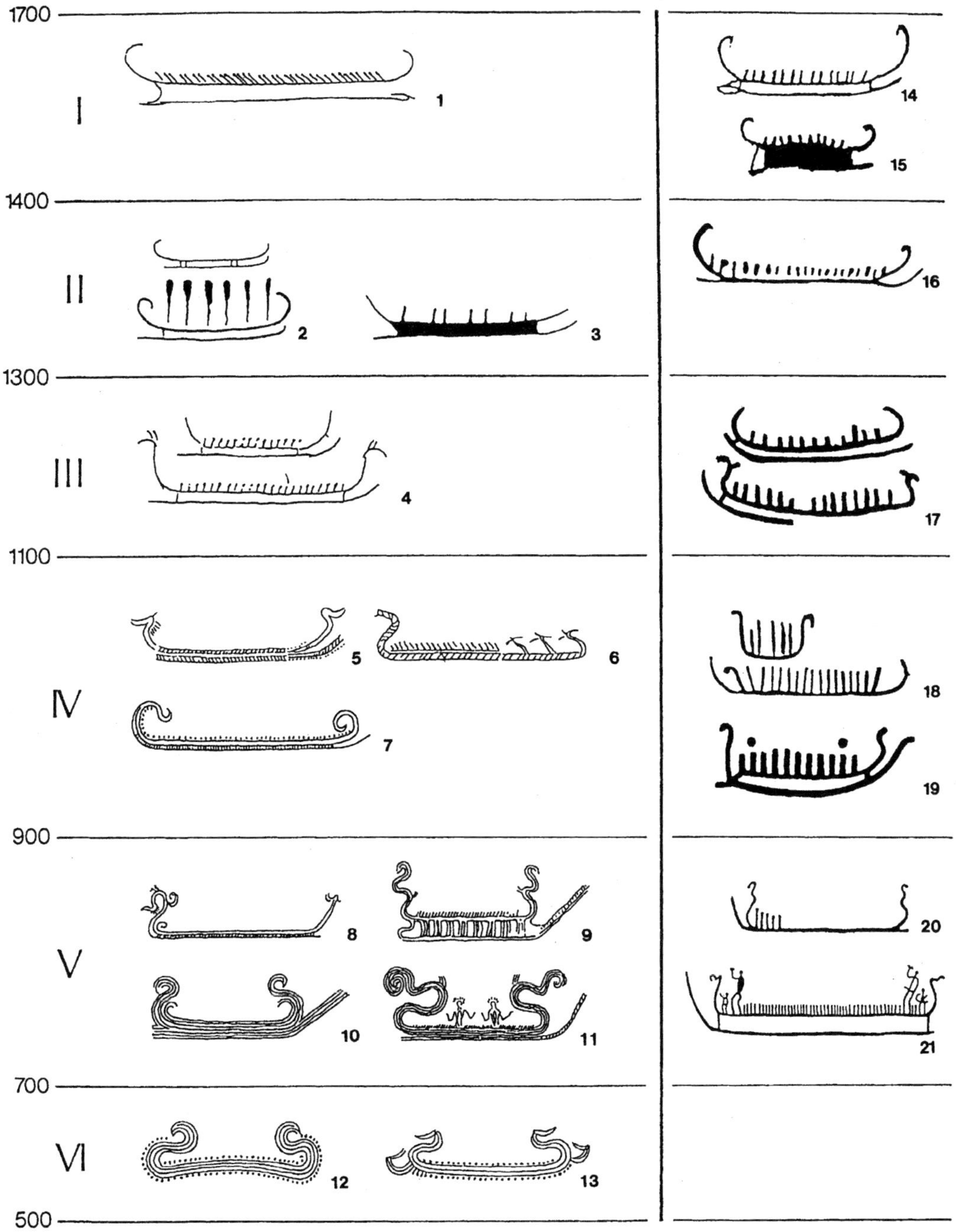

Fig. 14.3 Diagram showing the chronological typological development of Nordic Bronze Age ship renderings. Left column: datable ships, right column; ships on the rocks which can be dated by analogy with ships as those shown in the left column, after Kaul 1998.

(the earliest European rendering of *cosmos*) from a time equivalent to the Nordic Bronze Age period I (*c.* 1600 BC) gives us an impression that the movement of the heavenly bodies somehow had a relation to the ship – ship or ships of the sun, moon or perhaps even stars. This unique piece of religious art seems to demonstrate that at this time – only 400 km from the Baltic Sea – attempts were taken to create a new iconography related to the celestial bodies and to the ship. Furthermore, the Nebra disc seems to show peculiar traits related to Near Eastern or Egyptian iconography. It thus demonstrates some of the iconographical features that were in play in Northern Europe at a time when the Nordic Bronze Age (ship) iconography was at its advent.

However, it still seems difficult to explain the particular role of the ship in the Nordic cosmology and religion (as demonstrated by the Late Bronze Age bronzes), merely as reflecting contacts with Central Germany or Eastern Central Europe. We

Fig. 14.4 Naviform figures on one of the cult axes with disc-shaped butt from Hajdúsámson, Hungary, after Mathé 1996.

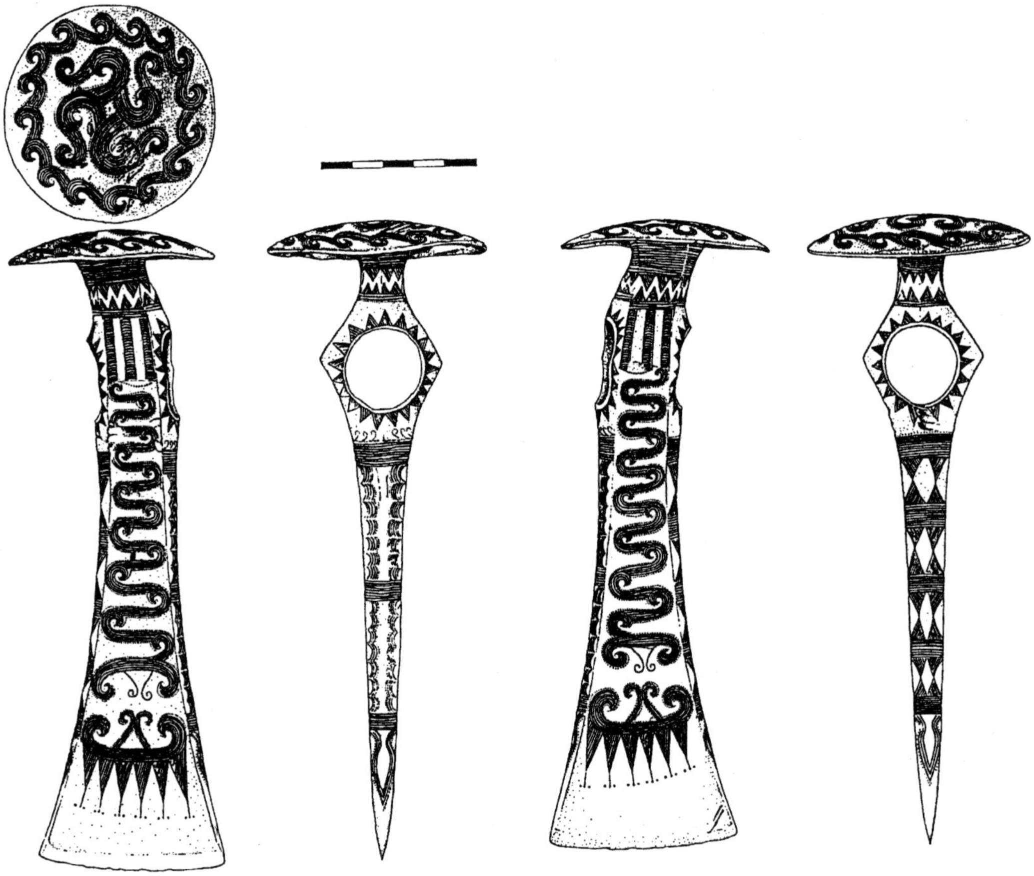

Fig. 14.5 Three gold discs from Graniceri, Western Rumania. On one of the discs horses and figures in the shape of ship stems are encircling a central zone. On the two other discs are ship-like figures, and on one of them what seem to be renderings of aquatic birds. The composition making a cross could be related to the wheel cross. After Randsborg 1993.

need to go further south. In the ('Greek') Mediterranean there does not seem to be evidence of a coherent and widespread ship iconography, even though some examples can be noted. But when we go to ancient Egypt, the picture is quite clear. Here the ship had a prominent role in cosmology and religion, primarily being the sun ship (Kaul 1998, 277–284). The structural, mythological role of the ship (the sun ship connecting zoomorphic manifestations of the sun, both night-ships and morning-ships, etc) and its use in cult and ceremonies seems to demonstrate some general common characteristics in each end of the 'world'. How these general notions made their way to the North is still difficult to explain, but we do find some other Eastern Mediterranean features that reached NW Europe. When the ship image turns up in the North, it has got its own particular character, and we should not talk of a take-over of Egyptian religion as such. On the other hand, the whole structure of the Nordic Bronze age cosmology seems somehow to be linked with Egyptian cosmology, as demonstrated on the bronzes of the Late Bronze age.

Other figural motifs or symbols of the Nordic Bronze Age related to the ship, and their appearance in the Early Bronze Age

The fan-shaped or mushroom-shaped symbol was a popular symbol in the Late Bronze Age, but it is also known from the Early Bronze Age. Structural analysis of the bronzes of the Late Bronze Age reveal that this symbol should be related to the sun and day-time, being found solely on right-sailing ships and often together with sun-images. This symbol should thus be associated with key words like *day*, *up*, *sun* and *light*. In the Late Bronze Age it is also found related to ship images on the rocks (Fig 14.7). The recently acquired cult axe from Bredebækgård in Northern Zealand further documents the presence of this symbol in the Early Bronze Age, *c.* 1500–1400 BC (Kaul 2001). Among different decorative elements the fan-shaped symbol is seen 'balancing' on top of a tall triangular figure (Fig 14.6). The earliest occurrence of this motif shows it in a very distinct, almost heraldic form, demonstrating that it was already fully 'developed' in the Early Bronze Age, in the formative phase of Nordic Bronze Age religious art, and that this motif was of importance almost all the way through the Bronze Age, as were the horse and the ship. We could choose to see the introduction of the fan-shaped symbol as something local – Nordic – built upon some of the basic values of the axe and the axe-shape. However, one could also ponder upon the possibilities of distant foreign influences. When searching for parallels to the composition seen on

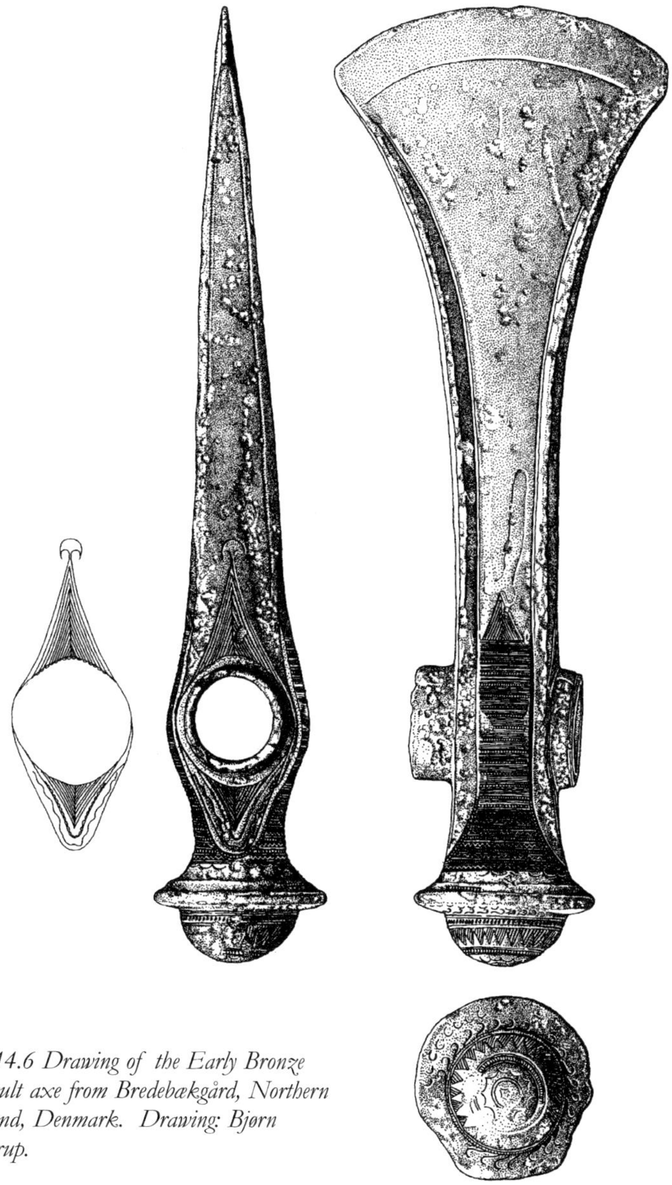

Fig. 14.6 Drawing of the Early Bronze Age cult axe from Bredebækgård, Northern Zealand, Denmark. Drawing: Bjørn Skaarup.

Fig. 14.7 Fan shaped symbol as an impressive stem ornament on a ship rendering from Blåholthus, Bornholm, Denmark, Late Bronze Age, Period IV or V (1100–700 BC). The whole ship among other rock carving ships and detail of the prow with the fan shaped symbol. Photograph: Kaul and Milstreu.

the cult axe from Bredebækgård, the closest similarities are on royal Hittite seals from the great period of the Hittite Kingdom around and before 1300 BC (Gurney 1962; Randsborg 1993). Among other motifs and symbols, these Hittite royal insignia carry a hemispherical shape with inturned lower ends 'balancing' on the point of a tall triangular figure. The meaning of this composition in its Hittite context is not quite clear; it has been suggested that it was a symbol of the prominent heaven and weather-god, and that it meant something good or positive.

Another important figural motif, the horse, was introduced after 1500 BC. On the 'Chariot of the Sun' from Trundholm, Northern Zealand (*c.* 1400 BC), we meet the horse in the most splendid manner, as a full plastic bronze figure, where the horse is seen drawing the golden image of the sun (Fig 14.8). The mythological role of this divine horse – the sun-horse – is thus documented in an early part of the Bronze Age. From the Late Bronze Age comes a number renderings of the sun-horse pulling the sun, (both on bronze objects and on rock carvings) documenting that the idea of this mythological horse continued through the Bronze Age. In many cases these horses are closely related to the ship (see below). The horse was something totally new at the time, and it seems reasonable that its introduction in iconography reflects connections with Greek or Southern/Central European areas. From where the notion of the horse being the divine sun horse came is difficult to say and at many places an underlying idea of the horse being related to the voyage of the sun could have existed.

The wheel cross also turns up in the Early Bronze Age. It could be assumed that the wheel cross was understood as a solar image, and also as a symbol of the movement of the sun and its eternal cyclical voyage. The wheel cross also carries the symbolism of the wheel, sometimes *being* wheels when seen used as such on images of two wheeled chariots. The wheel cross, the four spoked wheel, and the two-wheeled chariot could have been introduced in the north from Greece, probably via Central Europe. Miniature wheels from period II (*c.* 1500–1300 BC) are known as a single wheel from a grave at Tobøl, Western Jutland (Thrane 1963), and are seen as part of the vehicle of 'The Chariot of the Sun'.

Fig. 14.8 'The Chariot of the Sun', Northwestern Zealand, Denmark, c *1400 BC. It is the gilded, radiant side of the sun disc being pulled to the right. Photo: The National Museum of Denmark.*

The fish is seen on a splendid Early Bronze Age bronze spearhead from Valsømagle, Southern Zealand (period IB, *c.* 1600–1500 BC; Aner and Kersten 1976, no. 1098). Its introduction in the north may reflect influences from Crete or ancient Egypt. The snake seems to be found in an Early Bronze Age context on the rock carving Simris 19 (Fig 14.9). Here it is seen together with the horse and the ship, and this particular rock carving could be interpreted as a rendering of the divine agents helping the sun on its voyage at day and night, where the horse's position may reflect a day-time situation, while the snake's position lowermost may reflect its role during the night. The ship could be understood (already) here as the mediating transport between day and night. The introduction of the snake in the Nordic iconography could reflect contacts or influences from Minoan Crete and Egypt. The cosmological role of the snake in Egypt seems to demonstrate some similarities with its role as seen on some Nordic Late Bronze Age razors.

The general interest in the sun in Bronze Age religion and iconography could be perceived from a local perspective, where already in the Stone Age the orientation of the passages of some passage graves of the Funnel Beaker Culture seems to indicate a certain interest in particular positions of the sun. A number of small flat stones decorated with various line and circular ornaments from the final phase of the Funnel Beaker Culture (*c.* 2800 BC) found at a palisaded settlement at Rispebjerg, Bornholm, may hint at en earlier sun related iconography (Kaul *et al* 2002). Some of these 'miniature rock carvings' are round and carry circular ornaments that could be interpreted as solar symbols or images. But first in the Bronze Age with its many new motifs, a new and probably more codified cosmological system emerged related to religious ideas as to the eternal voyage of the sun.

If we accept that some of the symbols being introduced in the formative phase of the Nordic Bronze Age iconography and religion (Nordic Period I and Early Period II, *c.* 1700–1300 BC) did reflect distant foreign influences, then we should consider how and from where these influences came. Perhaps we should envisage this formative phase not merely as a phase were some diffusion took place, but rather as a time of an active and deliberate selection process as seen from the North.

The different figurative and symbolic elements of the iconography, and hence the religion, were deliberately picked up by a restricted elite group of the Nordic societies, who had been travelling and who knew 'the secrets of the world'. In this formative phase, the different elements were deliberately chosen and introduced, and shortly after, these elements became arranged in a new manner in accordance with and in relation to a Nordic cultural tradition, framework and perception. Seen in this light, the ship (the sun ship) reflects knowledge of Egyptian religion; the horse and the wheel-cross reflect familiarity with Mycenaean Greece and Central Europe; the snake knowledge of the religion of Minoan Crete or Egypt and the fan-shaped symbol knowledge of Hittite symbols. All these motifs soon came together in a new order and in a Nordic artistic tradition, forming the basic iconographical elements of the Nordic Bronze Age religion that persisted for 1000 years. The cosmological role of the ship and the basic structure of cosmology as demonstrated by the renderings of the Nordic Late Bronze Age razors, related to the eternal voyage of the sun, may point in the direction of Egypt. But without a local Nordic background, where the ship already had a great importance, it would probably never had achieved its divine status as the Sun-ship.

The (ship) iconography on bronzes of the Late Bronze Age, interpretation

It is the direction of travel of the ships, towards left and right, which form one of the most decisive clues to the structure and meaning of the iconography of the bronze objects. The ships (and the mythological sun ships) of the Nordic Bronze Age were not symmetrical, as were their southerly counterparts of the Central European Urnfield Culture (*Vogel-Sonnenbark*). The prows of the ships carry a marked and highly raised keel extension, whereas the keel extension aft is short and horizontal. By means of the direction of the ships and a systematic analysis of the motifs related to right direction versus left, significant patterns can be observed (Kaul 1998). Sun images never occur together with left-sailing ships. If we for at time forget that the earth is round, and forget everything related to map reading and compass directions of today, we realise that the observable 'travel' direction of the sun (in the Northern hemisphere) is always from left to right. This must indicate that ships sailing towards right, and associated with sun images are renderings of the sun's journey in day-time. To understand this world view or cosmology we must consider the earth to be flat, and when the sun sets in the evening, it has to return to its starting point of dawn, sunrise, by moving left under the water and through the underworld. In this way, the direction of sailing to the right in the structure of Bronze Age iconography can indicate day-time, up, the sky and light, while the direction to the left can indicate night, down, the earth (or sea), the underworld, and darkness.

The direction of sailing seems to indicate at what point in the daily cycle the various motifs had their main 'field of activity' and how far they were associated with the night or the day, the morning or the evening. The sun-horses are almost always moving to the right. The fish and the snake however, are more equally represented as regards their direction, indicating that their field of activity was close to the horizon, working over and below it, and that they could work both during day and night. With the aid of this left-right structure the mythological circumstances surrounding the journey of the sun on its daily cycle could thus be represented in iconographical form as a kind of cartoon-strip narrative on the bronzes. The zoomorphic helpers or manifestations of the sun thus had specific functions or 'finest hours'. This left-right-logic is demonstrated as early as *c.* 1400 BC by 'The Chariot of the Sun' from Trundholm, Northern Zealand (Kaul 1998, 185–187).

Let our starting point be the morning. One of the most illustrative razors gives interesting evidence as to how sunrise was perceived in the cyclical myth of the Bronze Age (Fig 14.10). By means of the raised keel extensions it is possible to read the directions of the two ships and to see the right-left logic work. The night-ship at the bottom is sailing to the left, and over that the day-ship (or morning-ship) is sailing to the right. It is seen that the night ship from the top of its prow has just handed over

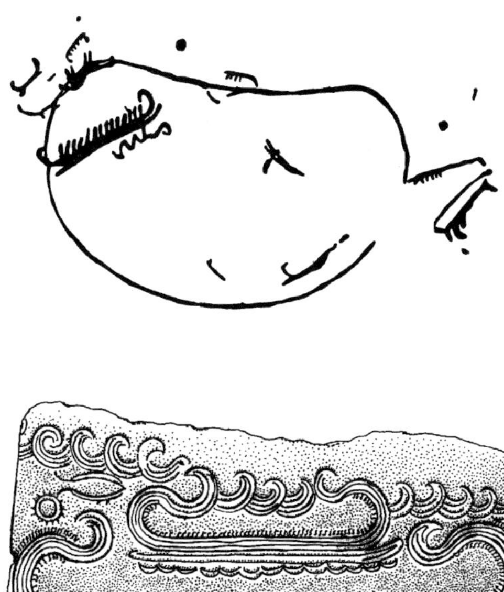

Fig. 14.9 (top) Part of the rock carving Simris 19, Scania, Southern Sweden. A snake-like figure is closely associated with a rendering of a ship and a horse, Early Bronze Age. The outline of the ships is similar to other ships assigned to Early Bronze Age; see Fig 14.2: after Burenhult 1973.

Fig. 14.10 (below) Razor without find provenance, Moesgård Museum, Denmark, c 800 BC. Here a ship is sailing to the right above a ship sailing to the left, where a fish is seen pulling the sun upwards and to the right from immediately above the ship sailing to the left to the ship sailing to the right. Note the raised keel extensions which indicate the sailing direction of the ships. Drawing: Bjørn Skaarup.

the sun to the fish, which is on its way upwards and to the right towards the day-ship. Other razors show that the fish then – for a time – was allowed to sail on with the ship. On a razor from Torupgårds Mark, Northern Jutland, the fish is to be devoured by a bird of prey, the sun now being on the ship. To the right a group of stylized sun-horses are ready to fetch the sun, which is also seen together with the sun horses. The role of the horse is best seen on a razor from Neder Hvolris, where a fine horse pulls the sun away from a ship. It is the sun-horse that at mid-day takes over the transport from the morning ship (Fig 14.11). On yet another Danish razor, from Vandling, the horse seems actually to land on a ship, and this motif is consequently interpreted as the sun horse landing on the afternoon-ship, giving over the transport of the sun to this ship (Fig 14.12). Finally, at sunset, a snake took over the sun from the afternoon ship as shown on a razor from Knuthenborg (Fig 14.13). This serpent was helping the sun down under the horizon, into its nocturnal travel, where also ships, the sun-horse, and the fish could assist the sun at its path through the underworld, and its left turned voyage. In some other cases the snake seems to work in one direction, while the related ship sails in the opposite direction. This confusion of directions may hint at how the circumstances at sunset or sunrise were rendered in the symbolic language of the Nordic Bronze Age, where the directions left and right and the orientation up and down were changing just when the sun meets the separating horizon, and where night -and day-ships change their direction and for a moment can work upside-down. Then, after sunset, during the nocturnal, sinister, and left-directed, voyage of the ship or ships of the night the fish can be seen following the ship, swimming to the left. The sun is not visible, extinguished and dark on its voyage through the underworld. The eternal cyclical voyage of the sun, helped by the sun ship and other divine agents, has been completed, and the sun can be born anew. Tentatively I have allowed myself to relate some of the motifs from Danish Late Bronze Age razors, where different points of the daily cycle are shown, to the wheel-cross, a symbol of the sun and its eternal voyage, thus in a graphic way illustrating this central myth of the Nordic Bronze Age (Fig 14.14).

This cyclical-mythological system seems to work well without the involvement of anthropomorphic gods (Kaul 1998, 242 ff.). The sun was not or only rarely represented in the shape of a human being; we are dealing primarily with the sun as a non-personified manifestation of the highest power. When humans or human-like figures occur in the rock carvings or as small figurines they can be regarded as human beings acting in rituals. The possibility should not be excluded, however, that gods were on their way to appear in the Late Bronze Age, in the Nordic period V, around 800 BC, not as a Parnassus of gods, but in the shape of one single deity, the sun god, though of a twin-nature.

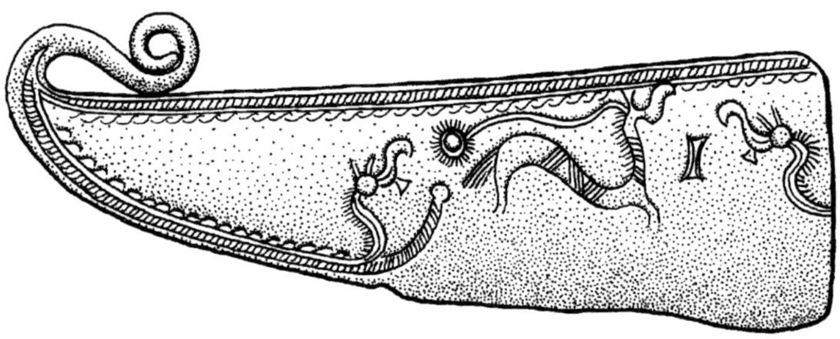

Fig. 14.11 (top) Razor from Neder Hvolris, Northern Jutland, Denmark, c *900 BC. The sun-horse is pulling the sun to the right just in front of the stem of a ship sailing to the right. The ship has a highly raised keel-extension and a stem with a horse head. The ship is folded, and the other stem is seen right. Drawing: Bjørn Skaarup.*

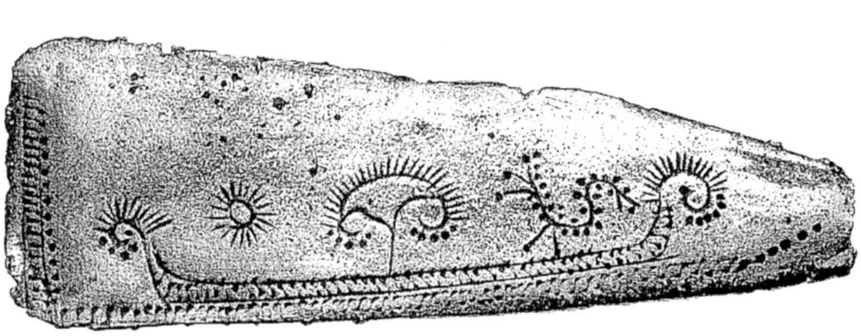

Fig. 14.12 (middle) Razor from Vandling, Southern Jutland, Denmark, c *900 BC. The sun-horse seems to be landing on the ship, where the sun is seen to the left of the fan-shaped symbol. The slightly raised keel extension to the right indicates the direction of sailing. Photo: National Museum of Denmark.*

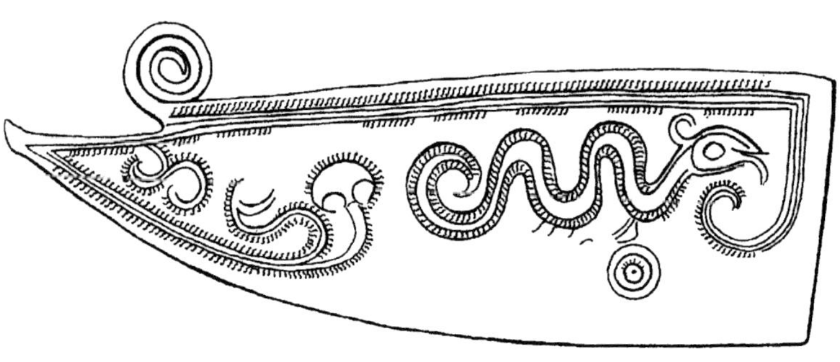

Fig. 14.13 (bottom) Reconstruction drawing of a razor from Knuthenborg, Lolland, Denmark, c *800 BC. A large snake is seen together with the sun in front of a ship with highly raised keel extension and a horse headed stem. The keel extension carries the fan-shaped symbol. Drawing: Bjørn Skaarup.*

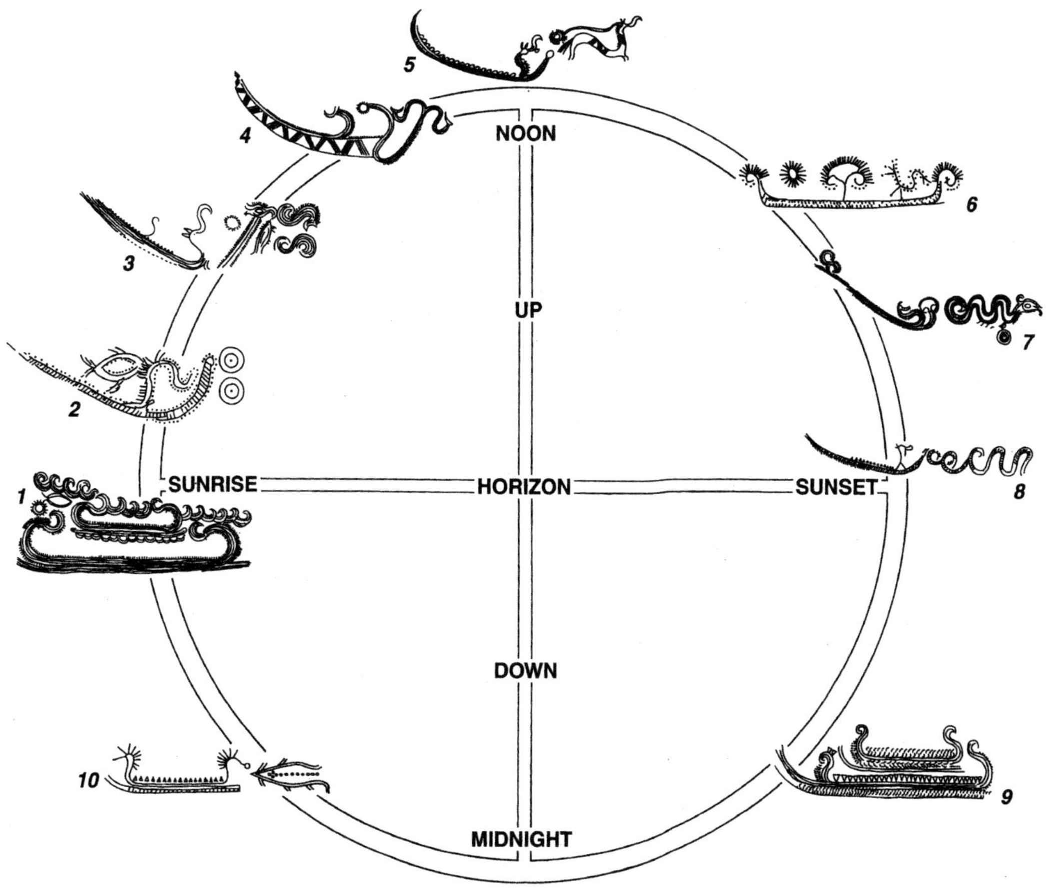

Fig. 14.14 Motifs from Danish razors, Late Bronze Age, 1100-700 BC, showing different points of the cyclical movement of the sun, here being placed in relation to a wheel-cross figure. 1: Sunrise. The fish pulls the rising sun up from the night-ship to the morning ship. 2: For a while, the fish was allowed to sail on with the ship. 3: The fish is to be devoured by a bird of prey. Stylized sun-horses (S-figures) are ready to fetch the sun. 4: Two sun-horses are about to pull the sun from the ship. 5: At noon the sun-horse has collected the sun from the ship. 6: In the afternoon the sun-horse lands with the sun on the sun-ship. 7: Some time after the sun-horse has landed, the sun is taken over by the snake from the afternoon-ship. 8: The snake is concealing the sun in its spiral curls. It will soon lead the sun down under the horizon. 9: Two night-ships sailing towards left. The sun is not visible, extinguished and dark on its voyage through the underworld. 10: A night ship followed by a fish swimming to the left. The fish is ready to fulfil its task at sunrise. The wheel has come full circle. Drawing after Kaul 1999.

Renderings of human-like figures on bronze objects are extremely rare. The most illustrative example of human-like creatures is seen on a razor from Southern Jutland. Here two men are apparently paddling the ship. Their heads are probably the sun, a twin day-and-a-night version (diuscuri) – they are paddling the sun-ship.

The ship did not alone play an important role in the transempirical facies of religion, where it is particularly the motifs on bronze objects that show us the mythological aspect, and where the ship had an important role. From the Nordic Bronze Age other phenomena of religion are also well represented. The active part of religion, the rituals, are depicted on rock carvings, where cult objects such as lurs and cult axes are shown in use, often onboard ships, where rituals were performed. Pictorial evidence of the rituals are particularly well represented in the West Swedish region of Bohuslän. In some cases we see cult axe-bearers on board ships. They may appear with persons who kneel in a praying position as well as with lur-blowers. Sometimes these performers of the cult are carrying horned helmets. In a rock-carving at Sotetorp near Tanumshede in Northern Bohuslän one can see cult axe bearers both fore and aft on some ships. Between the axe-bearers one sees the crew. Just above the ships one see one or more persons almost flying in a strange posture with bent backs (Fig 14.15). They are people who performed acrobatic dances on the ships as part of the rituals. Bronze figurines from Grevensvænge in South Zealand, Denmark, show similar rituals, with cult-axe bearers with horned helmets and acrobats (Gelling and Davidson 1969, 49; Kaul 2001). On the Grevensvænge figurines the costumes can be seen; in this case the female acrobats are 'topless', wearing only a corded skirt (Fig 14.16). Other rock carvings demonstrate that men could also perform such dances of acrobatic or gymnastic kind. Perhaps these acrobatics on or at ships could be seen as counterparts to the ritual acrobatics of Minoan Crete, here involving bulls instead of ships (Bengtsson 2001). One Bohuslän rock carving, however, shows such acrobatics involving a bull (Wanke 1997). Many other kinds of ritual dance postures are known from the vast rock carving material, as for instance on a stone from Engelstrup, Northern Zealand, Denmark (Fig 14.17).

The Nordic Bronze Age rock carvings have

Fig. 14.15 (above) Rock carvings from Sotetorp, Bohuslän, Western Sweden, showing cult axe bearers and persons performing an acrobatic dance, Tracing after Gelling and Davidson 1969, photo after Almgren 1963.

Fig. 14.16 (right) Figurine of 'topless' dancer in a 'bridge' or similar acrobatic posture or movement from Grevensvænge, Southern Zealand, Denmark. Photo: Danish National Museum.

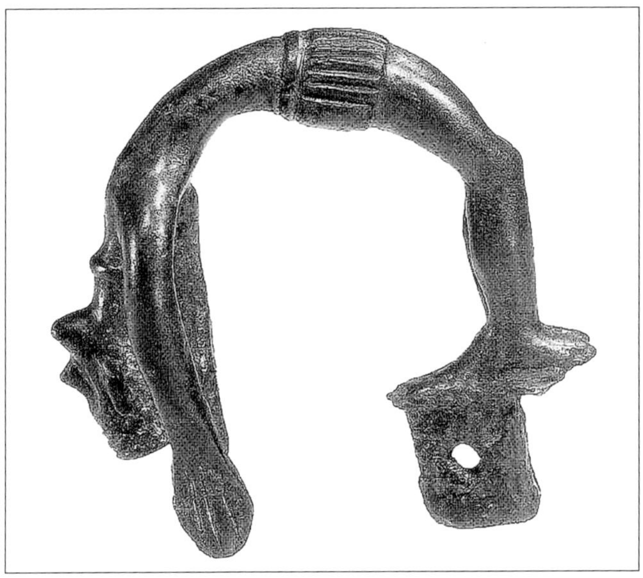

yielded a number of depictions of circular images – including the wheel-cross – on a pole or pedestal, sometimes carried by a person, sometimes placed on a ship (Fig 14.18). Such renderings on the rocks demonstrate that the ship was also used as a platform for carrying solar images and ceremonial devices in the rituals of the Bronze Age.

Thus, the ship of the Bronze Age also had a role as a transportable platform for rituals and ceremonial devices, the ship as symbol itself being sacred, related to basic cosmological myths. That the ship in this way served as both 'temple' and as a vehicle of this, seems to be rather practical, when considering the possibilities of Nordic Bronze Age rituals in some cases being carried out as larger 'festival-like' events, where people met from near and far, and where the sea and waterways were important connecting factors.

In the 'practical' or 'secular' sphere the ship could be the symbol of contacts and access to bronze in the cultic world – the ritual reality – ships could be moving platforms for performing rituals with lurs and cult axes (as seen on rock carvings), and in the divine or heavenly world the ship could be the transport or helper of the sun in its daily and nocturnal voyage (as seen on the razors). In other words, the ship became the paramount symbol of everything powerful, and an important vehicle in all spheres.

In the Late Bronze Age, we find an iconography

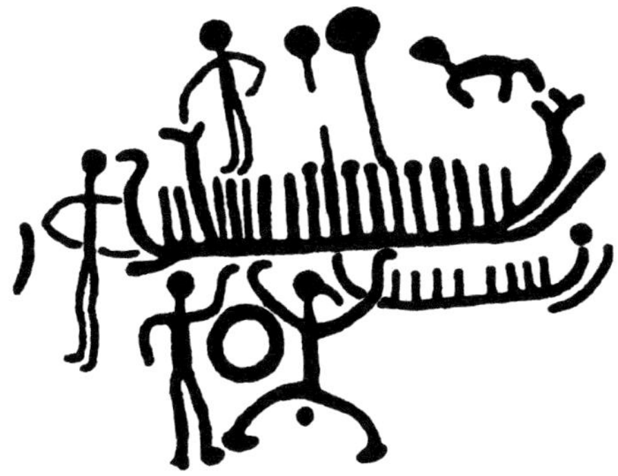

Fig. 14.17 (far left) Rock carving from Engelstrup, Northern Zealand, Denmark, showing a female and a male in a ritual dance, related to the sun and ships. One of the ships carry two circular figures on a stand or pedestal, probably images of the sun or images of the sun and the moon. Photo/graphic: Kaul/Milstreu.

Fig. 14.18 (left) Rock carving from Egely, Bornholm, Denmark, depicting a ship carrying two sun images or wheel crosses on a stand, Late Bronze Age. Photo/graphic: Kaul/Milstreu.

of Central and Southern Europe that also involves the ship. What is of import here is that the ship renderings are not as detailed as the Nordic ones. The most important animal related to the sun is the aquatic bird, the Central-European sun-animal or manifestation of the sun. The aquatic bird (being a diving duck or swan) could be envisaged as a 'combi-animal' that can follow the sun in all spheres of its cyclical voyage. It can follow the sun in the underworld during night (the neck of the swan); it can control the surface of the earth, the horizon and thereby sunrise and sunset, and it masters the heavens when the sun has reached its highest position at mid-day. The many qualities of the aquatic bird might be the reason for the Central European iconography being more simple. The aquatic bird could work in every sphere. As the horse and the ship mingled together into the horse-headed ship in the North, the aquatic bird and the ship grew together in the Urnfield Culture, creating the ship with stems in the shape of an aquatic bird. As an influence from the Urnfield culture, in the Late Bronze Age of the North we find some examples of ships with stems in the shape of aquatic birds. In many cases huge solar images are seen on the Central European sun ships, and these have given its name in German, *Vogel-Sonnenbarken* – bird-sunship). The bird-sunships do not mark any sailing direction; they are symmetrical, so it is not possible here to 'break the code' by means of analysing the sailing direction. All in all the bird-ship iconography of central Europe seems to be more simple or simplified, but of course we can not know whether the cosmological beliefs similarly were simpler than in the North. At any rate, the bird-sunship and the iconography of the aquatic bird tell us, that over wide European regions – as in the North – and as in Egypt – the basics of religion and cosmology was related to the transport of the sun on a ship, and that we have an important animal that could be seen as the helper of the sun or as a manifestation of the divine power of the sun. The bird-sun-ship also found its way further south into the Mediterranean and Balkan, where this divine ship is found in Northern and Central Italy, and also in Greece. It is still a matter of discussion where the amalgamation of the aquatic bird and the ship took place, the Mediterranean or in Central Europe. Anyway, the very emblemic form of the bird-sun-ship should not exclude the Hungarian area as a centre of iconographic development, but perhaps we should accept some feedback processes to Central Europe and the Mediterranean. In very few cases the ships of Northern Italy can carry horse-headed stems, and in this area we also find some rare evidence of the sun horse. That the ship with aquatic birds on the stems was not solely something of the supernatural world is documented by the reliefs of Rameses III's temple at Medinet Habu, where we see such ships in use as warships in the battle at the Nile Delta, here as an enemy to the forces of Egypt, the ships of the Sea people (Wachsmann 1998, 29–32).

The end of the ship iconography of the Nordic Bronze Age: Changes of the religious, political, and social role of values of the ship

The employment of the ship iconography on bronzes terminates at the end of the Nordic Bronze Age, *c.* 500 BC. The ships on bronzes demonstrate that the shapes of the ships of period V (*c.* 800 BC) continue into the last period, period VI (*c.* 700–500 BC), though a simplification of the ship design occurs. But on a few rock carvings, mostly in Bohuslän, Western Sweden (for instance the Litsleby site; Bengtsson 1998; Kaul 1998, 104–105), in Stjørdalen, North Trøndelag, Norway (Sognnes 1993; 1999) and on the island of Bornholm, Denmark are some ship representations which display features of the shaping of the stems and the hull that fall outside the typological developmental series indicated in Fig 14.3; ship representations which can not be paralleled with the well dated ship images on Bronze Age bronzes. These ships display special characteristics: they are symmetrical, the hull being slightly curved, the keel extension and the stem (being the extension of the gunwale line)

Fig. 14.19 Examples of symmetrical rock carving ships, attributed to the Early Pre-Roman Iron Age. From top to bottom: A ship from Bjørngård, North Trøndelag, Norway, two ships from Hammer near Steinkjer, North Trøndelag, Norway, Two ships form Varlös, Northern Bohuslän, Sweden, a number of ships from Askum Parish, Central Bohuslän, Sweden, and lowermost a ship from Hammersholm, Bornholm, Denmark. After Sognnes 1999, Gjesing 1936, Milstreu and Prøhl 1999, Bengtsson 1998: photo/graphic Kaul/Milstreu.

running almost parallel with each other and the keel extension is only slightly raised. It seems possible on the basis of the ship typology that these rarely occurring rock carving ships probably belong to the time after the Bronze Age (Kaul 2002). In some cases these ships carry steering oars (Fig 14.19).

The standard Late Bronze Age ship is marked by raised stems, often ending in an animal head. The keel extension fore is highly raised, sometimes almost horizontally raised, while the keel extension aft continues the keel line as a very short, horizontal or slightly downward turned excrescence. It is seen on Late Bronze Age ships on bronzes as well as on the rocks, when the rendering is sufficiently detailed. A horizontal projection of the keel line aft was a common feature through the whole of the Bronze Age. Summing up, the typical Bronze Age ship was asymmetrical, mostly with a raised keel extension fore, it had highly raised stems fore and aft, a horizontal 'dip keel like' stabiliser aft and no steering oar.

In the Early Pre-Roman Iron Age the animal head adornments disappeared, and the gunwale line and the keel line continued into parallel protrusions. The horizontal projection aft also disappeared, and steering oars took the place of this 'stabiliser'. Now the ship was truly symmetrical, and this symmetrical design could be interpreted as designed to a more martial role of the ship, where it was more necessary to leave the shore within seconds, or being in a river, to turn the whole ship, which is not possible with the asymmetrical Bronze Age ship, where the stabiliser could stick into stones or sea vegetation at the shore (Kaul 2002). This Early Pre-Roman Iron Age type of ship is of exactly that type or profile-shape which is found at Hjortspring together with the first of the larger weapon sacrifices, thus underlining the martial character of this type of ship (Figs 14.20–21).

These last rock carvings from Pre-Roman Iron Age with ships (and also showing armed horsemen in combat-like situations) seem to have lost parts of their religious character, with armed horsemen instead of religious ceremonies. As with the ship, the horse as a symbol seems to have lost aspects of its religious character. The ship and the horse were in the Bronze Age the most important religious symbols, both being intimately related to myths of the voyage of the sun, but here in the Early Pre-Roman Iron Age they both became somewhat 'secularised', apparently being (partly) moved from the sphere of religion into the sphere of warfare. Both motifs were brought from a heavenly sphere down to the ground, closer to man and the earthly world. With the 'secularisation' of these remaining rock carvings motifs from limited areas, the great old rock carving tradition of Scandinavia, covering more than 1000 years, was brought to an end during the Pre-Roman Iron Age.

At around 500 BC the ship iconography of the North came to an end; the venerable religious system seems somehow to have collapsed, followed by social and economical changes. The Early Iron Age boat or ship with its turning abilities and particularly its new symmetrical design enabling it to pull out of narrow waters and rivers without turning – to leave a beach quickly when mission was to be aborted immediately – seems to demonstrate that the basics of the design of this type of vessel was that of a warship. It is this type of ship that was found in the Hjortspring find, *c.* 350 BC, the first large weapon sacrifice of the North (Rosenberg 1937).

I shall not here suggest that Bronze Age ships could not have been used in warfare, but the differences between Bronze Age ships and Early Iron Age ships seem to underline that in the Early Iron Age choices in ship building and design (as regards the performance of the ships) related to warfare. This change in the use of the ship seems to mirror important changes in society. The time around and just prior to 500 BC represents an essential turning point for NW-Europe, Denmark and Southern and Central Scandinavia. The change or loss of iconography could suggest a change in religion. Also the settlement pattern changed, and the first true villages with a cluster of small farms appeared. Other values came into consideration; signs of status and of wealth changed, probably from the possession, use (and deposition) of cult objects into more 'profane' possessions. A social system, including the employment of cultic objects such as cult-axes, lurs and drinking vessels, as well as the related iconography, must have perished, and a different social structure would seem to have developed. A collapse, disruption or readjustment of the traditional (bronze) exchange network system in the period from *c.* 700 to 400 BC, which involved Western Atlantic Europe, Denmark, Scandinavia, Northern Germany and Poland, should also be taken into consideration (Cunliffe 2002, 293; Jensen 1988, 335; 1997, 200–203; Kaul 1998, 111). The performance of religion and the acquirement of objects for cultic purposes seems to have lost its overwhelming importance and a more 'material' approach in the set up of the ideology of the Early Pre-Roman Iron age could be proposed. It has been suggested that the economy of the Late Nordic Bronze Age was dominated by moveable wealth such as cattle and the exchange of prestige goods including objects related to the performance of religion, while in the Iron Age the economy was to a higher degree directed towards immoveable wealth such as land (Kristiansen 1998, 407; 1999, 185). Furthermore, the control of the access of an important metal (bronze (copper and tin)) was no longer as dependent on mostly peaceful sea and river transport, since the new metal (iron) was widely available locally. Focus of political power probably shifted from the control of exchange to the control of land and its produce. Thus the traditional (Bronze Age) system of legitimisation of power, based on exchange and ritualised rank, could be seen as being substituted by one based on land and the direct control of production and the producers (Kaul 1998, 111–112; Kristiansen 1994, 20).

Of course, this process taking place in the centuries around 500 BC was a gradual process. If we accept that these changes observed in many different aspects of the archaeological source material, such as structure of the farm, settlement patterns, land allotment, burial practises, ritual hoarding (mostly bronze objects, including weapons) and dramatic changes (disappearance) of the iconography do reflect fundamental changes in the structures of society and in the ideological set up of power, then evidence of changes of warfare and maritime warfare should be considered and included. The test trials of the replica of the Hjortspring boat have clarified its abilities as a war ship. Together with an assessment of the pictorial evidence of the ship profiles of Bronze Age ships and Early Iron Age ships respectively a consequential shift can similarly be observed when considering the role of the ship around 500 BC, from being a vehicle of peaceful transport, a divine vehicle of the sun helping or transporting the sun over the heavens in the beliefs of the Bronze Age, and a platform for religious rituals and dances, into being a true and agile warship of the following period.

The Hjortspring find itself, being the oldest large scale weapon sacrifice, evidences larger military units and thus also larger military operations than in the Bronze Age. The changes to be observed around 500 BC also seem to include changes in the concept of warfare and in the organisation of raids and warfare going from smaller units of warriors with swords to larger units of warriors with spears/lances (Randsborg 1995, 156). During the Bronze Age the chiefs of warrior (or priest) aristocracies had to organise trading and religious expeditions and to visit political allies, and secure their protection by warrior retinues. The chiefs would gain control over new 'clients', and part of the warfare was raiding and capturing cattle and perhaps also women or slaves (as suggested by Kristiansen 1999, 184–185).

Fig. 14.20 (top) The profile of the Hjortspring boat. Drawing: Leif Hammelev.

Fig. 14.21 (bottom) Photos of the replica of the Hjortspring boat, Tilia Alsie. *Photo: F. Kaul.*

In particular, cattle raids may be regarded as being a prominent aspect of Bronze Age and tribal warfare (Roymans 1999, 296–299) – cattle raids also being included in mythological, heroic aspects of warfare. When the focus of political power shifted from control of exchange to control of land, true conquering of larger areas including the takeover of the leadership apparatus became possible. In this period of social, religious, economical and military change the role of the ship also shifted. It never regained its former status as the paramount vehicle of everything positive in the religious and political sphere – being the companion of the sun in the heavens, and the vehicle for rituals, contacts, and exchange on the earth. The ship became an effective warship giving evidence of kinds of military operations other than securing passages of connections and cattle raids. A ship was of no use for cattle raids either in Bronze Age or Early Iron Age. The new role of the ship with a performance of a warship tells us about more mobile warfare, where strategies of conquering land and territories could have been employed – the weapon sacrifices of the Roman Iron Age giving its evidence – but the Hjortspring find demonstrates a change many centuries before, where larger armies could meet. The concepts of warfare seem to have changed dramatically around 500 BC, the ship from now on being part of the military history of the Baltic area.

The information given by recent test sailings by a newly built replica of the Hjortspring Boat named *Tilia Alsie*[1] shows us an agile landing craft, which easily can be pulled ashore by its crew of 20 paddlers/warriors (plus two helmsmen and a leader, a captain), and which within seconds – due to its symmetrical shape – can leave the shore. Its maximum speed over a short distance is about 8 knots; its 'economical speed' over longer distances is 4–5 knots (Kaul and Valbjørn 2003). This means that this boat or ship had a daily range of around or a little less than 100km, indicating the possibilities of long distance military operations (a mobile army of naval infantry could arrive at its target area well before any 'intelligence reports' could give warning; albeit the preparations for launching a military expedition force could have revealed plans). Test sailings were also undertaken in open water at winds of gale force, demonstrating that the sudden break out of bad weather was not necessarily crucial for the ship and its crew (Kaul and Valbjørn 2003).

Since it seems reasonable that the Hjortspring Boat and its construction principles reflects an old ship building tradition deeply rooted in the Bronze Age (Kaul and Valbjørn 2003) – a tradition of light sea going plank built vessels – the range and mobility of the Bronze Age ship should be somewhat the same, the most considerably difference being the symmetrical design as opposed to the asymmetrical design. Back in the Bronze Age, the range of such vessels could thus be regarded as similar, and also in this period the mobility of the ship in the Baltic-Scandinavian area was considerable. It is here suggested that during the Bronze Age the primary use of the ship was that of peaceful transport or communication, and one of the uses of the Bronze Age ship, as demonstrated by the rock carvings, seems to have been as a movable platform for rituals, a 'sailing temple'. Perhaps the ships of the Bronze Age were used for transport to larger religious festivals, where people from larger areas could meet and communicate notions as to religion and iconography, performing rituals, processions and cultic dances. At the end of the Bronze Age, at around 500 BC, the social and religious perceptions of the ship in Bronze Age Northern Europe seem to have changed drastically, and the ship gained other political and military roles. The fascinating topless dancers performing to the mysterious sounds of the bronze lurs while the sun glittered in the ceremonial bronze axes on ships with horse headed stems were replaced by warriors armed with iron weapons demonstrating quite another agenda.

Note

[1] Created by the private trust, *The Guild of the Hjortspring Boat.* The Danish National Museum wishes to thank *The Guild of the Hjortspring Boat* for the excellent cooperation during the fascinating test sailings, where also the present author were allowed onboard being part of its crew of paddlers; Kaul 2002, Valbjørn 2002, Kaul and Valbjørn 2003.

List of references

Almgren, B 1963 *Die Datierung bronzezeitlicher Felszeichnungen in Westschweden,* Uppsala

Althin, C-A 1945 *Studien zu den Bronzezeitlichen Felszeichnungen von Skåne*, Lund

Aner, E and Kersten, K 1976 *Die Funde der älteren Bronzezeit des nordischen Kreises in Dänemark, Schleswig-Holstein und Niedersachsen*, Band II, København/Neumünster

Bengtsson, L (ed) 1998 *Arkeologisk Rapport 4 från Vitlycke Museum, Hällristningar från Askums Socken Bohuslän*, del 2, Tanumshede

Bengtsson, N 2001 Att leva på hoppet, *Adoranten*, Årsskift 2001, Scandinavian Society for Prehistoric Art, Underslös, 84–95

Burenhult, G 1973 *The Rock Carvings of Götaland, Part II*, Acta Archaeologica Lundensia, Series in quarto, **8**, Lund

Coles, J 2000 *Patterns in a Rocky Land. Rock Carvings in South-West Uppland, Sweden, vol. 1–2*, AUN 27, Uppsala

Cunliffe, B 2001 *Facing the Ocean. The Atlantic and its Peoples 8000 BC–AD 1500*, Oxford

Engedal, Ø 1999 'Døderitual i nordisk bronsealder', *Arkæologiske Skrifter fra Universitetet Bergen*, **10**, Bergen

Gelling, P and Davidson, H E 1969 *The Chariot of the Sun,*

and other rites and symbols of the Nordic Bronze Age, London

Gjesing, G 1936 *Nordenfjelske ristninger og malinger av den arktiske gruppe*, Instituttet for sammenlignende kulturforskning serie B, **30**, Oslo

Gurney, O R 1962 *The Hittites*, (revised Pelican edition), London

Jensen, J 1988 *Gyldendals og Politikens Danmarkshistorie*, Bind 1, redaktion: Olaf Olsen, Copenhagen

Jensen, J 1997 *Fra Bronze- til Jernalder*, Nordiske Fortidsminder, Serie B, Bind 15, Copenhagen

Kaul, F 1998 *Ships on Bronzes. A study in Bronze Age Religion and Iconography*, Publications from the National Museum, Studies in Archaeology and History Vol. 3:1 and 3:2, Nationalmuseet, Copenhagen

Kaul, F 1999 'I Østen stiger solen op', *Skalk*, **5**, Højbjerg, 20–30

Kaul, F 2001 En sjælden kultøkse fra bronzealderen', *Nationalmuseets Arbejdsmark*, Copenhagen, 50–69

Kaul, F 2002 'The oldest war-ship sails again', in A Nørgård Jørgensen, J Pind, L Jørgensen and B Clausen (eds), *Maritime Warfare in Northern Europe, Papers from an International Research Seminar at the Danish National Museum, Copenhagen 3–5 May 2000*, Publications from the National Museum, Studies in Archaeology and History, **6**, Copenhagen, 7–19

Kaul, F and Valbjørn, K V 2003 *The Hjortspring Find. A Pre-Roman Iron Age Warship in Context*, Ships and Boats of the North, **6**, Roskilde

Kaul, F, Nielsen, F O and Nielsen, P O 2002 'Vasegård og Rispebjerg: To indhegnede Bopladser fra yngre stenalder på Bornholm', *Nationalmuseets Arbejdsmark 2002*, Copenhagen, 119–138

Kossack, G 1999 *Religiöses Denken in dinglicher und bildlicher Überlieferung Alteuropas aus der Spätbronze- und frühen Eisenzeit (9.–6. Jahrhundert v. Chr. Geb)*, Bayerische Akademie der Wissenschaften, Philosophisch-Historische Klasse, Abhandlungen, Neue Folge, Heft 116, München

Kristiansen, K 1994 'The emergence of the European World System in the Bronze Age', in K Kristiansen and J Jensen (eds), *Europe in the First Millennium BC*, Sheffield Archaeological Monographs, **6**, Sheffield, 7–30

Kristiansen, K 1998: *Europe before History*, Cambridge: Cambridge University Press

Kristiansen, K 1999 'The emergence of Warrior Aristocracies in Later European Prehistory and their Long-Term History', in J Carman and A Harding (eds), *Ancient Warfare: Archaeological Perspectives*, London, 175–189

Máthé, M Sz 1996 'The 'missing' axe of the Hajdúsámson treasure', *Studien zur Metalindustrie im Karpethenbecken und des benachbarten Regionen, Festschrift für Amália Mozsolics zum 85. Geburtstag*, Herausgegeben von Tibor Kovács, Budapest, 125–128

Meller, H 2002 'Die Himmelscheibe von Nebra', *Archäologie in Sachsen-Anhalt*, **1**, Halle, 7–20

Milstreu, G and Prøhl, H 1999 *Dokumentation och registrering av hällristningar i Tanum*, No. 2 Fossum, Tanumshede

Myhre, B 1981 *Sola og Madla i forhistorisk tid*, AmS-Småtrykk 10, Stavanger

Østmo, E 1990 *Helleristninger av sørskandinaviske former på det indre Østlandet*, Universitetets Oldsaksamlings Skrifter, Ny Rekke, 12, Oslo

Randsborg, K 1985 *Hjortspring. Warfare and Sacrifice in Early Europe*, Aarhus University Press, Århus

Randsborg, K 1993 'Kivik, Archaeology and Iconography', *Acta Archeologica*, **64(1)**, København

Rosenberg, G 1937 *Hjortspringfundet*, Nordiske Fortidsminder, III Bind, 1, Hefte, Copenhagen

Roymans, N 1999 'Man, cattle and the supernatural in the Northwest European plain', in C Fabech and J Ringtved (eds), *Settlement and Landscape, Proceedings of a conference in Århus, Denmark, May 4–7 1998*, Aarhus University Press, Århus, 291–300

Sognnes, K 1993 'The Role of Rock Art in the Bronze Age and Early Iron Age in Trøndelag, Norway', *Acta Archaeologica*, **63**, Copenhagen, 157–188

Sognnes, K 1999 *Helleristninger i Stjørdal*, Stjørdal

Solberg, B 1994 'Exchange and the Role of Import to Western Norway in the Late Neolithic and Early Bronze Age', *Norwegian Archaeological Review*, **27**, Oslo, 111–126

Thrane, H., 1963 'Hjulgraven fra Storehøj ved Tobøl i Ribe Amt', *Kuml*, 1962, Århus, 80–112

Valbjørn, K. V 2002 'Reconstruction of the Hjortspring Boat', in A Nørgård Jørgensen, J Pind, L Jørgensen and B Clausen (eds), *Maritime Warfare in Northern Europe, Papers from an International Research Seminar at the Danish National Museum, Copenhagen 3–5 May 2000*, Publications from the National Museum, Studies in Archaeology and History, **6**, Copenhagen, 21–27

Vandkilde, H 1996 *From Stone to Bronze: The metalwork of the Late Neolithic and Earliest Bronze Age in Denmark*, Jutland Archaeological Society Publications, **32**, Århus

Vandkilde, H 2000 'Material Culture and Scandinavian Archaeology: A Review of the Concepts of Form, Function and Context', in D Olausson and H Vandkilde (eds), *Form, Function and Context: Material culture studies in Scandinavian archaeology*, Acta Archaeologica Lundensia, series in 8, 31, Lund, 3–49

Wachsmann, S 1998 *Seagoing Ships and Seamanship in the Bronze Age Levant*, London.

Wanke, L 1997 Die Schiffshebung und die Sprünge über das Boot', *Adoranten*, Årsskrift 1997 för Scandinavian Society for Prehistoric Art, Underslös, 52–61

15. Finding 'new' boats: enhancing our chances in heritage management, a predictive approach

Thijs J Maarleveld

To the memory of Grahame Clark

The Dover Boat certainly ranks among the great discoveries of the twentieth century, even though we cannot be certain that it has as yet generally been recognised as such. For anyone whose perspective is biased by a maritime interest or a maritime outlook, the find is simply enthralling. It contributes to a much wider variability in composite boats than could be inferred from the early finds at Brigg and North Ferriby (McGrail 1987; Wright 1990). For many archaeologists, however, their world of experience is primarily land-based. Their archaeological outlook is qualified accordingly[1]. The Dover boat will probably not make them change their perspective fundamentally. Nevertheless, it forces them to open their eyes to the prospects that maritime technology offers. In fact, a widening of outlook, a shift to include the maritime perspective, the maritime cultural landscape, maritime constraints, maritime vistas and maritime liberty, maritime freedom in archaeological thinking is definitely occurring. A major contribution to this trend comes to the credit of Barry Cunliffe. What a pleasure to read his magnificent 'Facing the Ocean' (Cunliffe 2001). I did so in a very inspiring location as well: on a coastal holiday in North-western Spain, visiting some of the *castros* and other monuments that he integrates in his study. An extra bonus was meeting with Fernando Javier Costas Goberna, who led me and my family through the shrubs to a Bronze Age rock carving representing a boat that he discovered in the early nineties (Fig 15.1). This boat at 'Auga dos Cebros', near Santa María de Oia is the single Bronze Age boat engraving in Atlantic southern Europe to presently counterbalance the rich Scandinavian iconography (Bradley 1997, 209–210; Costas Goberna *et al* 1999).

Despite Cunliffe and Costas Gobierna, however, I would like to dedicate this contribution to the memory of Grahame Clark. The reason is not that Clark wrote on 'Water in Prehistory' (Clark 1944); however useful, that contribution deals with the management of water as a scarce resource rather than with its nautical uses. In fact Clark was not necessarily oriented towards the sea, but at least he did not exclude it from his thinking (e.g. Clark 1936, 1992, 14–39). The reason for acknowledgement is that very early on Clark realised that for recovering truly innovative archaeological information we have far better chances in waterlogged conditions than elsewhere. This line of thinking is crucial to my present contribution. Clark was at the basis of the 'Wetland Revolution in Prehistory' to use Bryony Coles's phrase (Coles 1992).

Clark inspired my teacher, professor Modderman in using geology, geo-archaeology as a tool to evaluate in what 'niches' archaeological sites might have formed and might have been preserved. He used them to get to grips with the riverine and delta area of the Netherlands, which at the time was *terra incognita* from an archaeological perspective: no finds, no recognised 'archaeological values'. The present situation with regard to underwater areas is more or less comparable to that. Modderman's assessments of the nineteen-fifties are of needs crude, but basically they are still valid today (Modderman 1955). That is to say, they are still valid for the questions they address. Modderman has a slight maritime bias himself – having excavated a medieval cog in 1942 (Modderman 1945) – but was nevertheless primarily concerned with identifying prehistoric settlement areas and settlement sites. Such, indeed was the main concern of archaeology at the time and long after. Water transport was not as yet a seriously considered matter in archaeological heritage management. This is gradually improving, although the process is slow. The entropy of set traditions in research as well as in the allotment of significance is definitely responsible[2]. In the Netherlands from the early eighties onwards it has been my commission to extend archaeological

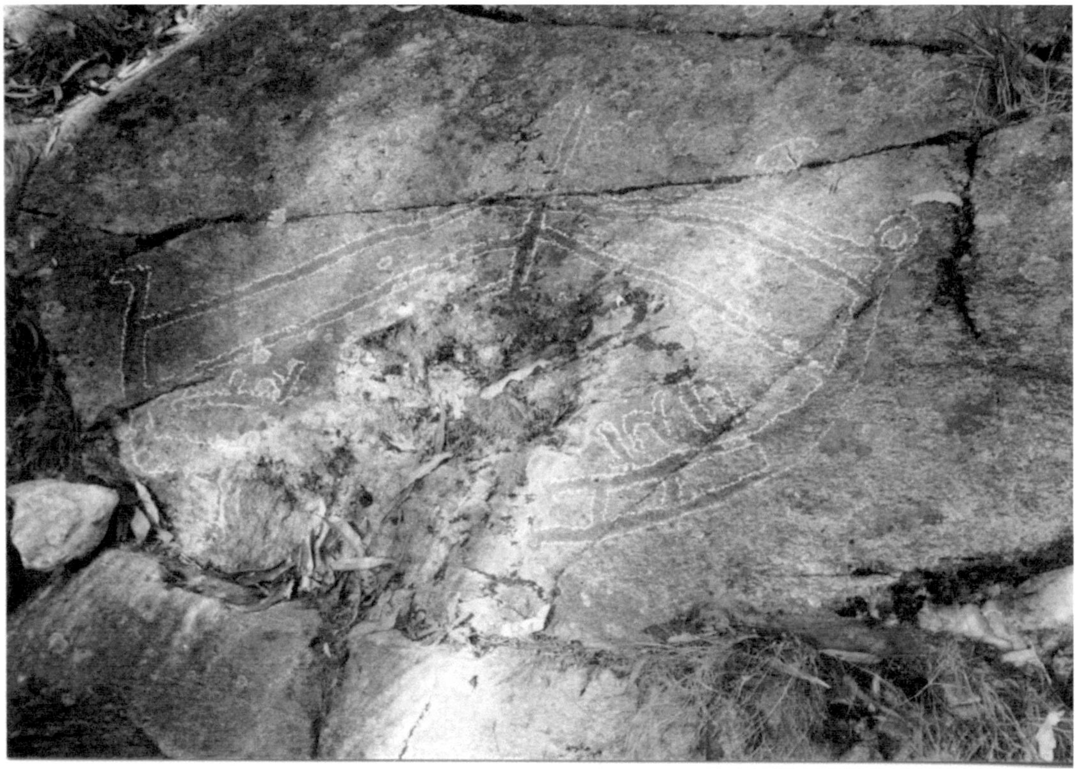

Fig. 15.1 Bronze Age rock engraving at 'Auga dos Cebros', near Santa María de Oia in Galicia, Spain. The engraving was discovered in the early nineties by Fernando Javier Costas Goberna, who published the find in Galician. It is the single Bronze Age boat engraving in Atlantic southern Europe to presently counterbalance the rich Scandinavian iconography.

heritage management one step further seawards: to embrace the maritime perspective and to develop archaeology under Dutch waters (Maarleveld 1998.). In doing so, I owe much to Grahame Clark's initial inspiration to which I had been exposed through my teachers. To bring the underwater world in the domain of archaeology means to bring the 'Wetland Revolution' to extremes.

A predictive approach?

Grahame Clark's realisation that we have far better chances for recovering truly innovative archaeological information in some conditions than in others is a relevant proposition. It is relevant to take into consideration when assessing the discovery of the Dover boat in a broader perspective. It is especially relevant to take into account if we want to enhance our chances of 'finding new boats' in the future. That is the subject on which I was asked to concentrate in my contribution. Is a predictive approach feasible? What kind of predictive models can we develop and take into account? Is predictive modelling a useful tool for the future? That, of course, remains to be seen. We all know how problematic predictions are, especially – as the saying is – if they concern the future. If they concern old boats from a very remote past, that does not make any difference. It is, after all, the future discovery of such ancient boats that we are concerned with. The reason to try and predict is actually to try and better our chances. It is to try and influence chance by serendipity. That we are missing something is quite obvious (Dean 1984; McGrail, this volume). If we want to find ways to miss less, inferences and predictive approaches seem to be ineluctable. The least we want to achieve is to reduce the chances of missing future finds. Influencing the chances and conditions for future discoveries of ancient boats is what counts. It is to that end rather than towards predicting *per se* that our efforts should be geared. From a maritime perspective this can be seen as one of the major challenges of archaeological heritage management. The scattered and disparate nature of our present maritime archaeological information is the more reason to try and combine it in theory, so as to be able to at least meet the challenge in some way. A predictive approach then serves the purpose of reducing our chances of missing something. It is a practical mission.

A predictive map

In The Netherlands as elsewhere, the integration of archaeology in spatial planning has given impetus to the development of a series of tools. One that we developed at the National Service for Archaeological Heritage (ROB) is an indicative, predictive map (Fig 15.2). The overall map has its roots in predictive pre-assessments of the archaeological impact of

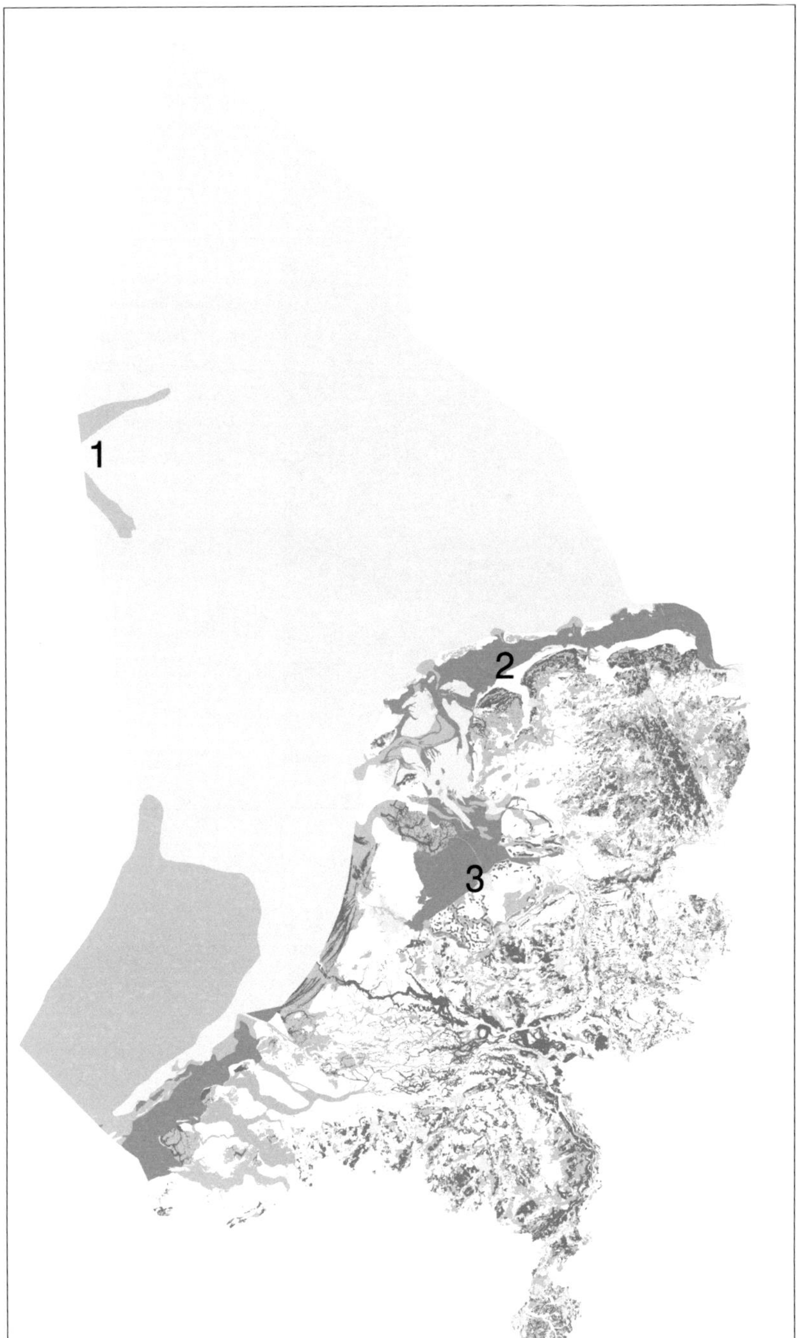

Fig. 15.2 Indicative Map of Archaeological Values (IKAW, 2nd generation). Dark shades represent high potential value. Specific areas mentioned in the text are the subglacial valleys in the Northwest of the Dutch Sector (1), the border between Wadden Sea and former Middelzee (2) and the former Zuiderzee (3).

large-scale planning projects. Under various conditions, various methods and techniques have been utilised. Field-walking, coring, sampling and quantitative extrapolation come to mind. Quantitative analysis on the basis of analogies with find-densities known from previously researched areas is another approach. Analysis of historical geographical information can be helpful, whereas physical geography produces indispensable information for understanding the genesis, development and potential uses of a particular area. Some of these methods and techniques can readily be utilised both inland and under water, both for the assessment of occupation floors and maritime remains. Others are more apt for specialised approaches.

The demand for predictive pre-assessments specifically addressing maritime environments has been felt since the early nineteen-eighties (Maarleveld 1989). In consequence a few pilot-studies have been carried through (Afdeling Archeologie Onder water 1995; Maarleveld 1986). The experience and testing of such 'pre'- assessments in practice gave rise to a crude consolidation at a more general level (Maarleveld 1995). Simultaneously, a first effort at producing an indicative, predictive map concentrating on terrestrial information and settlement archaeology was undertaken (Deeben *et al* 1997). Recently, along with quite a few other improvements the two approaches have been integrated. The 'second generation' of the map was prepared. As it stands now the indicative map of archaeological values (IKAW) encompasses both land surfaces and the maritime zones, up to the border of the Dutch sector of the continental shelf (Deeben *et al* 2002). The map, of course, is nothing more and nothing less than a tool, and indicative at that. It integrates present perceptions and insights, but needs constant critical scrutiny. It will need refinement at a more detailed scale for any specific project-area for envisaged developments. It will need updating whenever our understanding evolves. An improve-ment towards a 'third generation' is already under way.

I will try and explain some of the reasoning behind the map, insofar as it relates to the 'finding of new boats'. This reasoning includes basic assumptions and modelling. I will not refrain from stressing both assets and weak points. That we are missing something is quite obvious. No predictive map will ever guarantee that we will not be missing important finds in the future.

Significance and Awareness

That we have been missing something may be obvious, in a way it is also unavoidable. The biases of our outlook, the scope of our various outlooks guarantee that we miss time and again what we are not looking for, in the past as in the future. This is not a trivial factor at all when we consider the coastal and underwater expanses of the globe and not trivial either when we consider prehistoric boats in such environments. Hardly anyone has ever been looking for them. It is definitely to the credit of the person who at lunchtime of the 28th of September 1992 noticed some odd pieces of wood in a deep contractor's pit and to the credit of the Canterbury Archaeological Trust team that we do have a Dover Boat at all. The odds were not favourable. Another person might not have seen the significance.

Another team might not have been aware of the – possible – implications. We might well have missed it altogether. From a probabilistic point of view we may infer that on many similar occasions we have indeed collectively missed the boat. Undoubtedly many have been removed and destroyed unnoticed.

No use crying over spilt boats, however. In a maritime society some will inevitably be spilt. The challenge is to reduce the chances. It is a challenge for us all, but especially for the curator with a remit to make sure that adequate mitigation is being negotiated for the inevitable loss of archaeological deposits in development and planning. The challenge is to increase the probability that the possible discovery of such remains is taken into account and to increase the probability that such remains are then indeed discovered and recognized for what they are. Consciousness is the first step. We can be certain to miss everything when nobody is consciously paying attention.

Processes and transforms

What happens upon disclosure is a process we can consciously influence. In order to do so it is essential to dispose of theories informing our approach. It is therefore useful to try and analyze what the mechanics of loss and deposition are, what environmental factors cause immediate or gradual decay and what sedimentary 'niches' may have warranted optimal preservation. To do so means pushing Clark's and Modderman's approach ahead; bringing that approach to include deep sedimentation and the underwater world on the one hand and the maritime uses of land- and seascape on the other. In a general sense this is extremely straightforward. There is a good body of theoretical work and many regional or local archaeological curators are used to translating prior information into predictive models and maps in order to influence future planning processes in the best possible way. Looking closer, such an approach means quite a bit more. Much of the archaeological theory developed at present, such as for instance Schiffer's influential 'Formation Processes of the Archaeological Record' (Schiffer 1987), is useful for the purpose, but only as a starting point. Such work does not specifically address marine geological or oceanographical information. Where its approach is behavioural – a strong point in Schiffer – it is not nautical or maritime behaviour that is being addressed.

To pursue a predictive approach for the maritime archaeological record consequently means marrying traditional and new approaches and trying to find a workable balance in adopting, adapting and developing models and in collecting and interpreting relevant data as an input and feedback. There are, however, two good reasons to do so. One is purely scientific and epistemological. It is the justified wish to know what happened and the justified wish to understand what factors, behavioural and otherwise, have filtered and influenced the material evidence that we as archaeologists can study. In other words: to understand the relationship between what was, what we are able to observe and what we can effectively infer on the basis thereof. The second reason is the fact that archaeology, rescue archaeology and archaeological mitigation have not only become an acceptable pastime for learned and specialized interest groups, but have been accepted as a must in present-day society, an anchoring point that cannot be skipped in spatial planning. This latter factor puts us archaeologists under a range of obligations. One obligation, for instance, is to clearly assess which areas are to be considered archaeologically important and which are less so. Where, in other words, an activity like aggregate extraction will create limited damage to archaeological values and where extensive research is to be – or can reasonably be – negotiated as a useful and acceptable measure of mitigation. Even if not an exalted scientific purpose in itself, this second reason certainly aims at the optimisation of pre-eminently scientific results.

Balancing of interests is the basis of such negotiation. As in all negotiation, asking too much is counterproductive in the end, and so is asking too little. If we want to convince and commit others, we have to accept that we often have to judge alternatives even before we can start to collect adequate information in the area concerned. Nevertheless, even if imperfect, we can refer to prior knowledge. We can start to model probabilities and that will help us to develop our intuition or expertise. It will give our prior judgements some sort of basis and some sort of controllable credibility. We will still make mistakes. We will still miss and spill boats, but we may improve our models by discussions and the feedback of new and ever more detailed information.

In practice we evidently need models and theory at three levels:

what happened originally,
what happened in the meantime,
what happens upon discovery.

Nautical Uniformitarianism

With regard to the first question, 'what happened originally', a lot of maritime information, maritime rules of thumb and maritime human behaviour that traditionally escaped land-based curators and archaeologists, can be taken into account. Muckelroy, McGrail, Irwin and others have indicated this since the nineteen-seventies (e.g. Irwin 1992; McGrail 1993; Muckelroy 1978). The approach to translate common sense and seamanlike behaviour into the past is something we can call Nautical Uniformitarianism (Deeben *et al* 2002, 28). It is the proposition that a mariner's interaction with environmental factors like tides and winds may be variable according to his experience and according to the size and propulsion of his craft, but will essentially be the same, regardless of his position in time or culture. Of course there is bound to have been cultural preferences and differences. Nevertheless, 'Nautical Uniformitarianism' is probably the best approach to predictive assessment at this level. Risk management and curative behaviour are unifying trends in all traditions of seamanship and the risks themselves have always been the same.

In day to day heritage management this first level of thinking may not prove to be the most discriminating one. In the Netherlands I experienced that the second level of analysis – preservation in the meantime – simply overrules it. Likewise, this probably applies in many other regions. It is mainly for that reason that our approach can be seen as some sort of continuation of Clark's and Modderman's work. A major difference, of course, is that we do not now concentrate on habitable space, but include navigable space in our analysis.

Where navigable space occurred, it will have been used ever since a more sedentary way of life made investment in complex vessels feasible and attractive[3]. And we are in luck as it is the human fate that anything that can go wrong will go wrong and that anything that can submerge will submerge (Deeben *et al* 2002, 27)

Potential Preservation

The second question, 'what happened in the meantime?' is at least as important. In order to model and predictively map the present-day potential of finding 'new' ships in Dutch inland, riverine, estuarine, coastal and marine sediments we have even chosen to make 'preservation in the meantime' the dominant level. The choice is informed by the specific circumstances of the Netherlands: a subsiding subsoil and a rising sea level offset by rapid sedimentation. It is a choice for quality rather than quantity, and I am fully aware that for the Neolithic or Bronze Age we would all be very happy with a quantity of bad quality finds. On the other hand the major challenge is perhaps to try not to miss the really good quality ones. Anyway, in devising a general strategy in The Netherlands we made the quality aspect leading in our approach to management and mitigation. Such a general approach is never to be taken as gospel. Nor is it meant to be. It is always missing out on exceptions. Nevertheless it is useful to develop some idea of where 'the greatest density of high quality' might be present.

As a consequence, what we are trying to express in maps is those areas where ships may have entered the sediment as integrally as possible and where subsequent environmental influences have been such that – if they have – they have been optimally preserved. In practice this means one of the following two environments and processes:

- silted, but relatively deep gullies that have originally been dynamic enough to adjust their course and scouring on sinking of a ship, thereby ridding and covering the wreck that is blocking the flow;
- sheltered bodies of water with a relatively soft, sheltered bedding, in which foundered (or laid up) ships have sunken in.

This again is a generalization for the Dutch situation, where we are literally dealing with an 'embarrassment of riches', an embarrassment of well-preserved wreck-finds from a variety of periods. The phrase 'entered the sediment' is used on purpose. Under Dutch conditions that seems to be the main preserving factor. The substratum is soft or clastic and never solid. The occurrence of rot and other biological, chemical or biochemical degradation is directly related to the measure of embedding in sediments. A third determining factor, exposure to hydraulic and mechanical energy, is also directly related.

Discovery

'What happens upon discovery' is the third level of consideration. Predictive tools are used to try and improve what happens at that stage. A chance discovery can sometimes be dealt with appropriately, but in any planning process it is preferable that discoveries should be anticipated. Anticipation improves decision-making on the basis of regulations. Anticipation informs responsibilities. The growing social role of heritage and archaeological heritage as its most surprising and debunking factor has been codified in the European Convention on the Protection of Archaeological Heritage [Revised] of 1992, as well as in national and local regulations. Detailed procedures now generally rule what happens, if at least a discovery is recognised as such. Procedures and perceptivity are both a function of anticipation and expectations. Awareness is the key, but little more needs to be said about it in the present context.

The Netherlands example

The above means that the dominant factors in the model can be assessed on the basis of geology and uniformitarian principles. Scale, of course, plays a major role.

On a general scale the quaternary geology of The Netherlands and the Dutch sector of the continental shelf are well-studied and we have been able to analyze the situation and to identify areas of major maritime archaeological importance. The dark shade in the indicative maps corresponds with a high indicative value. In order to cartographically distinguish between land and water different colour sets have been used. These reflect the slightly different methodologies followed for both areas, but have mainly been chosen to keep the map readable. In both sets, however, the dark shade corresponds with a high indicative value. The light shade is assessed as less important...... It should, however be stressed that this does not equate with archaeologically sterile. An expectation of low density of high quality does not mean that none occurs. The high energy zone where stranding has frequently occurred and where finds abound, is nevertheless rated lowly. None of the Dutch beaches are sheltered. A specific flag has been put out for two deep sub-glacial valleys of Weichselian age in the extreme North of the Dutch sector (Fig 15.3). Reaching to depths of around 20 m below the seafloor and presently filled with younger silts, these valleys must truly have been a very protective receptacle for anything submerging at that spot. Other areas with a truly high value are those areas, where filled-in gullies have been preserved under other sediments, for instance convexly built-up ebb-tidal deltas.

At a more detailed scale the information is more equivocal, but it starts to guide choices, for instance regarding the extraction of large quantities of building material for the seaward extension of the port of Rotterdam (Fig 15.4). If we zoom in to the construction area itself the border between a high indicative value and a middle or low one is rather arbitrary. The border is not exactly the western limit of fossilized gully deposits in which shipwrecks can be embedded, which it means to indicate on the basis of previous surveys. Nevertheless it enables us to convince the developing authority to carry through more detailed mapping with shallow acoustics, a process in which 'new' fossilized gullies are discovered and mapped. Feedback from experience shows that the chances of finding 'new' ancient boats occur in pockets just below the erosive interface of migratory filled gullies (Adams *et al* 1990, 150–151). Inshore, information is more detailed, but not necessarily easier to assess. The peat bogs in the east of the country may have produced the Pesse logboat, reputedly the oldest boat in the world, but have to a large extent been cleared and will not preoccupy us from a maritime perspective.

The Wadden Sea proves to be extremely rich, but I will not enlarge on that now, other than pointing out two things. For one, the part of the basin that we know relatively well is the western part and it is of relatively recent date. It is therefore irrelevant for finding 'new' Prehistoric boats. This is different from the eastern bits, where a similar land- and seascape of an earlier period has become well

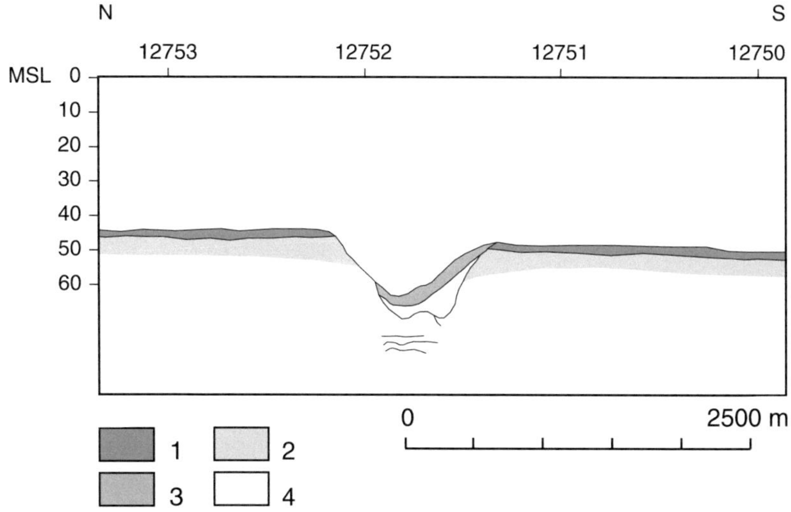

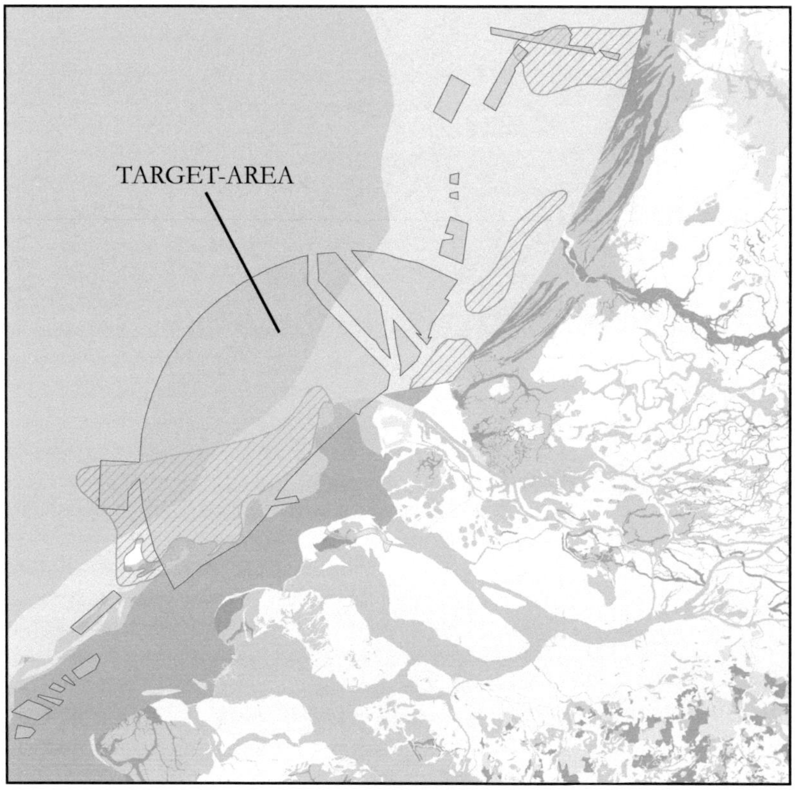

Fig. 15.3 (top) Section of a partly open subglacial valley of Weichselian age in the extreme north of the Dutch sector of the North Sea. Such valleys reach to depths of 20 to 40 meters below the present seafloor. Partly filled with younger silts, such valleys must truly have been a very protective receptacle for anything submerging. After Laban 1995. Legend: 1 Bolders Bank Formation; 2 Dogger Bank Formation; 3 Holocene sediment; 4 Botney Cut Formation.

Fig. 15.4 (bottom) Part of the Indicative Map of Archaeological Values (IKAW, 2nd generation) that is relevant for the seaward port extension of Rotterdam. The semi-circle delineates the target-area for the extraction of 400,000,000 m³ of sand.

Fig. 15.5 Excavation in 1998 of lime wood log boat alongside the late Mesolithic- early Swifterbant site Hardinxveld-Giessendam De Bruin at a depth of 9.35 m below ordnance datum. The boat is 5.59 m long and 0.49 m wide.

embedded in a thick layer of more recent anaerobic sediments. That is an important area indeed. For two, there is a nice methodological bias in predictive modelling, which shows where the maritime approach based on navigable space and preservation is confronted with the terrestrial model in which habitable space and superficial archaeology are predominant. An inland extension of the tidal basin 'the Middelzee' (Fig 15.2) was reclaimed at the end of the Middle Ages. It was settled only afterwards and is considered to be more or less sterile archaeologically on the basis of the terrestrial model and terrestrial information. Deep down, however, it is to be considered as important from a perspective of preservation of old vessels as the other parts of the eastern Wadden Sea, possibly even more so, as it has long been the main entry point to an extended hinterland.

In the western river area, the analysis of the complex geology and archaeology has been refined enormously since Modderman's efforts of the fifties. The Leiden research group of Louwe Kooijmans and the Utrecht physical geography group of Berendsen are to be held responsible (Berendsen and Stouthamer 2001; Louwe Kooijmans 1974; 1985). An indicative approach, combined with detailed survey for the specific mitigation within the framework of the construction of a new cargo railway (the so-called Betuwe-route) has been the occasion for unparalleled excavations. The swamp adjacent to a small island that had been settled in late Mesolithic and early Neolithic times, revealed an inland vessel, a nearly six meter long lime logboat, dated 6310 ± 90 BP (5473–5057 cal BC; 2s; GrN-24395), at a depth of nine metres below datum (Fig 15.5; Louwe Kooijmans 2001). The cofferdam and infrastructure that you see, was put up specifically for the archaeological excavation and not for any other reason. This site, at Hardinxveld, is at some 60 km from the present coast and the further we go westward, the deeper 'new' boats are to be expected to be embedded. A lot remains to be done in the estuarine areas.

An exceptional area on the indicative map is the distal part of the former Zuiderzee (Fig 15.2). It used to be more or less lagoonal. No gullies. Ships in this environment have proved to be well preserved because they sink through the unsettled mud. That

was shown to be the case with subrecent vessels that were located in the deeper part of the reclaimed area adjacent to it (Fig 15.6). However, this area, the present Markermeer, not only belonged to the Zuiderzee. It also belonged to a much earlier, Atlantic, tidal basin that had its inlet on the western shore (Fig 15.7). During the Atlantic the area presented a similar occasion for both transport and shipwreck and similarly ideal circumstances for optimal preservation. In the meantime, unlike the presently reclaimed areas, it has always remained open water, a lake or several lakes, Lake FLEVO probably in Roman times. In other words boats and ships from Neolithic through early medieval times have plied this ideal preserving environment. Combine this with the theorem that anything that can submerge will submerge and it becomes evident that it is an important area indeed.

Conclusion

Cursorily and in summary I have presented you with some aspects of predictive mapping and predictive modelling that we presently explore. Several fossilized 'niches' of high potential have been identified. Inland it is the filled in swamps and river gullies. In the coastal area it is the extensive tidal basins that have intermediately been filled. Such basins have two optimal preservation environments: the dynamic gullies close to the inlets, featuring relatively coarse embedding material and the weak and soft, lagoonal, distal parts. Last, but not least, the gullies that are preserved under the outbuild of present or earlier ebb-tidal delta's constitute an important area of attention. These occur all along the Dutch coast, but are most prominent in the South. They are likely to contain very early wrecks. If a 'Dover boat' be found in such an environment it will be complete with tackle, cargo, lot, stock and barrel.

That remark evidently brings me to the third level of analysis and one of its aims: influencing what happens upon discovery. Development of adequate detecting devices, which will prevent the often destructive process of 'hard detection', is getting more and more attention, but still has a long way to go (e.g. Gregory and Hocker 1999; Kinneging 2002).

In our approach to scale down the challenge, to

Fig. 15.6 Soft lagoonal sediments at the distal part of the former Zuiderzee tidal basin have warranted good preservation. Wrecks have sunk vertically through the soft sediments, like this 16th century fishing vessel at site KZ47 near present-day Almere. On discovery in August 1978 her deck lay just below the surface. Her hull extends below.

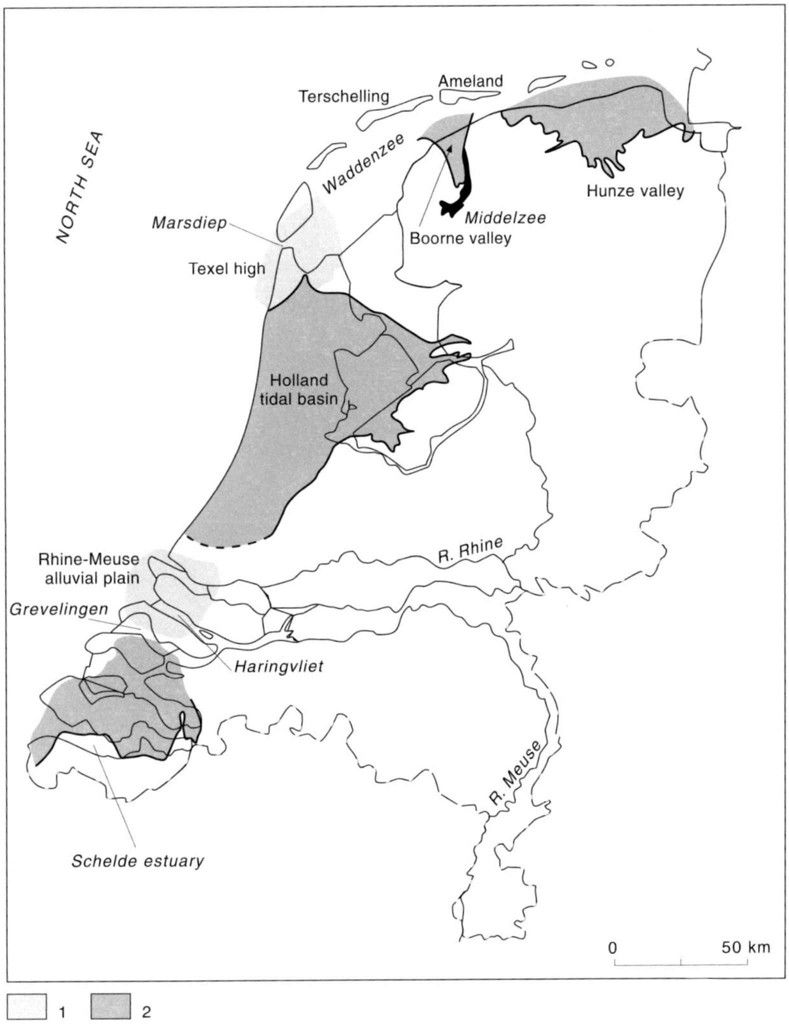

Fig. 15.7 Map showing subsequent tidal basins that are fossilized in the Holocene sediments of the Netherlands. After Van der Spek 1994. Legend: 1 former eroding headlands, seaward extent uncertain; 2 former tidal basins.

make underwater heritage management less of a '*mer à boire*' we have chosen to put preservation conditions first. Will it be enough to meet the challenge of not missing important 'new' ship-finds? That would be too optimistic. The most important asset of predictive mapping so far is that it helps us to formulate priorities and that it helps us to convince others, who are potentially responsible for destruction on how to invest in mitigating the loss of maritime heritage.

Notes

[1] On the general bias of archaeology towards regional, that is non-maritime, history and the bias of salvage inspired underwater research towards consolidation of 'national' metaphors of maritime pride and prowess see Maarleveld 1997; 1998, 37–54; Cederlund 1997.

[2] Cf. note 1; cf. Firth 2002.

[3] The exploitation of marine resources at early habitation sites proves the point. The Mesolithic in Europe is just one example. Pleistocene sites as Klasies River, the Pleistocene occupation of 'Greater' Australia and (parts of) Oceania (e.g. Irwin 1992; Kirch 2000) and even Terra Amata are at least as important; cf. Maarleveld 1994.

List of references

Adams, J, van Holk, A F L and Maarleveld, Th J 1990 *Dredgers and Archaeology, Shipfinds from the Slufter*, Alphen aan den Rijn

Afdeling Archeologie Onder water, 1995 *Vooronderzoek archeologie: rapport van de begeleidingscommissie archeologische aspecten baggerspecie-bergingslocatie Ketelmeergebied*, Alphen aan den Rijn

Berendsen, H J A and Stouthamer, E 2001 *Palaeogeographic development of the Rhine-Meuse delta, the Netherlands*, Assen

Bradley, R 1997 *Rock Art and the Prehistory of Atlantic Europe: Signing the Land*, London/New York

Cederlund, C O 1997 *Nationalism eller vetenskap? Svensk marinarkeologi i ideologisk belysning*, Stockholm

Clark, G 1944 'Water in Antiquity', Antiquity, **69**, 1–15

Clark, G 1992 *Space, time and man: a prehistorian's view*, Cambridge

Clark, J G D 1936 'Early Navigation in North Western Europe', *Proceedings of the Prehistoric Society*, **2**, 146

Coles, B (ed.) 1992 *The Wetland Revolution in Prehistory*, Exeter

Costas Goberna, F J, Hidalgo Cuñarro, J M and de la Peña Santos, A 1999 *Arte Rupestre no sur da Ría de Vigo*, Vigo

Cunliffe, B W 2001 *Facing the Ocean, The Atlantic and its Peoples 8000BC–AD1500*, Oxford

Dean, M 1984 'Evidence for possible prehistoric and Roman wrecks in British waters', *International Journal of Nautical Archaeology*, **13.1**, 78–80

Deeben, J, Hallewas, D P and Maarleveld, Th J 2002 'Predictive modelling in Archaeological Heritage Management of the Netherlands: the Indicative Map of Archaeological Values (2nd Generation)', *Berichten van de Rijksdienst voor het Oudheidkundig Bodemonderzoek (Proceedings of the National Service for Archaeological Heritage in the Netherlands)*, **45**, 9–56

Deeben, J, Hallewas, D P, Kolen, J, and Wiemer, R 1997 'Beyond the cristal ball: predictive modelling as a tool in archaeological heritage management and occupation history', in: W J H Willems, H Kars and D P Hallewas (eds), *Archaeological Heritage Management in the Netherlands, Fifty Years State Service for Archaeological Investigations*, Assen/Amersfoort, 76–118

Firth, A 2002 *Managing Archaeology Underwater. A theoretical, historical and comparative perspective on society and its submerged past,* British Archaeological Reports (International Series), **1055**, Oxford

Gregory, D and Hocker, F 1999 *Marine Archaeological Reconnaissance and Site Mapping using an AUV*, Roskilde

Irwin, G 1992 *The Prehistoric Exploration and Colonisation of the Pacific*, Cambridge

Kinneging, N A 2002 *Innovatief Meten Aan Gezonken Objecten, Rapport informatiestrategie Projectgroep IMAGO*, Lelystad

Kirch, P V 2000 *On the Road of the Winds, An Archaeological History of the Pacific Islands before European Contact*, Berkeley/Los Angeles/London

Laban, C 1995 *The Pleistocene glaciations in the Dutch sector of the North Sea: A synthesis of sedimentary and seismic data*, University of Amsterdam

Louwe Kooijmans, L P (ed) 2001 *Hardinxveld-Giessendam De Bruin een kampplaats uit het Laat-Mesolithicum en het begin van de Swifterbant-cultuur (5500–4450 v. Chr.)*, Amersfoort

Louwe Kooijmans, L P 1974 *The Rhine/Meuse delta, Four Studies on its Prehistoric Occupation and Holocene Geology*, (diss) Leiden

Louwe Kooijmans, L P 1985 *Sporen in het land, de Nederlandse delta in de prehistorie*, Amsterdam

Maarleveld, Th J (ed) 1986 *Vooronderzoek archeologie. Rapport van de werkgroep archeologisch onderzoek in het kader van de voorbereiding/uitvoering van de aanleg van de Grootschalige Locatie voor de berging van baggerspecie uit het Benedenrivierengebied*, Rotterdam

Maarleveld, Th J 1989 'Marine Archaeology and the planning of large-scale sand-extraction. An example from the Netherlands', in G Trotzig and G Vahlne (eds), *Archaeology and Society. Large scale rescue operations – their possibilities and problems*, Stockholm, 247–256

Maarleveld, Th J 1994 'Het ruime sop of wanneer de mens ging varen', *Spiegel Historiael*, **29–7/8**, 277–282

Maarleveld, Th J 1995 'Environmental factors in underwater cultural heritage management. A reflection on the Dutch situation', in O Olsen, J Skamby Madsen and F Rieck (eds), *Shipshape. Essays for Ole Crumlin-Pedersen*, Roskilde, 313–328

Maarleveld, Th J 1997 'Nautical Archaeology in the Netherlands: Developments and Cultural Appraisal', in W J H Willems, H Kars and D P Hallewas (eds), *Archaeological Heritage Management in the Netherlands, Fifty Years State Service for Archaeological Investigations*, Assen/Amersfoort, 35–57

Maarleveld, Th.J., 1998: Archaeological heritage management in Dutch waters: exploratory studies, (diss) Leiden

McGrail, S 1987 *Ancient boats in NW Europe*, London/New York

McGrail, S 1993 'Prehistoric Seafaring in the Channel', in C Scarre and F Healy (eds), *Trade and Exchange in Prehistoric Europe*, Oxford, 199–210

Modderman, P J R 1945 *Over de wording en de beteekenis van het Zuiderzeegebied, dissertatie*, Groningen

Modderman, P J R 1955 'De bewoonbaarheid van het rivierkleigebied in de loop der eeuwen', *Tijdschrift van het Koninklijk Nederlandsch Aardrijkskundig Genootschap*, 31–38

Schiffer, M B 1987 *Formation Processes of the Archaeological Record*, Albuquerque

Spek, A J F van der 1994 *Large-scale evolution of Holocene tidal basins in the Netherlands*, (diss) Utrecht

Wright, E V 1990 *The Ferriby boats, Seacraft of the Bronze Age*, London/New York

16. Facing the sea in Bronze Age Norway: the ship, the sea and society

Frode Kvalø

The Institute of archaeology, art history and conservation at the University of Oslo, and the Norwegian Maritime Museum are planning a joint project concerning the ship, the sea and the society in Bronze Age Norway.

The main objective is to explore the institution of travel by sea and its significance for the societies on land: to ask new questions and find new material. A special point on our agenda is to assess the possibility that the trips themselves had there own intrinsic value in the creation of Bronze Age societies in Southwest Norway.

The title of the project 'Facing the sea in Bronze Age Norway' stresses the point that engaging the sea requires cultural strategies and communal organising – and that inquiries into, and disclosing the content of, these strategies is our objective.

Furthermore, surveying for remains of seagoing ships as well as research on field methods for surveying under water will also be an important part of the project. We need to know more about the complexity in construction and the capacities of the ships to better grasp the cultural processes they were a vital part of. We also want to gain experience in and develop the methods most suitable to identify material from the Bronze Age in Norwegian waters.

This will not only benefit the status of knowledge today or research in the future; it will also be beneficial to the management of cultural heritage and especially rescue archaeology. This is a task that by legislation is delegated to the National Maritime Museum, and results from this project can immediately be implemented in their daily work.

We have a broad scope in this project, but I will focus on the part were we will make a survey for remains of seagoing ships as well as research on field methods for surveying under water in this presentation connected to the Dover Bronze Age boat. We have identified several bodies of water in Lista (southwest Norway) were we believe, based on a host of archaeological, natural and technical data, that an underwater survey has unusually good chances of identifying a Bronze Age boat and other maritime remnants.

Background

The Nordic Bronze Age embraces fascinating stories in the history of sea travel – though stories often overlooked or only implicitly told. Ideas, raw materials and material culture were spread far and wide through the use of seagoing vessels. The institution of travel brought together different local groups and established networks of interaction along the coasts of Scandinavia – and as such is a fundamental condition and premise for the Nordic Bronze Age.

This maritime aspect is a very important component of the Bronze Age communities' engagement with the material world. When the Bronze Age came to a close there had been continuous and often intense contact through nearly two millennia. During this period the ship and the sea had become important elements in social and ideological strategies. The organisational resources of the emerging social elite were to a considerable degree an integrated part of the networks, and the vessel was a striking ideological, economic, political and technological mechanism in this scenario. This maritime aspect raises major issues concerning the emergence of the political economy, and the whole idea of networks and of different kinds of networks.

There has been little research on the maritime aspects of the Nordic Bronze Age. The research has mainly focused on the terrestrial milieu: agriculture, livestock and exchange of prestige objects are portrayed as the foundations of Bronze Age society. One effect is that a transport-economic perspective has dominated interpretations of travel. The travels have become an anonymous by-product of the economic system.

The approach

The American anthropologist Mary Helms has convincingly demonstrated that geographical distance is not just a technological obstacle to overcome. In her book 'Ulysses' Sail: An Ethnographic Odyssey of Power, Knowledge, and

Geographical Distance' (1988) she explores the ideological nature and political significance of geographic distance and long-distance contacts. She bases her studies on data taken from the general ethnographic record.

She argues, among other things, that we should not interpret the activities of travelling in other times and places within 'practical' or 'secular' contexts, as we often do by the almost ritual invocation of very pragmatic terms such as 'trade' and 'exchange' when we describe long-distance activities. Maybe the tale of Odysseus is the archetypical story of a chieftains travels far away in the Bronze Age. Arriving is important, but so are the stories woven around the journey itself.

Against this background it is reasonable to ask the questions, as professor Barbra Bender does in a recent issue of 'Social archaeology' (2001):

What real or fictive kinscapes and clanscapes are crated to ease the journeys?
What song-lines or sacred topographies are woven to embrace the unknown?
What webs of exchange (of people, things, information and ideas) are spun?
And who does the travelling?
Who is left behind?
Who is/are encountered?
Who tells the stories?
Who get to hear the tale?

An important question in our project is: Did travellers in the Bronze Age express their stories in a way that is recognizable in the archaeological record today?

An important premise for the project is that long distance sea travel requires knowledge and skills. The local communities needed trained mariners and shipbuilders to maintain communications in a certain geographical area, on the level of intensity that the archaeological material demonstrates. Only then would they have a reasonable chance of reaching their destination and survive the journey back on a regular basis.

This maritime realisation must have required a local network of social co-operation where the passing on and control of knowledge, tools and techniques were central. This certainly included division of labour and specialisation within different domains of knowledge and skills.

So what were the effects of this on local communities and the way they were organised? The sociologist Michael Mann (1986) says that when collective aims, like long distance travels, are translated into organisational means, networks are created that make social stratification an institutionalised part of social life. This happens because organising and functional partition has an inherent tendency to distribute power, on the basis of control, co-ordination and specialisation.

We would like to explore how the kind of networks made in the planning, organizing and realisation of the journeys coincided with the overall hierarchical network of the communities.

In this project we therefore intend to search for material above and under water in a selected geographical area. Above water we will inquire into the remains of the social, economic and symbolic activities – through systemising the traditional archaeological record.

The Bronze Age communities of what is now Norway were 'saturated' with many aspects orientated towards the sea. This is expressed through burial cairns and mounds with topographical relations to the sea, many also with seashells and other material from the sea in the burial chamber. Indeed, the chamber wall rocks in some graves were decorated with engraved wave patterns. The pattern of settlement, as well as the deposition of prestige objects, show strong ties to water. The study of this record constitutes one line of inquiry in the proposed project.

Another line of inquiry is the search for a specimen of a seagoing ship. Actual seagoing vessels have not yet been recovered or in other ways satisfactorily empirically identified in the archaeological record from the Nordic Bronze Age. Portrayals of large seagoing vessels are presented through ship motifs in rock art and on bronzes, stone ships settings and ship-shaped razors. One has to assume that the ship represented a considerable technical and social achievement within that cultural context. But to further our understanding of the technology of seafaring and of the socio-cultural processes to which the ship belonged we need more specific material and a more comprehensive record.

Project organisation

The Institute of archaeology, art history and conservation at the University of Oslo, and the Norwegian Maritime Museum are cooperating on this project. The university will direct and administrate the project. The maritime museum will contribute with maritime perspectives, its knowledge of survey and excavation methods under water, and will make available equipment for conducting underwater archaeology.

This project will be a part of the archaeological institute's strategic program on 'Man and Landscape'. It will be closely tied to recruiting and educating new researchers in both the fields of Bronze Age and maritime research. It is planned to last 5 years; 2 years of fieldwork, and 3 years of research within PhD scholarships. The duration of the fieldwork may be expanded, depending on the nature and extent of the results from the survey.

The total budget is approximately £800.000. The cost of larger excavations and conservation will be additional. We are counting on the Norwegian

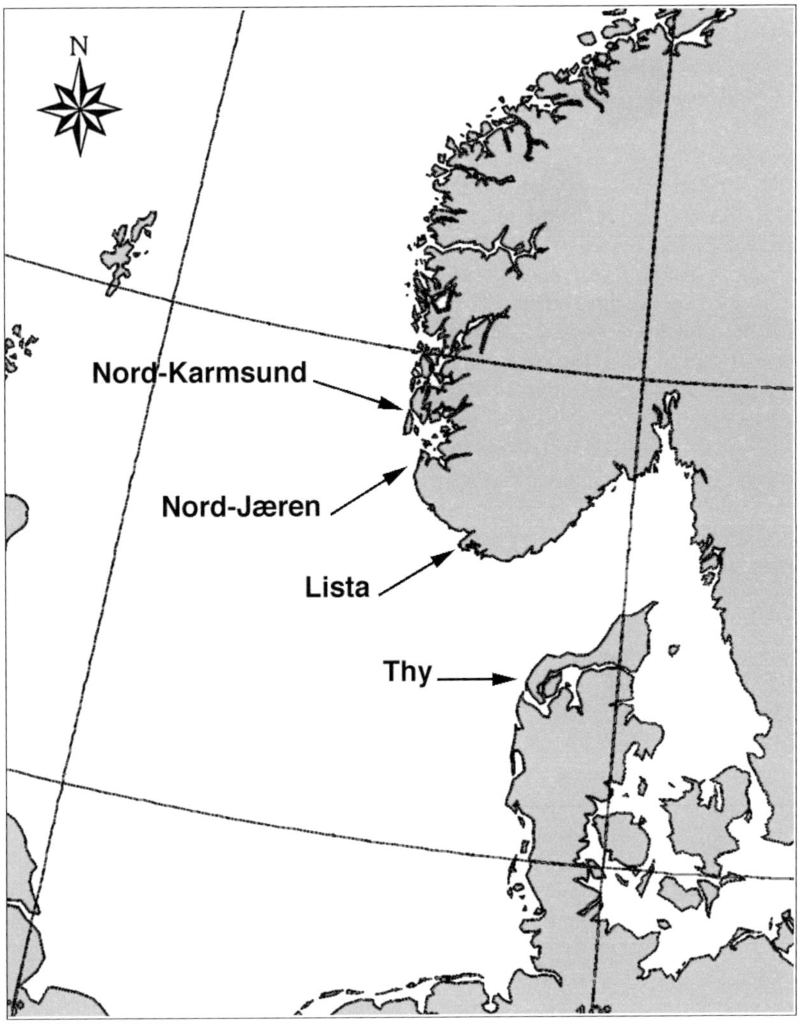

Fig. 16.1 Southwest Norway: The core areas in the Bronze Age.

Research Council to be the largest financial contributor; in 2001 they concluded that the project was worth supporting, but we had to wait for a strategic program with the necessary means. As it looks today the Council may start a suitable program in 2003, which we of course will apply to.

The project leader will be associate professor Christopher Prescott. He will have three months each year for his own research within the project. The main part of the project will be assigned to three PhD - scholarships. These will be open to applicants with their own theoretical perspective within the framework of this project. Those who get the three scholarships will to a large extent be able to define their own perspectives.

The intention is that the PhD dissertations, together with the final project publication, will contribute to the project's main objective by describing new material, generating new interpretation within a broad perspective on long distance travel activities, as well as analysing the possibilities and limitations of the underwater archaeological field methods used.

We have, so far, concluded that we will not make the assignments more concrete and specific. One reason for this is that the underwater survey and, hopefully, the following excavations, have a potential to give surprising results for further research. Another reason is that it might be advantageous for the recruitment of new scientists to allow the attention around the underwater survey stimulate competitive theoretical creativity and development. The scholarships will be advertised during the two years of underwater survey.

In case of a no-find situation at the end of the survey, the evaluation of the field methods and the research on the shore based cultural remains may still yield interesting results. It is also highly probable that the fieldwork will give useful results in regard to cultural remains from other archaeological periods. The geographical area of investigation we have selected has had a considerable degree of cultural activity from the end of the Ice Age up till today.

The geographical area of investigation

We have selected a geographical area of investigation where the archaeological record indicates a high level of activity that is clearly defined as a part of the Nordic Bronze Age culture.

The survey under water in this pilot project necessitates an area where conditions and the potential for finds are optimal. These conditions include an area where there must have been considerable shipping activity in the Bronze Age, and the conditions for preservation must be the best. In addition, the body of water should represent a range of different environmental factors, so that the field methods can be evaluated under a variety of conditions.

Through a systematic analysis of available data we have concluded that all the relevant cultural historical and physical environmental factors are represented in a small geographical area at Lista, in the county of Vest-Agder in Southwest Norway (Fig 16.1).

Southwest Norway: The core areas in the Bronze Age

As early as the end of the 3rd millennium BC, large quantities of flint were transported by ship to southwest Norway from North-Jutland, Denmark. This importation continues into the 2nd millennium BC and throughout the Bronze Age, but encompasses metal objects as well. Rich archaeological material from the Bronze Age has made the literature emphasise Lista as one of three core areas in the southwest.

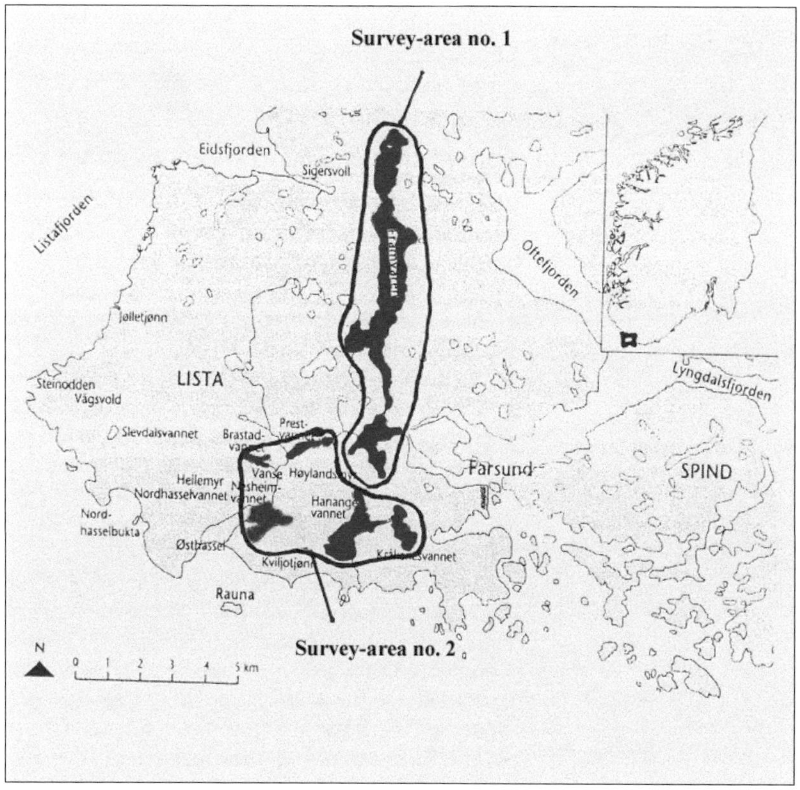

Fig. 16.2 The survey areas.

Lista, and the other two core areas: Jæren and Karmsund, had extensive overseas contacts. The Thy-area in Jutland was an important point of contact in this scenario. The three core areas have many similarities in the archaeological record, but they also differ in many aspects. This makes the Southwest an especially interesting area to study.

An important factor all three areas have in common, a factor stressed in the literature, is the strategic positioning as a crossroad for communication and interaction. This involves overseas travels, travelling along the coast and travels into a system of fjords to the hinterland.

The travels to Jutland are best viewed as expeditions, that is, the ships and crews were planned, organized and equipped to be away from home under difficult conditions for a longer period of time. Along the coast the distance from Karmsund to Jæren is about 40 nm, or 74 km, and from Jæren to Lista about 80 nm, or 148 km. The direct distance overseas from Lista to Jutland is about 100 nautical miles, or 185km.

The fieldwork: Lista-area

When we started to think about this project we did a preliminary analysis of possible travelling routes from the available data relevant to the general sea condition, related to palaeo-environmental studies, prehistoric and historic information on seafaring, the visibility of topographical elements from the seaside, and so on.

On these grounds we have argued that one of the most important voyaging corridors for travel both ways along the coast in the Bronze Age probably followed the system of fjords on the inside of Lista. This argument is corroborated by finds of import on land. The corridor inside of Lista is also connected to a freshwater system in the region of Lista.

This voyaging corridor is well-known from historic times, because the lanes outside of Lista are among the roughest on the Norwegian coast. Even in our time ships are frequently lost in this area.

Survey area 1: The fjords

The fjord gives access to well protected harbour areas close to the central Lista. Framvaren, Helvigsfjorden and Kjørrefjordsbukta have been chosen as the initial survey area (Fig 16.2). This voyaging corridor includes a historically well-known boat portage over Listeidet, between Framvaren and the sea northwest of Lista.

Framvaren has four thresholds, with depths from 2 to 18 metres, which separates the fjord from costal water. The maximum depth is approximately 180 metres. Minimal supply of both fresh- and saltwater makes Framvaren brackish, and it has constant rotten water beneath 15 m depth. The rate of sedimentation is low. Framvaren has been the subject of hydrographical and biological research because it has the lowest content of oxygen measured in a natural body of water anywhere in the world. An effect of this is that there is virtually no bio-activity in the sediments on the seabed.

The conditions for *in situ* preservation of organic material are assumed to be exceptionally promising. There is poisonous hydrosulphide, an absence of oxygen, great depth, and almost no human initiated activity in the water area. All this gives a potential for a minimal biological and mechanical break down of most organic cultural remains.

Helvigfjorden and Kjørrefjordsbukta have several of the same characteristics as Framvaren, but not to the same extreme extent. Helvigsfjorden has a threshold of 3.5 m, and 36 m as its maximum depth. There is critical oxygen content beneath 14m, with hydrosulphide below 18 m. Kjørrefjordsbukta is proportionally a small and shallow basin. A threshold at about 4 m and maximum depth of 13m. The oxygen conditions in the deeper parts are critical, with periodical anoxic conditions. Inside of Kjørrefjordsbukta is an area on land which formed the inner part of the fjord in the Bronze Age, and as such as a potential for finds.

The situation in regard to the preservation of archaeological material in these three fjords are due to much of the same chemical conditions that now make the amazing finds in the Black Sea possible.

Earlier fieldwork by the Norwegian Maritime Museum has shown that organic material in these fjords is broken down at an unusually slow rate.

Survey area 2: The freshwater system

The lakes in the central part of Lista made up a larger water system in the Bronze Age. From the seaside at Lundevågen there was a short portage to Kråkenesvannet, which is connected to Hanagervannet and further on with Prestvannet, Nesheimvannet and Brastadvannet.

Around this water system there have been numerous finds of cultural remains from the Bronze Age. Deposited in the lake Brastadvannet was also a bronze sword, found by accident. In this water system a rare structure dated to the Bronze Age, interpreted as a bridge, has also been reported and investigated.

In modern times the farmers have drained wetlands and lakes. Traditionally the water systems have been more extensive and travelling thus easier – and maritime solutions more necessary. The likelihood that larger vessels, possibly seagoing ones, were used –and lost – in this water system is great. As the lakes stand today, the remaining lake beds have been subjected to little direct, modern human activity. These lakes have been selected as the second survey area.

As the potential for preservation is supposed to be very good for organic material, a Bronze Age vessel deposited in these lakes has a very good chance of being preserved. Lakes in general have not been given much attention in archaeological investigations in Norway; a survey on the proposed scale will therefore break new ground in Norwegian archaeology.

To our knowledge, these two areas on Lista are the most likely places to expect a find of larger vessels. We expect the material we are searching for to be closely integrated in the depositional environment. This means it will be very difficult to detect and identify it.

Methods and surveying techniques in the salt/brackish water

Both the fresh and salt water areas present a wide range of particular environmental factors to an underwater survey. So far we have proposed a suite of different geophysical methods to confront the challenge.

In the salt/brackish water we plan to use a Side-scan sonar, a ROV (remote operated vehicle) with a horizontal sonar, a vertical seabed-penetrating sonar and a magnetometer with the capability of recognizing metals with a low-magnetic signature. And finally we will use SCUBA diving archaeologists to check out anomalies in the data from the geophysical survey.

In the freshwater area we plan to use a GPR (ground penetrating radar) and the same side-scan sonar, ROV and magnetometer mentioned above. And of course SCUBA-diving archaeologists will also be an integral part.

GPR will also be used on land inside of Kjørrefjord, in an area that was submerged in the Bronze Age and may have been used as a landing place.

Each of the techniques might not alone provide adequate detection, but by complementary use of the data from different techniques, we expect to get results. The fieldwork will also give valuable experience in regard to identifying the most useful methods for surveying cultural remains from other periods. We expect surprises will crop up, given the environmental conditions and as some sites are already known under water in this area, and more will certainly be found, we have no doubts concerning the value of the proposed excavations.

If the project succeeds, we will provide results beneficial – potentially path breaking – to future research in the field of the Nordic Bronze Age and in the development of prehistoric seafaring. We hope to develop the understanding of travel in, to and from a periphery of the European Bronze Age, and contribute to a developing socio-political anthropology of the Bronze Age.

And certainly, we want to find a Bronze Age boat, too.

List of references

Bender, B 2001 'Landscapes on-the-move', *Journal of Social Archaeology*, **1(1)**, 75–89

Helms, M W 1988 *Ulysses' Sail: An Ethnographic Odyssey of Power, Knowledge, and Geographical Distance*, Princeton University Press

Mann, M 1986 *The sources of social power: Vol. 1*, Cambridge University Press